Essays and Studies 2018

Series Editor: Elaine Treharne

The English Association

The objects of the English Association are to promote the knowledge and appreciation of the English language and its literatures, and to foster good practice in its teaching and learning at all levels.

The Association pursues these aims by creating opportunities of co-operation among all those interested in English; by furthering the recognition of English as essential in education; by discussing methods of English teaching; by holding lectures, conferences, and other meetings; by publishing journals, books, and leaflets; and by forming local branches.

Publications

The Year's Work in English Studies. An annual bibliography. Published by Blackwell.

The Year's Work in Critical and Cultural Theory. An annual bibliography. Published by Blackwell.

Essays and Studies. An annual volume of essays by various scholars assembled by the collector covering usually a wide range of subjects and authors from the medieval to the modern. Published by D. S. Brewer.

English. A journal of the Association, *English*, is published four times a year by the Association.

English 4–11. A journal supporting literacy in the primary classroom, published three times a year

The Use of English. A journal of the Association, *The Use of English*, is published three times a year by the Association.

Newsletter. Published three times a year giving information about forthcoming publications, conferences, and other matters of interest.

Benefits of Membership

Institutional Membership

Full members receive copies of *The Year's Work in English Studies, Essays and Studies, English* (4 issues) and three *Newsletters*.

Ordinary Membership covers *English* (4 issues) and three *Newsletters*.

Schools Membership includes copies of each issue of *English* and *The Use of English*, one copy of *Essays and Studies*, three *Newsletters*, and preferential booking and rates for various conferences held by the Association.

Individual Membership

Individuals take out Basic Membership, which entitles them to buy all regular publications of the English Association at a discounted price, and attend Association gatherings.

For further details write to the Membership Administrator, The English Association, The University of Leicester, University Road, Leicester LE1 7RH.

Essays and Studies 2018

English: Shared Futures

Edited by
Robert Eaglestone and Gail Marshall

for the English Association

D. S. BREWER

ESSAYS AND STUDIES 2018
IS VOLUME SEVENTY-ONE IN THE NEW SERIES
OF ESSAYS AND STUDIES COLLECTED ON BEHALF OF
THE ENGLISH ASSOCIATION
ISSN 0071-1357

First published 2018
D. S. Brewer, Cambridge

D. S. Brewer is an imprint of Boydell & Brewer Ltd
PO Box 9, Woodbridge, Suffolk IP12 3DF, UK
and of Boydell & Brewer Inc.
668 Mt Hope Avenue, Rochester, NY 14620–2731, USA
website: www.boydellandbrewer.com

ISBN 978-1-84384-516-4

A CIP catalogue record for this book is available
from the British Library

The publisher has no responsibility for the continued existence or accuracy of
URLs for external or third-party internet websites referred to in this book, and
does not guarantee that any content on such websites is, or will remain, accurate
or appropriate

This publication is printed on acid-free paper

Printed and bound in Great Britain by
TJ International Ltd, Padstow, Cornwall

MIX
Paper from
responsible sources
FSC
www.fsc.org   FSC® C013056

Contents

Notes on Contributors

James Annesley is currently Head of the School of English Literature, Language and Linguistics at Newcastle University. A Senior Lecturer in American Literature, he is the author of *Blank Fictions* (1998) and *Fictions of Globalization* (2006).

Katherine Isobel Baxter is Reader in English Literature at Northumbria University and General Editor of *English: Journal of the English Association*. She works on colonial and postcolonial law and literature, and has also published extensively on the works of Joseph Conrad, including *Conrad and Language* (2016; with Robert Hampson), *Joseph Conrad and the Swan Song of Romance* (2010) and *Joseph Conrad and the Performing Arts* (2008; with Richard Hand). More recently she edited, with Ann-Marie Einhaus, *The Edinburgh Companion to the First World War and the Arts* (2017).

Barbara Bleiman was, until 2016, Co-Director at EMC, a development centre for English and Media teachers at secondary level. She now works there as an Education Consultant, editing *emagazine*, running training courses and engaging in special projects and initiatives. She has written, and co-written, many books for the secondary English classroom, developing practical approaches to support learning in the subject, particularly at A-Level, as well as writing many articles and chapters in books on English teaching. She is also a fiction writer, with two published novels.

Elleke Boehmer is the Professor of World Literature in English at the University of Oxford, Director of OCLW, the Oxford Life Writing Centre, Wolfson College, and a founding figure in the field of colonial and postcolonial literary studies. She is the author, editor or co-editor of over twenty books, including monographs and novels. Her monographs include *Colonial and Postcolonial Literature* (1995/2005), *Stories of Women* (2005), *Indian Arrivals* (winner ESSE 2015–16 Prize), and *Postcolonial Poetics* (2018). Her novels include *The Shouting in the Dark* (long-listed *Sunday Times* Prize, 2015), and *Screens against the Sky* (short-listed David Higham Prize, 1990).

Kirsti Bohata is Professor of English Literature and Director of CREW, the Centre for Research into the English Literature and Language of

Wales, at Swansea University. She is Co-Chair of the Association for Welsh Writing in English and Co-Editor of the Writing Wales in English series of monographs and essays published by University of Wales Press. She has published widely on women's writing, postcolonial theory and queer writing from Wales. She is currently completing a co-authored interdisciplinary book on Disability in Industrial Britain 1880–1948 and a monograph on the queer fiction of Amy Dillwyn.

Benjamin A. Brabon joined the Higher Education Academy in February 2016 as head of Arts, Humanities and Social Sciences. Prior to this he was Academic Courses Manager within the executive team of the School of Arts and Humanities at Nottingham Trent University. A former Reader in English Literature and Digital Education with five books to his name, he is recognised within the sector for his work on Digital Education, Gothic fiction and Gender Studies. The convenor of the UK's first undergraduate credit-bearing MOOC, he has worked with the QAA, HEFCE and the Swedish Ministry of Education in this area, and his pedagogic research has been cited by the former Universities Minister, David Willetts.

Linda Bree was until early 2018 Senior Executive Publisher and Head of Humanities at Cambridge University Press, and is now a Senior Member of Wolfson College, Cambridge. She has extensive commissioning experience in British and European literature, and her own publications include essays on a range of eighteenth- and early nineteenth-century writers together with editions of Jane Austen's *Persuasion* and Daniel Defoe's *Moll Flanders*; she is co-editor with Janet Todd of the *Later Manuscripts* volume in The Cambridge Edition of the Works of Jane Austen.

Susan Bruce read English at the University of Cambridge and took her MA and PhD from Cornell. She is currently a Professor of English at Keele, and between 2014 and 2017, she was Chair of UE and a member of the Higher Education Committee of EA. The idea of English: Shared Futures was mooted at the meeting that elected her to the Chair of UE, and planning it and seeing it materialise was an important (and very enjoyable and rewarding) part of her role as Chair.

Billy Clark is Professor of English Language and Linguistics at Northumbria University. His research and teaching interests cover a wide range of topics in linguistics and stylistics, with a particular focus on semantics and pragmatics. This has included work on lexical and syntactic meaning, semantic change, phatic communication, prosodic meaning, multimodality, and pragmatic processes involved in the reading, writing and evaluation of texts. He has a long-standing interest in connections between work at school and at university. He was a founding member of the UK Linguistics Olympiad committee and, with Marcello Giovanelli and Andrea Macrae, coordinates the Integrating English project (http://integrating english.org).

Stefan Collini is Professor Emeritus of Intellectual History and English Literature at Cambridge University, and a Fellow of the British Academy. He is the author of, among other books, *Public Moralists* (1991), *Matthew Arnold: a Critical Portrait* (1994), *Absent Minds: Intellectuals in Britain* (2006), and *Common Writing: Literary Culture and Public Debate* (2016), as well as a frequent contributor to *The London Review of Books*, *The Times Literary Supplement*, *The Guardian* and other publications. His 2012 book *What Are Universities For?* and its sequel *Speaking of Universities* (2017) have become points of reference in international debates about higher education. He does not go to many conferences.

Jane Davis is Director of The Reader (www.thereader.org.uk), which she founded in 1997 while teaching English in the Department of Continuing Education at the University of Liverpool. In 2011 she was elected as the UK's 20th Ashoka Fellow and received an MBE for services to reading. The Reader sells Shared Reading to a wide range of commissioners in the NHS and across HM Prison Estate, as well as to local authorities, housing providers and employers. With sister projects developing across Europe, Australia and New Zealand, The Reader is currently building the International Centre for Shared Reading at Calderstones Mansion, in Calderstones Park, Liverpool.

Sarah Dillon is University Lecturer in Literature and Film in the Faculty of English at the University of Cambridge. She is author of *The Palimpsest: Literature, Criticism, Theory* (2007) and *Deconstruction, Feminism, Film* (2018). She is currently a Senior Research Fellow at the Leverhulme Centre for the Future of Intelligence, where she is co-Project Lead for the AI Narratives project, in collaboration with the Royal Society. She is committed to reaching audiences outside of the academy, and broadcasts regularly on BBC Radio 3 and BBC Radio 4; she writes and presents the BBC Radio 3 documentary series, Literary Pursuits.

Robert Eaglestone is Professor of Contemporary Literature and Thought at Royal Holloway, University of London, and was co-chair of 'English:

Shared Futures'. He works on contemporary literature and literary theory, contemporary philosophy and on Holocaust and Genocide studies. He is the author of six books, including The *Holocaust and the Postmodern* (2004), *The Broken Voice* (2017) and *Doing English* (4th edn, 2017), and the editor or co-editor of seven more, including *Derrida's Legacies* (2008) and *The Future of Trauma Theory* (2013). His work has been translated into six languages, and in 2014 he won a National Teaching Fellowship.

Clare Egan is a Lecturer in Medieval and Early Modern Literature at Lancaster University. Her research interests include libel and defamation, drama, performance, and spatial and digital humanities approaches. She was previously a Research Assistant in Early Modern Literature at the University of Huddersfield, working on an anthology of ecocritical sources for the early modern period. She completed her PhD in February 2015 at the University of Southampton where she was then briefly a Visiting Lecturer in Early Modern Drama and the Law.

Elizabeth English is a Lecturer in English Literature at Cardiff Metropolitan University in Wales. Her research focuses on modernist and early twentieth-century popular fiction with a particular interest in women's writing. Her first monograph, *Lesbian Modernism: Censorship, Sexuality and Genre Fiction*, was published in 2015 (paperback in April 2017). In addition, she is the author of a number of published essays and articles, the latest of which, 'Tired of London, Tired of Life: The Queer Pastoral in Alan Hollinghurst's *The Spell*', was published in *Sex and Sensibility in the Novels of Alan Hollinghurst* in 2017. She is also the Treasurer for the newly formed Modernist Network Cymru (MONC), which brings together scholars and professionals working on modernism in Wales to encourage collaboration and communication.

Emily Ennis recently completed her AHRC-funded PhD at the University of Leeds after taking her bachelor's and master's degrees there. Her PhD explored the connections between four key authors – Thomas Hardy, Bram Stoker, Joseph Conrad and Virginia Woolf – and the rise of popular photography between 1880 and 1920. She is now a Short-Term Postdoctoral Fellow at the Leeds Humanities Research Institute at the University of Leeds, where she also works part time as an Admissions Officer. She also works as an hourly paid Postdoctoral Teaching Assistant at the University of Leeds and Newcastle University, teaching Modern Literature and Close Reading.

Martin Paul Eve is Professor of Literature, Technology and Publishing at Birkbeck, University of London. He is the author of five books, including *Open Access and the Humanities: Contexts, Controversies and the Future* (2014), and the forthcoming *Close Reading with Computers: Textual Scholarship, Computational Formalism, and David Mitchell's 'Cloud Atlas'* (2019).

Corinne Fowler is an Associate Professor in Postcolonial Literature at the University of Leicester. She is the author of *Chasing Tales: Travel Writing, Journalism and the History of British Ideas about Afghanistan* (2008), co-author of *Postcolonial Manchester: Diaspora Space and the Devolution of Literary Culture* (2013) and co-editor of *Travel Writing: Theory and Practice* (2013). She has edited a number of creative anthologies and is director of the Centre for New Writing.

Bárbara Gallego Larrarte (barbara.gallegolarrarte@wolfson.ox.ac.uk) is a DPhil candidate at Wolfson College, University of Oxford. Her dissertation explores intergenerational relationships between writers during the interwar period in Britain, with a focus on Virginia Woolf, T. S. Eliot and E. M. Forster. Wider themes addressed in her doctoral work include the role of friendships in intellectual development, the dynamics of intergenerational networks, and the workings of affective and intellectual influence.

Marcello Giovanelli is Senior Lecturer in English Language and Literature at Aston University, Birmingham, UK. He has research interests in stylistics, cognitive poetics, reader response theories, and English education. Recent books include *Text World Theory and Keats' Poetry* (2013), *Teaching Grammar, Structure and Meaning* (2014), *Knowing About Language* (2016, with Dan Clayton), and *Cognitive Grammar in Stylistics: A Practical Guide* (2018, with Chloe Harrison) as well as publications in stylistics and applied linguistics in a number of leading international peer-reviewed journals. He is Chair of Examiners for A-Level English Language and Literature at a major English examination board.

Diya Gupta (www.diyagupta.co.uk) is a PhD researcher at the English Department, King's College London. Her project provides the first literary and cultural examination of Indian soldiers' experiences in the Second World War, looking at life-writing and visual culture sources, and war responses in Indian literature and intellectual thought. Her article for The Conversation entitled 'Why Remembrance of Indian Soldiers who fought for the British in World War II is so political' was the most read piece in November 2017, with over 150,000 hits. A short film on her research, called 'The Indian Soldier's Experience of WW II', can be viewed on YouTube. She was awarded the 2017 Barbara Northend Prize for academic excellence by the British Federation of Women Graduates.

Rob Hawkes is Senior Lecturer in English at Teesside University. He is author of *Ford Madox Ford and the Misfit Moderns: Edwardian Fiction and the First World War* (2012) and editor (with Ashley Chantler) of *Ford Madox Ford's 'Parade's End': The First World War, Culture, and Modernity* (2014), *War and the Mind: Ford Madox Ford's 'Parade's End', Modernism, and Psychology* (2015), and *An Introduction to Ford Madox Ford* (2015). His current work includes a forthcoming monograph: Trusting Texts: Literature, Money, and Modernity, 1890–1990; and a book chapter on trust and uncertainty in Stewart Lee's Comedy Vehicle.

Ann Hewings is Director of Applied Linguistics and English Language at The Open University. She teaches and researches disciplinary variation in academic writing and online pedagogy in English language and applied linguistics. She is series editor for Worlds of English (Routledge), and co-editor of *Futures for English Studies* (Palgrave) and *The Routledge Handbook of English Language Studies*.

Keith Jarrett writes poetry and fiction. He is a PhD candidate at Birkbeck, University of London, completing his practice-led research under the Bloomsbury Studentship scheme. His book of poetry, *Selah*, was published in 2017 and his monologue, 'Safest Spot in Town', was aired on BBC Four the same year. He is a former UK Poetry Slam Champion, and was international slam champion at FLUPP favela literary festival. He was also one of the pioneering members of the Spoken Word Educators programme – the first of its kind globally – teaching in a secondary school while studying for an MA at Goldsmiths University.

Clara Jones is a Lecturer in Modern Literature at King's College London. Her research focuses on the politics of modernist and interwar women writers. She is the author of a series of articles focusing on the class and gender politics of Virginia Woolf's writing, and her monograph is *Virginia Woolf: Ambivalent Activist* (2016, paperback 2017). She is currently at work on a project about the political and literary practice of interwar women writers.

Seraphima Kennedy writes poetry, memoir and comment. From 2011–14 she taught Creative Writing at Goldsmiths while studying towards a PhD in Life Writing. In 2016, she was short-listed for The White Review Poets' Prize, and in 2017–18 she was mentored through the Jerwood/ Arvon mentoring scheme. In 2018 she received a grant from the Arts Council Developing your Creative Practice Fund. She is Director of NAWE.

Ben Knights, Emeritus Professor of English and Cultural Studies at Teesside University, is a former director of the HEA English Subject Centre. His research interests include the cultural history of masculinities, Humanities pedagogies, and the relationship between fields of academic enquiry and their associated teaching styles. His latest book (which contextualises and explores in more detail the ideas touched on here) is *Pedagogic Criticism: Reconfiguring University English Studies* (2017).

Simon Kövesi is Professor of English Literature at Oxford Brookes University, and has been Head of its Department of English and Modern Languages since 2011. He studied at the universities of Glasgow, North Carolina at Chapel Hill, and Nottingham Trent. He specialises in Romanticism and working-class literature, and has written the monographs *James Kelman* (2007) and *John Clare: Nature, Criticism and History* (2017). He has been Editor of the *John Clare Society Journal* since 2008 and is honorary lifetime member of the British Association for Romantic Studies. His current book project is called *Literature and Poverty, 1800–2000*.

Clare A. Lees was Professor of Medieval English at King's College London. In 2018 she became Director of the Institute of English Studies, School of Advanced Study, University of London. Her research interests include gender, literature and relationships between modern and medieval culture. She was the founding Director of the London Arts and Humanities Partnership (LAHP), an AHRC DTP (2013–16); she is a member of the Higher Education committee of the EA, and helped support the Early Career Strand of English: Shared Futures.

Alison Lumsden holds a chair in English literature at the University of Aberdeen. She has published on many aspects of Scottish literature, including Nan Shepherd, Lewis Grassic Gibbon and Robert Louis Stevenson. The main focus of her research is Walter Scott, and she was a General Editor of the Edinburgh Edition of the Waverley

Novels. She is now the lead editor for a critical edition of Walter Scott's Poetry. She co-directs the Walter Scott Research Centre at Aberdeen, is Honorary Librarian at Abbotsford, Scott's home in the Scottish Borders, and is currently President of the Association for Scottish Literary Studies.

Andrea Macrae is a Senior Lecturer in Stylistics at Oxford Brookes University. She specialises in deixis and has published research in several books and journals, most recently in a volume she co-edited with Alison Gibbons entitled *Pronouns in Literature* (2018). She also works in charity communications. She teaches stylistics, cognitive poetics, world literature and metafiction. With Billy Clark and Marcello Giovanelli, she works on the Integrating English project, which advocates a holistic, text-centred approach to English studies.

Gail Marshall is Head of the School of Literature and Languages, and Professor of Victorian Literature and Culture, at the University of Reading. She was co-chair of English: Shared Futures, and is the author and editor of books on Victorian fiction and theatre, including several on Shakespeare and the Victorians. She recently completed a manuscript on 1859, and is planning a new project on George Eliot.

Lewi Mondal is a PhD student and module lecturer at Teesside University, funded by the Graduate Tutor Scheme, where he teaches a module on short fictions of the nineteenth century. His thesis explores liminality and excess as defining features in Neo-Victorian Representations of Race and Masculinity, and he is currently working on a chapter on the physical body and time travel. He was alerted to the opportunity to gain an insight into the workings of a conference by interning at English: Shared Futures by his supervisor Rob Hawkes (a member of the organising committee for the conference).

Paul Munden was Director of the National Association of Writers in Education (NAWE), the UK subject association for creative writing, from 1994–2018. He has, for the past three years, been postdoctoral Research Fellow at the University of Canberra, working within the International Poetry Studies Institute and running the annual Poetry on the Move festival. He is the author of *Beyond the Benchmark* (2011), the research report on creative writing in the UK commissioned by the Higher Education Academy. He has published five poetry collections, most recently *Chromatic* (2017).

Daniel O'Gorman is Lecturer in Twentieth and Twenty-First Century Literature at Oxford Brookes University. He is the author of *Fictions of the War on Terror: Difference and the Transnational 9/11 Novel* (2015), and has published articles in *Textual Practice, Critique: Studies in Contemporary Fiction*, and the *Journal of Commonwealth Literature*. He is currently co-editing the *Routledge Companion to Twenty-First Century Literary Fiction* (with Robert Eaglestone), and is an Associate Editor at the *Journal of Postcolonial Writing*. Daniel has taught English Literature to a diverse range of students across four very different higher education institutions.

Lynda Prescott is Associate Dean (Learning and Teaching Innovation) in the Faculty of Arts and Social Sciences at the Open University. As a former head of the OU's Department of English she has been extensively involved in the development of curriculum in Literature and Creative Writing, and has collaborated with colleagues in English Language on numerous projects, including a 2016 collection of essays, *Futures for English Studies: Teaching Language, Literature and Creative Writing in Higher Education*, edited with Ann Hewings and Philip Seargeant. She is a Principal Fellow of the Higher Education Academy.

Ilse A. Ras completed her PhD in English Language at the University of Leeds. She also holds an MSc in Criminology from the University of Leicester and is a co-founder of the Poetics and Linguistics Association Special Interest Group on Crime Writing. Her work and teaching often crosses the boundaries between English language and Criminology, focusing on the use of language to express, maintain and reinforce (capitalist) power structures, using corpus-assisted critical discourse analysis and critical stylistics to examine this language.

Catherine Redford is a Career Development Fellow in English at Hertford College, University of Oxford, and has published on Mary Shelley, Lord Byron, H. G. Wells, and the Gothic. She has a long-standing interest in outreach work with school children, and regularly runs enrichment workshops and seminars for GCSE and A-Level students. During her time as a British Academy Rising Star Engagement Award holder (2016–17) she developed a project to bring together teachers and academics, with the aim of encouraging a dialogue about how universities can best work with younger students to help foster a love of English.

Rick Rylance is Dean of the School of Advanced Study at the University of London. He previously served as Director of the Institute of English

Studies in the School. Before that he was Chief Executive of the Arts and Humanities Research Council (AHRC) and Chair of Research Councils UK. His most recent book is *Literature and the Public Good* (2016).

Helen Saunders completed her PhD, on the relationship between fashion and literary modernism in the work of James Joyce, at King's College London in 2017. While at King's, she taught courses on city literature and the philosophy of language; she has articles either forthcoming or published in the *Journal of Victorian Culture, James Joyce Quarterly* and *Irish Studies Review*. Currently working in academic publishing, she has been a postgraduate representative on the Executive Council of the British Association of Modernist Studies (BAMS) since 2016. She participated in the postgraduate panel on the Futures of Modernist Studies at English: Shared Futures.

Jenny Stevens is a Fellow of the English Association and convener of its University Transition Special Interest Group. She is an external subject expert for Ofqual and has worked on a variety of assessment-related projects, including the 2015 reform of both the GCSE and A-Level qualifications. A former Head of English in an inner London school, she has taught at both secondary and undergraduate level and currently combines part-time teaching with educational consultancy and publishing.

Marion Thain is a professor of arts and literature in New York University's school of the interdisciplinary global liberal arts (Liberal Studies), and is Director of Digital Humanities for NYU. She began her career as a Junior Research Fellow at Cambridge, and then worked in English departments at Russell Group universities in the UK as Junior Lecturer, Senior Lecturer and then Reader, before moving to NYU. She publishes primarily on aestheticism; poetry and poetics; technology and the production of cultural knowledge. Book publications include: *The Lyric Poem and Aestheticism: Forms of Modernity* (2016); *The Lyric Poem: Formations and Transformations* (2013); *Michael Field: Poetry, Aestheticism, and the Fin de Siècle* (2007); and *Poetry of the 1890s* (1998).

Stephen Watkins is an AHRC-funded PhD student in English at the University of Southampton. His thesis, 'The Revolutionary Theatres of Sir William Davenant, 1650–1668', examines the political and cultural conditions under which Davenant wrote and staged his dramatic works during the middle decades of the seventeenth century. He is currently preparing articles on Davenant's 1650s entertainments as well as on the print and performance afterlives of his Restoration adaptation (with John Dryden) of Shakespeare's *Tempest*.

Harry Whitehead is Associate Professor of Creative Writing in the School of Arts at the University of Leicester. He is the author of the novel *The Cannibal Spirit* (2011), numerous short stories, and articles on subjects ranging from the global proliferation of creative writing as an academic subject, to the ethnography of the Northwest Coast of Canada. He has sat on the National Association of Writers in Education's Higher Education Committee, and was principal editor of the journal *Writing in Practice*. His current research interests include Cold War Creative Writing programmes in the Soviet Bloc.

Acknowledgements

The editors would like to thank the contributors to this volume, who both presented their work at the English: Shared Futures conference in Newcastle in July 2017, and have re-worked and re-presented their work in written form here. It has been a great pleasure to work with them and to see the book evolve with their help.

We also need to acknowledge the hard work of the many people without whom the conference could not have taken place. As organisers, we were indebted especially to Helen Lucas and Atiqa Rehman of the English Association for their extraordinary commitment, professionalism, and that unfailing good humour which is often cited in acknowledgements but rarely seen in such abundance as here. The staff of Newcastle and Northumbria Universities, the Newcastle Conference Bureau, and everyone at the Newcastle Civic Centre, especially James Thomas, were generous in their hospitality, and helped to make the conference a landmark event.

As conference organisers, we were brilliantly supported by the English: Shared Futures planning committee, which consisted of Clare Lees and Clara Jones (who curated the Early Career Academics strand), Seraphima Kennedy and Paul Munden (who curated the NAWE strand), Ben Brabon (who curated the HEA sessions), James Annesley and Katherine Baxter (who curated the Cultural Fringe events, and liaised with local organisers), Andrea Macrae (who put together our digital programme), Rob Hawkes, Fiona Douglas, Rick Rylance, Nicole King, Simon James, Alex Thomson, Susan Bruce and Martin Halliwell.

We are especially indebted to Susan Bruce and Martin Halliwell, who were at the time the Chairs respectively of University English and the English Association, for their unwavering support of the conference, which demonstrated the close working relationship between the two bodies. We are grateful too for the collaboration of the Institute of English Studies (whose Director at the time was Rick Rylance), the Higher Education Academy and the National Association of Writers in Education. The fruitful and generous working relationships established between these bodies bodes well for our shared futures.

We thank Seren Books for permission to quote Peter Finch's poem 'Partisan', from his collection *Useful* (Bridgend: Seren Books 1997). The quotation from 'Simultaneous Translation' appears in *Talkies* by Robert Crawford, published by Chatto & Windus. Reproduced by permission of

The Random House Group Ltd. © 1994. We also thank Carcanet Press Limited for permission to quote Hugh MacDiarmid's poem 'The Eemis Stane', from *The Complete Poems of Hugh MacDiarmid*, edited by Michael Grieve and W. R. Aitken (1985).

Abbreviations

Every ecosystem within education is full of acronyms: our niche is no different. Citations from the relevant website.

AAH	Arts and Humanities Alliance	'an association of learned societies that work together to promote the interests of the arts and humanities, particularly with respect to higher-education and research policies at UK and EU level'.
AdvanceHE	AdvanceHE	'AdvanceHE was founded in 2017 through a merger of the Equality Challenge Unit, the Higher Education Academy and the Leadership Foundation for Higher Education'.
AHRC	Arts and Humanities Research Council	The quango that 'funds world-class, independent researchers in a wide range of subjects from history, archaeology, digital content, philosophy, languages, design, heritage, performing arts, and much more': includes English.
Alt-Ac	Alternative Academic	The movement which, given the shortage of academic jobs and the large number of people with PhDs, promotes alternative careers for those with doctorates.
ASLS	Association for Scottish Literary Studies	learned society
AWWE	Association for Welsh Writing in English	learned society
BA	British Academy	'the UK's national body for the humanities and social sciences – the study of peoples, cultures and societies, past, present and future'.
BAAL	British Association for Applied Linguistics	learned society
BAAS	British Association for American Studies	learned society
BACLS	British Society for Contemporary Literary Studies	learned society

BAIS	British Association for Irish Studies	learned society
BAMS	British Association for Modernist Studies	learned society
BARS	British Association for Romantic Studies	learned society
BAVS	British Association for Victorian Studies	learned society
BCLA	British Comparative Literature Association	learned society
BS18S	British Society for Eighteenth-Century Studies	learned society
BSA	British Shakespeare Association	learned society
BSLS	British Society for Literature and Science	learned society
CEF	Common English Forum	A lobbying and advocacy group which brings together various disciplinary organisations.
CWWA	Contemporary Women's Writing Association	learned society
DfE	Department for Education	Government department for education
EA	English Association	A national body, set up in 1906, which aims to 'further knowledge, understanding and enjoyment of the English language and its literatures and to foster good practice in its teaching and learning' at primary, secondary and higher education levels. It runs a range of conferences and prizes, and undertakes policy for the discipline. It has a primary, secondary and Higher education committee.
ECA or ECR	Early Career Academic or Early Career Researcher	Common abbreviation for an academic within five years of their PhD. We prefer *Academic* to *Researcher* because many of these early career staff are in demanding and often precarious teaching posts.

EMC	English and Media Centre	'an educational charity providing CPD and innovative & award-winning teaching materials to secondary English & Media teachers'. Publisher of *emagazine*.
ESSE	European Society for the Study of English	'a European federation of national higher educational associations for the study of English… The aim of the Society is to advance the education of the public by promoting the European study and understanding of English languages, literatures in English and cultures of English-speaking peoples'.
HEA	Higher Education Academy	The 'national body which champions teaching excellence. We work with governments, ministries, universities and individual academics in the UK, and around the globe. We provide value to the HE sector by focusing on the contribution of teaching as part of the wider student learning experience.' The HEA supports initiatives in teaching and has a Fellowship scheme that academics can join. Now part of AdvanceHE.
HEFCE	Higher Education Funding Council for England	Closed in September 2018, this was the quango that funded many aspects of Higher Education in England.
IES	Institute of English Studies	Part of the University of London's School of Advanced Study (SAS), the IES is 'an internationally renowned research centre, specialising in the history of the book, manuscript and print studies and textual scholarship'. It is developing a national remit to support the discipline.
KEF	Knowledge Exchange Framework	'The framework is intended to increase efficiency and effectiveness in use of public funding for knowledge exchange (KE), to further a culture of continuous improvement in university KE by providing a package of support to keep English university knowledge exchange operating at world class standard. It aims to address the range of different KE activities.'

LATE	London Association for the Teaching of English	Formed in 1947, 'LATE is an active branch within the London and Hertfordshire region of NATE'. Mainly for teachers in Secondary English and in English in education.
MLA	Modern Language Association of America	Founded in 1883, the Modern Language Association of America has works to strengthen the study and teaching of languages and literatures in the USA. It runs a number of journals (including its *Proceedings*, PMLA) and conventions, including the annual MLA convention.
NATE	National Association for the Teaching of English	Mainly for Primary and Secondary level teachers, NATE promotes 'standards of excellence in the teaching of English from Early Years to University... innovative and original ideas that have practical classroom outcomes' and 'support teachers' own professional development'. In addition, it runs conferences, collaborations and advocacy for the discipline.
NAWE	Nation Association of Writers in Education	NAWE's mission is to 'further knowledge, understanding and enjoyment of Creative Writing' and to 'support good practice in its teaching and learning at all levels'.
NSS	National Student Survey	Taking place in the Spring term, and focusing on final-year students, the National Student Survey 'gathers students' opinions on the quality of their courses' and so helps to 'inform prospective students' choices; provide data that supports institutions in improving the student experience; support public accountability'.
OA	Open Access	Open Access is the movement to make academic research free to access online.

OfS	Office for Students	'We regulate English higher education providers on behalf of all students. Our regulatory framework explains how we do this, and our strategy describes our objectives and priorities.' Successor to HEFCE, and (at the time of writing) its powers are still under discussion in Parliament.
OLH	Open Library of Humanities	'a charitable organisation dedicated to publishing open access scholarship with no author-facing article processing charges (APCs). We are funded by an international consortium of libraries who have joined us in our mission to make scholarly publishing fairer, more accessible, and rigorously preserved for the digital future. All of our academic articles are subject to rigorous peer review and the scholarship we publish showcases some of the most dynamic research taking place in the humanities disciplines today... Our mission is to support and extend open access to scholarship in the humanities – for free, for everyone, for ever.'
PALA	Poetics and Linguistics Association	learned society
PGR	Postgraduate, Research	A postgraduate undertaking a research degree (e.g. PhD, MPhil etc).
PhD+	Phd plus	Academics who have got their doctorates, but are not yet in full-time employment
PSA	Postcolonial Studies Association	learned society

QAA	Quality Assurance Agency for Higher Education	'an independent, not for profit organisation, we check that students working towards a UK qualification get the higher education they are entitled to expect'. Crucially, QAA offers 'subject-specific guidance' in the 'Subject Benchmark Statements', which 'set out the skills and knowledge that graduates are expected to have at the end of specific degree courses'. There is one for English (2015) and for Creative Writing (2016).
REF	Research Excellence Framework	The REF 'is the system for assessing the quality of research in UK higher education institutions' and so determining research funding. It is a regular periodic exercise (the next one is 2020).
SRS	Society for Renaissance Studies	learned society
SSML	Society for the Study of Medieval Languages and Literature	learned society
TEF	Teaching Excellence and Student Outcomes Framework	TEF 'recognises excellent teaching in UK higher education providers by rating them as gold, silver or bronze. The results help prospective students choose where to study. The TEF was developed by the Department for Education and is carried out by the Office for Students. The ratings are judged by an independent panel of students, academics and other experts.'
UE	University English	The main professional body for University departments of English. Formerly the Council for College and University English (CCUE), it was 'founded in 1993 to promote the study of English in higher education, and to provide opportunities for English lecturers to meet colleagues from other institutions and discuss matters of shared concern'.

Introduction

ROBERT EAGLESTONE AND GAIL MARSHALL

'English: Shared Futures', the event after which this volume is named, was a huge celebration of the intellectual strength, diversity and dynamism of the English Language, Literature and Creative Writing community, held in Newcastle in the summer of 2017. Part-conference, part-festival, part-professional meeting, it brought together 600 academics, writers, publishers, teachers and students.

Like a more traditional conference, it had around 150 panels on a range of intellectual matters from Old English to contemporary literature and theory to creative writing; plenary lectures from Deborah Cameron (English Language), Bernardine Evaristo (Creative Writing) and Brian Ward (on Martin Luther King's honorary degree from Newcastle University, to celebrate our local connections) and a plenary panel on literary biography from Martin Stannard, Kathryn Hughes and Andrew Hadfield. Sixteen of our learned societies ran sessions. And all the major UK academic publishers attended, as did many of the smaller local publishers in this vibrant and creative part of the country.

Like a professional meeting, there were sessions on advocacy, collegiality, diversity, management, broadcast media, harassment, employability, TEF, mentoring and calibration. Well aware of the consequences of precarity in the profession, there were sessions organised by and for early career academics and PhD students, and the English Association used the conference to pilot a large, site-specific mentoring scheme, putting junior and senior academics in touch. There was a special interest too in pedagogy across the discipline, focusing on the curriculum, creativity, new approaches and on crossing the HE/Secondary school divide. Specially sponsored by University English, there was an international panel on 'The Discipline of English and the Work of the Humanities' with Stefan Collini, Helen Small, Amanda Anderson and Chris Newfield.

And like a literary festival, we had a feast of readings, talks and exhibitions. For many, the highlight was the 'Night of Three Laureates' with readings from Carol Ann Duffy and Lorna Goodison, respectively Britain's and Jamaica's Poets Laureate, and Jackie Kay, the Scottish Makar, and there were readings from 'The Cold Boat' project and other local poets. 'English: Shared Futures' also featured a series of 'salons' in which leading figures were interviewed about their life in literature and the literature in their life: the award-winning poet Helen Mort talked with Mary Jean Chan (who, since the event, has also won awards[1]); Elleke Boehmer spoke with Diya Gupta and Barbara Gallego (and this interview is included here); John Mullan talked with Sarah Dillon; Dinah Birch with Hilary Fraser; and Marina Warner with Shahidha Bari.

But, as Simon Kövesi one of our contributors, notes in his chapter, 'Can Wisdom be put in a silver rod? / Or Love in a golden bowl?', while 'English: Shared Futures' 'certainly had a celebratory and affirmatory atmosphere' it was 'born of uncertainty about the future of English'. There had been considerable unease in and about the English subject community for some time. Some of this disquiet is intellectual: for example, in English literary studies, Rita Felski's widely discussed and lively attack, *The Limits of Critique*, responds to what she calls a 'legitimation crisis, thanks to a sadly depleted language of value that leaves us struggling to find reasons why students should care about Beowulf or Baudelaire'.[2] In terms of pedagogy, and English Language, a similar dissatisfaction emerges in Marcello Giovanelli – another contributor to this volume – and Jess Mason's article ' "Well I don't feel that": Schemas, worlds and authentic reading in the classroom'.[3] They discuss the impact of what they call 'Manufactured reading', in which the student simply provides what the teacher (or exam schema) asks for. Of course, this kind of intellectual 'crisis' might be seen to suit a responsive and responsible discipline (after all, 'criticism' and 'crisis' have the same etymological root). But the concerns about English and Creative Writing that led to 'English: Shared Futures' were also about the less flashy, more workaday problems that face our discipline.

Some of these problems are down to the image the disciplines of English Literature, English Language and Creative Writing fashion both for themselves and for the world outside. For example, the ingrained subdivisions in the discipline (language, creative writing, literature) and within these bands (say, for example, Shakespeareans, Medievalists, Victorianists, Modernists; specialists in corpus linguistics and those in

[1]   Mary Jean Chan is the winner of the 2017 Psychoanalysis and Poetry competition, and the 2017 PSA/Journal of Postcolonial Writing Postgraduate Essay Prize.
[2]   Rita Felski, *The Limits of Critique* (Chicago: Chicago University Press, 2015), p. 5.
[3]   'Manufactured reading' comes from M. Giovanelli and J. Mason, '"Well I don't feel that": Schemas, worlds and authentic reading in the classroom', *English in Education*, 49:1 (2015), 41–55.

stylistics; poets, playwrights and novelists) mean that these smaller groups all have their own courses, conferences and journals, and rarely talk to each other. The national subject bodies are arguably not as well-known as they should be, and sometimes seem a bewildering array of acronyms: EA (the English Association), CCUE (the Council for College and University English), who very sensibly rebranded as UE (University English), NAWE (National Association of Writers in Education). There is also a rich array of learned societies, which reflects discrete areas of the discipline, but no central online forum or body to act as a 'clearing house' for conference calls, new books, announcements and papers. Part of the point of 'English: Shared Futures' was to help unify a disparate discipline.

There is also a divide between English at secondary school level and English in higher education. Despite the wonderful work of the English Association, many English colleagues at secondary level feel abandoned by English in HE and look enviously at organisations like the Institute of Physics, Classical Association or the History Association, which not only lobby for their disciplines nationally, but help to bridge this divide. And this link needs to be strengthened considerably at this moment. For example, in 2013, by working together bodies in the discipline headed off a terrible GCSE reform in relation to student choice. However, the new GCSE content is dispiriting: the Literature syllabus rigid and overly traditional; the Language closer to 'composition'. This seems to have led to a downturn in A-Level applications (Barbara Bleiman discusses this in her chapter). The A-Level in Creative Writing was discontinued, and the amount of Creative Writing at secondary level cut, and numbers taking A-Level English Literature and A-Level English Language are falling.

This is worrying enough for English in Secondary Education: but applications to English at HE have also been falling. English has a skewed gender imbalance (over 70% of the students who take the A-Level are women) and is developing a pronounced class imbalance too. The removal of the 'numbers cap' has exacerbated the disparities in the sector: Russell Group universities have been 'hoovering up' students, leaving many other departments with depleted numbers. In terms of recruitment of academics, English and Creative Writing have, like many other subjects, created a precariat of highly trained academics who have short-term contracts, or temporary jobs, or zero-hours contracts. Again, part of the point of 'English: Shared Futures' was to respond to this by helping to rebuild webs of information, contacts and communication across the discipline. Some of these challenges are easier to address than others: some we need imagination and hope to address as we consider the bigger picture within which English as a discipline operates.

Writing on 1 January 2018, the future for English, for British universi-ties, and indeed for Britain, contains a number of challenges that were not foreseen at the turn of the century. They descend to us from those economic upheavals of ten years ago that have caused such widespread and deeply felt tremors across whole swathes of Britain's political, cultural, educational, professional and social life. The austerity politics of recent years, the dif-ferent horrors of Grenfell and terror attacks, the uncertainties of global economics, the rise of voices of popular protest, and the election of leaders new to the front-line of politics have combined to produce a set of cir-cumstances in which traditional expectations and assumptions have been re-calibrated. Governments in recent years have concentrated on promoting STEM (Science, Technology, Engineering and Maths) subjects to counter perceived skills shortages, and students have increasingly been turning to Economics, presumably retrospectively to understand 2008's crash and to be well-placed to prevent its repetition, and to IT, to ensure their part in a digital future. These responses make a certain amount of sense, par-ticularly in a context of rising tuition fees, and in light of Destination of Leavers from Higher Education (DELHE) data, which shows the high earn-ings generally available to graduates with STEM, Economics and Medical degrees. However, that data measures prosperity and value only in one way; an important way, but not the only measure of value. DELHE does not measure contribution, non-monetary value or job satisfaction, and impor-tantly it only works retrospectively: it cannot predict future earnings or areas of developing employment, nor can it foresee the potential paradigm shifts involved in a future where robotics and AI may re-shape the world of work entirely, and where lucrative legal, medical and scientific careers may be changed irredeemably, even effaced, by the advent of new technologies. In this future, the arts and humanities will be even more important than ever; as Robert Peston writes in his succinctly titled *WTF?*:

> What machines can't do – and quite possibly never will be able to do – is negotiate, build relationships, empathise, instil confidence, win trust, create great art, write moral philosophy, dream or any of the other emotional and intuitive activities that are central both to highly paid careers and the sheer joy of being alive.[4]

As many of the essays in this book make clear, new technologies give us the ability to open up new fields of research, and to answer unprecedented research questions, but theirs are not the only answers to our future. And

---

[4] Robert Peston, *WTF?* (London: Hodder and Stoughton, 2017), p. 223.

nor is the atomistic pursuit of salary measured by DELHE. The future of English, as our conference showed, is a shared one, characterised by the invigorating pursuit of knowledge, the sharing of that knowledge with students, colleagues and the wider public, and the conviction that English matters. The Royal Society of Literature's newly launched campaign, 'Literature Matters',[5] is just one manifestation of this shared conviction, which in fact goes beyond the bounds of literature, to take in creative writing and language work.

English matters because it creates links that enhance understanding, of each other, of the past, and of the power of language. It matters because a literate, articulate population is a population less likely to be uncomprehendingly stymied by its own frustrations, and less likely to be unable to see beyond its own preoccupations to the troubles of others. That population will also be more analytical, creative, critical, and capable of reflection and perspective. And it will be more resilient. English is fundamental to personal and national well-being; it is not an optional add-on, or a box-ticking measure of literacy, or a flurry of cultural references that designate a good education, but an inherent right that demands the best teaching at all stages in order to be nurtured and relished. It offers an alternative means of measuring value, and contribution.

We hope that the conference, and this book, which reflects the conference through its miscellany of voices and vectors rather than as a more formal 'proceedings', can leave a trace. We hope that some part of its legacy might lie in small but significant disciplinary shifts: encouragement to undertake innovative forms of conference session and academic dissemination; more ambitious forms of professional engagement, mentoring, networking; a sense that discussing our pedagogy more formally is worthwhile and significant intellectually. More ambitiously, we hope that the event may help build with others to develop responses to academic and political issues like precarity, harassment and inequality within and around our discipline. Perhaps most of all, and most intangibly, we hope that 'English: Shared Futures' might help us talk to each other beyond our more traditional subdisciplinary divisions in order to generate a stronger sense of a discipline that 'thinks together': collaboratively and with a further developing feeling for its own disciplinary identity. This will become increasingly necessary.

As 'English: Shared Futures' the conference, and *English: Shared Futures* the book demonstrate, English is fundamentally a shared venture,

[5] See https://rsliterature.org/2017/09/literature-matters-campaign/ for more details.

based in the collaborative acts of reading and writing. These may be, and indeed often are, practised in isolation, but are in essence communicative acts, depending on transaction, understanding and the belief that gaps between readers and writers can be bridged. In any setting where readers come together – be it in a book group, a Reader group or university seminar – that act of communication grows, and we experience, as George Eliot wrote, 'the extension of our sympathies' both to other readers, the writer and his or her characters, and to each other. It matters that we share ideas and a language in which those ideas can most effectively be communicated, and that we understand fully the ramifications of the language that we use. No matter what our future looks like, we will need to communicate, to understand, to be as fully and richly human as we can be, and English is integral to those ambitions.

Robert Eaglestone and Gail Marshall
January 2018

The Changing Picture of School English

BARBARA BLEIMAN

The story of English in schools over the past few decades has been one of constant change. At every level, from KS3 to AL, successive governments have made it their mission to reform the system, sometimes just tinkering with the examinations, but more often than not introducing major changes that require significant re-thinking and re-structuring. Some of the changes have been content-based – for instance, prescribing or proscribing content (as in the case of former secretary of state for education, Michael Gove's determinations for GCSE English). Others have been concerned with assessment (as in strictures over coursework, requirements for exams without access to texts, or approaches to examining using assessment criteria), and still more have revolved around structures (linear, modular, with or without AS- Levels, re-sittable or not). As a result, teachers' attention has been skewed to focus most of all on getting to grips with the new, different content, structures and ways of assessment, rather than on practices – what we mean by doing English, what kinds of pedagogic practices are associated with our subject and how we might best introduce students to what it means to be a student of English. This has also been hugely exacerbated by the most damaging elements in governments' attempts to 'raise standards' in schools – the use of league tables, OFSTED inspections and the mining of data on individual pupils and their progress, which have resulted in an overbearing, threatening accountability culture. In 2017 760,277 students sat English Language and 574,358 sat English Literature.[1] Only Maths has comparable figures. Exam success has become all-important, and schools have inevitably become overly focused on how to get the best grades at any cost. Even if English teachers have wanted to resist this, risk-averse senior management have brought them in line. The pressures on Heads of English over student exam performance have been immense. As a result, some of the conventional approaches and ways of thinking that have been the bedrock of our practices, have become supplanted by more unfamiliar, sometimes perverse 'shortcuts' to success.

---

[1] Figures from Joint Council for Qualifications Results 2017, https://www.jcq.org.uk.

This is the broad sweep of what has been happening in schools. I hope to show in more detail how some of this has played out more recently, at GCSE and at A-Level in particular, but also to demonstrate how, despite a culture that is hostile to best practice, many teachers and teacher-educators have continued to develop excellent and innovative approaches, against the odds.

Changes at GCSE

When I first started teaching in the 1970s there were two exams at 16, O-Levels and CSEs. CSEs were 100% coursework and a top grade at CSE was equivalent to a pass at O-Level. The introduction of GCSEs in 1988 provided a single, unitary exam for all abilities, with most students following specifications with 100% coursework. In 1991, tiering was brought in, with a Foundation and Higher tier providing slightly different requirements for students of different abilities. In 1994, coursework was reduced to a maximum of 40% (20% of which was oral assessment). In 2009, coursework was replaced by 'controlled assessment', where students wrote under controlled conditions and there was strong guidance about task setting. This was a DfE response to concerns about authenticity and reliability of coursework assessment. In 2015, with the introduction of a new reformed system designed by Michael Gove, tiering was abolished but alongside this, the requirements for study in English Language and English Literature were changed, with new content requirements and forms of assessment that were thought by many teachers to be inappropriate for the full range of students. The key changes were:

- The abolition of coursework (or controlled assessment) altogether.
- Speaking and listening being assessed in English Language but no longer having any contribution to the final grade.
- The loss of a discrete language component, involving knowledge *about* language. (The previous 2010 GCSE included the study of spoken language and an investigation that required some explicit knowledge of how language in use works.)
- The requirement for all students to study a complete nineteenth-century English novel.
- The proscription of American texts, including Gove's bugbear, *Of Mice and Men*, which had been studied by vast numbers of students up and down the country.
- Examination without having any of the texts available in the exam room, with all that implies about learning and memorising quotations and information.

- A requirement to answer questions on unseen texts.
- Adjustments to the, by now, well-established use of assessment objectives (AOs), as the basis for examining. Despite the Awarding Bodies stressing that they will take an holistic approach, questions in all the papers are devised with particular AOs in mind.
- Changes in the overall grading system, from a well-understood A*–G, to numerical grading 9–1, supposedly to counter grade inflation. (The future introduction of 10, 11, 12 and so on would supposedly allow for this.)
- Language and Literature GCSEs made entirely distinct, rather than overlapping. (In the past, requirements for the two subjects allowed elements to count in both exams.)
- New formulae, Progress 8 and Attainment 8, for judging achievement in schools' League Tables. Double weighting is awarded to English Language or Literature, depending which is the higher, so long as students are entered for both.

A few of these changes are worth spending more time on. First, the abolition of coursework. This had always been a powerful form of developmental work for students – a chance to work on sustained writing, rather than shorter examination responses, with the potential (admittedly not always realised by teachers) to allow students an element of choice and self-initiated study. Plagiarism issues made it problematic, as did the belief that teachers weren't to be trusted in determining marks, particularly given how high the stakes had become. These are both undoubtedly issues in universities as well, but rather than address these directly, by tackling the underlying reasons for pressure on teachers, or by attempting to reform the assessment of coursework by the Awarding Bodies, Gove decided to abolish coursework altogether. This has major implications for the nature of student work at GCSE and the development of their writing and autonomy as learners. It will also have a possible knock-on effect at A-Level, where students are likely to arrive with limited experience of self-directed work, and no experience or understanding of the process of drafting.

Second, the changes to the content of the subject. The study of a nineteenth-century novel and the proscription of all American texts have posed fresh problems for teachers of English and their students. Shakespeare, modern drama or fiction and poetry have all seemed like very sensible mainstays of study at this level and remain on the specifications. However, a full nineteenth-century novel is a less than obvious *requirement*, unless going on to study English at A-Level and beyond. Given the prevailing climate, awarding bodies and teachers have been weighing up the question of length and difficulty against that of quality, and unsurprisingly, though *Jane Eyre*, *Great Expectations* and *Frankenstein* are on the list of choices for most specifications, the vast majority of teachers have chosen either *Jekyll and Hyde* or *A Christmas Carol* for obvious pragmatic reasons. As a result, this is the experience of nineteenth-century fiction that most students are having. Are these the novels to set students' interest alight, to make them want to read more nineteenth-century fiction and go on to study English at A-Level? Though both have their merits, they are not the choices one would leap to make in order to win students over to the subject, nor are they suitable for less able students who have no interest in pursuing the subject further. A similar issue emerges in relation to American texts. While Arthur Miller's plays may not rock the world with their originality as a choice for study, they're more interesting and 'iconic' than the British equivalents that have replaced them. *A Taste of Honey*, *An Inspector Calls* (always a staple of GCSE) and *Blood Brothers* versus *The Crucible*, *A View from the Bridge* or *Death of a Salesman*? I know which would set my pulse racing, whether at the age of 15, or now.

The loss of any explicit study of language is a very disappointing development, given that the earlier requirement to investigate an aspect of language provided a significant opportunity for students to discover the pleasures it could afford. It was also a key step in the ladder of progression into Language A-Level, giving students a taste of that particular discipline within the suite of English subjects. The curriculum at Key Stage 3 and 4 now reduces knowledge about language to learning a set of linguistic terms and then, at GCSE, applying them to particular texts.

Third, the position of English Literature. At one point in the reform process, it looked as if English Literature would be a casualty of the new Attainment 8/Progress 8 system of accountability. As an ordinary subject, rather than a double-weighted core one, it would have become like any other subject, open to student choice, and given the heavy new requirements, it seemed possible that schools would advise a proportion of students not to take it. Given the new splitting of content, with no overlap between Language and Literature, students not taking Literature would have had virtually no experience of any complete literary texts beyond the age of 14. Ironically, this would have had the opposite effect to that desired by Michael Gove himself, which was to offer all students a version of our rich literary culture. When this was pointed out to the DfE, by myself and by members of the Common English Forum (a loose umbrella group of organisations with English and education at their heart), a formula was arrived at whereby English Language would only be double-weighted if it were accompanied by entry to the Literature exam, and vice versa – the double weighting applies to Literature if a student achieves a higher grade in it. The effect of this has been to secure the future of English Literature, with more students than ever before being entered for it (over 574,000 in 2017, as compared with 414,000 in 2016[2]). However, it is not without its problems. Changes to systems almost always have unforeseen consequences. Literature for all is undoubtedly a good thing, but offering a 'Gove-style' canonical Literature course to all students, regardless of ability, is already proving to be a struggle for some, and it is possible that, if results are poor, schools will reconsider the policy of entering so many pupils for it.

Finally, the continuing (mis)use of assessment objectives. I say continuing, as there is nothing all that new in this. What started in 2000 as a way of defining the key knowledge and skills of the subject (devised originally by QCA through significant consultation with teachers and university colleagues), the use of the AOs as a tool for assessment has had unforeseen consequences and become an inadvertent rod for our backs. The accountability culture has contributed to their importance growing out of all proportion. Even when Awarding Body Subject Officers and Examiners' Reports suggest flexibility and an holistic approach, anxious teachers have felt impelled to pin them down more and more closely and drill students in what is expected in ever more formulaic ways. Students are schooled in procedures for constructing paragraphs and sentences, offering students an array of acronyms: PEE (Point, Evidence, Exploration), PEEL (Point, Evidence, Exploration, Link), PETAL (Point, Evidence, Technique, Analysis, Link) and other such 'procedural', formulaic approaches to writing a literary critical response. The Assessment Objective for contextual awareness has been particularly problematic. Where marks are given for this, students (and their teachers) feel obliged to 'prove' coverage of this objective and do so, all too often, by teaching far too much 'distant' context rather than 'adjacent context' (very helpful terms supplied by Professor Peter Barry to distinguish between contextual information that is only vaguely relevant and information that is directly related and really illuminates the text under discussion). Students have been encouraged to draw examiners' attention to their coverage of the AO by starting sentences with 'Contextually,' or making other explicit uses of the word 'context', while not always making apposite use of that information. Happily, the Awarding Bodies are urging against such approaches,

---

[2] Figures from Joint Council for Qualifications Results 2017, https://www.jcq.org.uk.

and there's been a growing recognition that the best results are being denied to pupils by such routinised ways of dealing with texts in writing. Among English consultants and bloggers, there are also increasing moves to 'go beyond PEE'. There are, of course, many excellent teachers who have never regarded this as a good road to go down and have maintained sound practices throughout, but for many teachers pressure from senior management and others makes this very difficult. EMC, seeing well over a thousand teachers on its training courses every year, has always countenanced against going down the formulaic route.

Changes at A-Level

For the A-Level itself, 2015 also brought a raft of changes. The biggest has been the change to the structure of AS and A-Level, whereby AS is no longer the first half of an AL but rather a stand-alone qualification. This has had major implications for the organisation of subject teaching in schools. Initially schools continued to offer AS exams, but after the first year recognised the limited value of putting students through an exam that wouldn't count towards the full A-Level, yet would require a revisiting of the same material studied in a different context and with different exam questions. Exam entries are also expensive, which has quickened the pace of the abandonment of AS and, as of 2017, AS entries have dropped dramatically. The linear A-Level has many benefits – a two-year course, less examining that shrinks the time for teaching, students assessed at the end of two years when they've had a long run at the subject and more flexibility to organise the course as teachers see fit. One downside is the way in which doing three A-Levels is now, once again, becoming the norm. Costs of entries and of providing teaching mean that many schools and colleges are no longer offering an additional subject at AS in the way that was previously the case. This is a narrowing of breadth and also means that where students sometimes took on English as their fourth subject and then decided to pursue it further, this is no longer the case. It's an additional factor in the possible shrinkage of English candidates at AL in the future, with a potential knock-on effect for applications to university.

English as a subject now has just one piece of coursework (now called Non Examined Assessment or NEA) and only in the full A-Level course rather than the one-year AS course. What this effectively means is that a student studying English at school will have no opportunities for extended writing on a topic of their choice at GCSE and only one at A-Level. In what ways this adequately prepares them for university study, where almost all degree courses now involve dissertations and elements of continuous assessment, is a puzzle. Equally, in working life, in professional jobs, they are more likely to be expected to work on something requiring their own research and initiative, over a period of time, than the kind of instant, short, one-draft writing that is done under exam conditions. Another aspect of this is the question of equality. Exam-only assessment works to the benefit of some students more than others. Girls are often said to profit more from coursework than boys, because of their work habits and preference for this kind of work over high-stakes exams. (Interestingly, results in the June 2017 exam cycle show boys doing better than girls in top grades for the first time.)

The 'unseen texts' issue, as with GCSE, has been one other major change in the 2015 iteration of A-Level Literature. This has caused mixed feelings. At GCSE, there has been concern about less able students and the impact on them. At A-Level, however, there has been a stronger recognition that an unseen element can help to shift practices away from rote learning, formulaic approaches and over-teaching towards teaching of more authentic close reading as a cornerstone of the subject. The tendency to try to cover every base, and tell students exactly what to say and do, is countered by exams where they will come across texts they *can't* be taught in advance, where they have to apply knowledge gained over two years, and rely on their own skills and practices in reading critically. Given the shift towards drilling, I personally welcomed the enforced inclusion of unseen texts as one practical way of countering this tendency. At EMC, we have long been teaching approaches to texts, both unseen and studied, both close reading and broader brush, that encourage students to develop their own critical faculties and independence of thought. These stand them in very good stead, not only in approaching an unseen text, but also in any future study in the subject at university level. Students studying in this way are learning how to 'do' the subject. They are being introduced to the practices of the various disciplines of English, recognising that it has its own discourses and underpinning concepts and methods. If school students encounter English in this way, they are, in my view, much more likely to see the value of continuing to study it at university level, and recognise that it is a serious discipline with much more to it than just reading a pile of books and writing about them.

Concerns about Take Up of the Subject – All Three Englishes

Successive governments introduce changes but without necessarily realising that every change is likely to have unforeseen consequences. Of course, the more often you change things and the more you change at once, the greater the likelihood of seismic shifts and volcanic eruptions, with greater uncertainty about cause and effect. In the summer of 2017 there were worrying signs that enrolment for all the A-Level Englishes would be significantly lower than the previous year. In September 2017, once enrolment was well under way, EMC undertook a survey of English departments,[3] to find out exactly what had happened and elicit views about the reasons why. A total of 105 schools and colleges took part in the survey. Nearly 68% of those who responded had fewer students enrolling for A-Level Literature in September 2017 than the previous year, and this had led to nearly 29% reducing their numbers of classes or removing the offer altogether. For Language, the figure was similar, 67%, with 32% reducing the number of classes and for Lang/Lit, 61% had fewer students, with 45% reducing the numbers of classes. The reasons for this are complex, for the reasons suggested above. The teachers, unsurprisingly, suggested that the loss of AS-Levels, with students commonly now taking three rather than four (or even five) subjects was a key factor. With fewer subjects being studied overall, all subjects will inevitably shrink, so this is not just confined to the English subjects. However, other factors may well have led to English numbers dwindling more than others. The emphasis on STEM subjects, and encouragement to take them at school (as well as in student perceptions of university subjects and employability), was often quoted by respondents. But even more important was the teachers' belief that the experience of GCSE English itself had had a negative impact on students' perception of the subject. While 55% stated that they believed that the new GCSEs had prepared students for A-Level quite well (and 17% very well), many were much more troubled by the students' response to the GCSEs – even that of the most able. The content was regarded as off-putting, the subject was perceived as being difficult and highly pressurised, and this, combined with a perception that students are no longer reading for pleasure, was quoted as a major reason for the fall in numbers signing up for A-Level English subjects.

In terms of Language, Literature and Lang/Lit, all three seem to have seen a reduction in recruitment, and the main causes quoted seem to be similar (the overall drop in subjects studied, the content of GCSE English Literature and English Language, the lack of reading for pleasure and the competition from STEM subjects). However perhaps one additional issue (not explicitly questioned in the survey), is the Russell Group's 'facilitat-

---

[3] Barbara Bleiman, 'Decline and Fall? A Level English – The Figures', *Teaching English*, 15 (Autumn 2017).

ing subject' guidelines, which continues to have an effect on students' willingness to enrol for English Language.

Is English in crisis in our schools? It's perhaps too early to say, but there are warning signs, which the whole subject community needs to pay attention to. Both in the practices of the subject (under threat from a form of 'examination English' that is proving hard for teachers to resist) and in the changes to the content and structures of the subject brought about by recent government intervention, there are worrying developments. Holding on to the fundamental practices of the discipline and finding ways of ensuring that the subject remains exciting, challenging and engaging for students are two vital elements in making sure that English continues to thrive.

From A-Level to HE: Working Towards a Shared Future?

JENNY STEVENS

Student transition from post-16 to higher education is a well-established and active area of research, engaging education specialists as well as those working within university and, more rarely, secondary English departments. It is also an issue that has prompted several cross-sector initiatives, many of which serve to put schools and universities in direct touch with one another. My own interest in the interface between the two sectors came from observing the frustrations of a colleague who spent half of her week teaching A-Level English Literature and the other half teaching undergraduates at a pre-92 university: a dual role that was, and still is, highly unusual. Her accounts of some of the misunderstandings, misinformation and mythologizing that persisted on both sides of the divide, prompted me to form the English Association's University Transition Special Interest Group with the aim of fostering and sustaining dialogue between A-Level and university teachers.

I was fully aware when I initiated the group back in 2007 that we were entering potentially choppy waters. Carol Atherton, one of the leading schoolteacher-figures in transition, spoke for many in the teaching profession when she remarked: 'I get very twitchy about the issue of transition. I am uneasy with the deficit model that it seems to set up: the assumption that students are not adequately prepared for degree level study and that this is because teachers aren't doing their jobs properly.'[1] Such wariness is not without justification. In the Foreword to David Ellis's illuminating report *In at the Deep End?* (2008), Jonathan Gibson observes:

> In the past, English departments seem, on occasion, almost to have relished the discomfort of new students, seeking to induce a kind of existential trauma. Freshers were told that doing English literature at university would involve a radically new approach to texts, disturb-

---

[1] Carol Atherton, 'Coming of Age in Shakespeare: A Levels to university', *English Drama Media*, 16 (2010), 56–57 (p. 56).

ingly different from the old-fashioned nonsense they had been taught at school: it was time to grow up.[2]

Nowadays, with undergraduate recruitment and retention high on most universities' list of priorities, adopting the *de haute en bas* attitude noted above would seem more than a little unwise and, while there are doubtless some academics who hold fast to the belief that students arrive stuffed with 'old-fashioned nonsense', most manage to hold back from issuing what used to be fairly standard advice to new undergraduates: 'Unlearn everything they taught you at A-Level.'

The 'sink or swim' approach to settling in new undergraduates has its attractions, especially considering the complexities inherent in inducting a socially, educationally and culturally diverse group of students. Even in institutions where most entrants arrive clutching three or four straight A/A* grades, there is no guarantee that their readiness for degree-level English will be as comparable as their examination grades. Although all five A-Level specifications are underpinned by a compulsory core of study laid down by the Department for Education, each has its own choice of texts and approaches to assessing them – its 'unique selling-point', if you will. Once a specification has been chosen, a school department will develop its own approach to delivering it, tailored around the needs, interests and ability profile of its student body. It is, then, only reasonable to expect differing states of 'readiness' within a new undergraduate cohort. Prior learning environments add an extra layer of diversity: the student who has attained starry A-Level grades after being nurtured in groups of ten or so is likely to arrive with quite different expectations and learning habits from one who has attained the same grades in a class of twenty-five. In addition to accommodating the diverse starting-points of a typical first-year intake, universities must factor in educational reform and the impact that this can have on students' preparedness for university study. And it is at times of curriculum change that dialogue between the sixth-form and higher education sectors is especially crucial. Secondary teachers can, for example, pass on up-to-date knowledge of popular A-Level texts, thus flagging up to those tasked with designing undergraduate programmes the works best avoided (freshers may welcome the comforting familiarity of A-Level texts on their undergraduate reading list, but those who teach them are unlikely to welcome the recycled sixth-form essays in their marking pile).

---

[2] David Ellis, *In at the Deep End? The First Year in Undergraduate English Literature* (London: English Subject Centre, 2008), p. 2.

The education reforms of 2000 and 2008 offered opportunities to ease the transition from Key Stage 5 to university English by reframing and reconceptualizing the way the subject was assessed at A-Level. However, judging by reports from those currently teaching in higher education, these reforms have had relatively little impact on how readily first-year students adapt to undergraduate study. How far this can be put down to Awarding Organizations failing to wholeheartedly embrace the spirit of the changes in their specification designs, or to an unwillingness on the part of teachers – and indeed students – to move away from traditional approaches, is a matter for debate. The fact remains that there are several distinct difficulties that students continue to encounter: the amount of prescribed reading; engaging with secondary sources (especially theoretical writing); dependency on assessment objectives, often viewed as an unfortunate consequence of 'teaching to the test'. While there are several other common 'complaints' that could be added to the list, those around students' reluctance to develop as autonomous readers and writers seem to be the most enduring.

One of the driving principles behind the 2015 large-scale reform of A-Level was that universities should take an active role in qualification development. In a letter to Ofqual's Chief Regulator, the then Secretary of State, Michael Gove, wrote:

> It is essential that new A levels command the respect of leading universities: I would therefore expect that Awarding Organisations should draw on the expertise of university academics in making any changes to curriculum content[.]³

Leaving aside the implication that only 'leading' universities need have faith in A-Level, Gove's pronouncement did at least ensure that universities had a say in the qualifications which determine the applicants they select. As it turned out, all three English A-Levels were placed in 'Category 2' of Professor Mark Smith's report to Ofqual ('a subject with minor, but substantive changes'), and the subsequent alterations made to the subject content and assessment methods were, indeed, relatively 'minor'.⁴ Yet if the changes made at subject level were modest, those introduced at quali-

³ Rt Hon Michael Gove MP to Glenys Stacey, 14 March 2013.
⁴ Mark E. Smith, *Independent Chair's report on the review of current GCE 'specification content' within subject criteria*, July 2013, p. 8, <http://webarchive. nationalarchives.gov.uk/20141111122712/http:/ofqual.gov.uk/files/2013-09-06-smith-review-of-specification-content-july-2013.pdf> [accessed 16 September 2017].

fication level were anything but. The move back to a linear model has brought with it a narrowing of the sixth-form curriculum, with the typical A-Level profile now being three, rather than four, subjects. The stand-alone AS qualification, which could serve to maintain breadth, appears to be dead in the water. On A- Level results day 2017, the General Secretary of the ASCL, Geoff Barton, pronounced some stark truths:

> Against a funding crisis, which is especially severe at post-16 level, few schools can afford to run a separate suite of AS levels – hence the big decline we have seen in entries this year. Any school and college leader will tell you that if you make cuts, you target the smallest courses first. Thus the rejection of the broadening principles of the AS and the need to reduce costs means that small subjects are in spiralling decline at A level.[5]

The 'small subjects' that Barton mentions here include Film Studies, Drama and Theatre Studies, and Media Studies, all of which introduce students to ways of thinking that they may well encounter in English undergraduate courses. Moreover, the reduction in subject range that comes with linearity does little to promote student confidence when they encounter the interdisciplinary approaches of many university modules.

Focusing specifically on the transition implications of the new English Literature A-Level, the reduction of mandatory texts for study from twelve to eight, looks unlikely to equip students better for the breadth of reading required at university. And while, ideally, it frees up time for wider sixth-form reading, the pressures exerted on teachers by account-ability measures mean that the more probable scenario will be that 'doing' eight prescribed books will fill up most of the scheduled learning time, with students continuing to be overly dependent on assessment objec-tives. The assessment-facing mindset, often considered an impediment to transition, can be traced back to Curriculum 2000 when a set of state-ments defining the knowledge, skills and understanding that candidates needed to demonstrate in the final examinations and coursework formed a compulsory framework for all specifications. As with most innovations in education, responses to this new millennium approach ranged from warmly welcoming to downright hostile. Back in 2010, I was invited to take part in a BBC Radio 4 programme, *How to get an A**, a media

---

[5] Geoff Barton, 'As our country becomes more insular, so, it seems, does its curric-ulum', 2017, <https://www.tes.com/news/school-news/breaking-views/results-day-our-country-becomes-more-insular-so-it-seems-does-its-curriculum> [accessed 16 September 2017].

project that veered more towards the hostile than the welcoming. Its central gimmick was that an experienced A-Level marker (namely me) would grade answers on *Hamlet* produced in examination conditions by two celebrity Shakespeareans: an eminent theatre director and a rather less eminent stage actor. Applying an authentic mark scheme, I awarded both candidates middling B grades, and then steeled myself to announce the results on air. That the actor received the news with good grace and the director rather less so is beside the point. What became clear to me, as I explained why a straightforward description of the play and its characters no longer cuts the mustard, was that assessment objectives have done more good than harm. To quote Robert Eaglestone, they are an attempt 'to make the subject transparent (rather than hidden, confusing and "passed down from master to student", as it were)'.[6] The challenge for today's A-level teacher is to strike a balance between making assessment objectives the departure point for all classroom activities and neglecting them entirely, thus putting candidate outcomes in jeopardy.

Another aspect of university English frequently identified as problematic for new undergraduates is reading and applying literary theory. As Gary Snapper observes of the first-year theory course that he attended as part of his doctoral study of the relationships between A-Level English Literature and university English:

> The anthology of literary theory, which constituted the core set text of the module, was simply too difficult for students to negotiate without considerable mediation, which was not forthcoming [...]. A Level English Literature has, until very recently, provided little in the way of precedent; indeed, many students have gone through an entire A Level Literature course without encountering literary criticism, never mind literary theory.[7]

Although two of the current assessment objectives (AO4: 'Demonstrate understanding of the significance and influence of the contexts in which literary texts are written and received' and AO5: 'Explore literary texts informed by different interpretations') encourage a theorized approach, the style-character-theme paradigm remains alive and well in some English classrooms. This is puzzling, given that a sizeable proportion of today's

---

[6] Robert Eaglestone, 'What Do We Teach When We Teach English?', *The Use of English*, 67 (2016), 4–12 (p. 11).
[7] Gary Snapper, 'Beyond English Literature A Level: The silence of the seminar?', *English in Education*, 43:3 (2009), 192–210 (p. 205).

teachers will have taken core literary theory modules as part of their degree programme, learning that one might expect to inform and influence their teaching practice. Perhaps what prevents any direct feed-through is teachers' reluctance to leave behind the security that comes from following ready-made departmental schemes of work. At a time when pay and promotion depend to a large extent on examination results, branching out from tried-and-tested methods, geared towards examination success, is not for the faint-hearted. Yet even those A-Level teachers who *are* willing to risk bringing their university training into the classroom might well be working towards assessment tasks that have barely changed in decades. Take, for example, three questions on *The Tempest* set by the same board over a period of twenty years:

June 1997 (pre-Curriculum 2000)
'A strange mixture of the poetical and the absurd, the pathetic and the savagely evil.' How far do you agree with this analysis of Caliban?
June 2007 (Curriculum 2000)
Discuss the significance of Stephano and Trinculo in *The Tempest*.
June 2017 (current curriculum)
'Caliban is a troubling mixture of brutality and sensitivity.' Using your knowledge of the play as a whole, show how far you agree with this view of Caliban.

While it is only fair to register that there are other questions on offer, which invite a broader, more conceptually based response, it is evident from this snapshot that the 'character question' remains a safety net for those candidates schooled in traditional ways of reading.

Modes of assessment, like some question-setting, have also remained static. Recent research into the differences in assessment between A-Level and university English found that

> Despite the reforms, the range of assessment types used in the reformed A level was very similar to the current [pre-2015] A level. Although there is some increase in the number of assessments students would encounter, there is little increase in the variety. Overall, at university, there was more variety in comparison to A level English literature.[8]

---

[8] Frances Wilson *et al.*, 'Assessing the transition between school and university: Differences in assessment between A level and university in English', *Arts and Humanities in Higher Education*, 16:2 (2017), 188–208 (p. 199).

It is true to say that while universities have gone some way to expanding their assessment methods beyond the traditional essay, A-Level, if anything, has gone into reverse. The reduction of non-examination assessment (formerly known as 'coursework') from 40% to 20% has limited students' opportunities for independent work and, as this reduction applies to subjects across the board, it is bound to impact on the research and writing skills of new undergraduates. Oral assessment, a feature of the International Baccalaureate for many years, has never, to the best of my knowledge, been given any serious consideration for A-Level; if anything, with oracy now downgraded at GCSE, the possibility of adopting any non-written form of assessment looks even more remote. And while there are still recreative writing options on offer in two specifications for the non-examination component, the relative lack of teacher support for this alternative to the conventional essay makes it a daunting choice for the risk-averse.

At a time when English A-Level numbers are falling about 6–7% year on year, a decline that will undoubtedly affect future undergraduate numbers, it is more important than ever that those in the post-16 and university sectors work together to promote the health and strength of the subject. One key imperative is to protect the status of all three qualifications that make up the suite of English subjects. Gove's exclusion of English Language and English Language and Literature from the list of 'facilitating subjects' was a deeply regrettable move, not least because, as one Admissions Tutor points out, this list 'sets up an implicit hierarchy of "hard" and "soft" subjects.'[9] In an educational climate that sees students and parents carefully weighing up the 'value' of their A-Level and degree choices in terms of employability potential, 'hard' subjects will usually win out. The consequences of a decline in take-up of qualifications involving English language study should not be overlooked. As Andrea Macrae and Billy Clark point out in their report on integrating language and literature:

> Though undergraduate Literature courses increasingly involve some language study [...], many graduates of Literature courses studied language explicitly only at GCSE level, and even at this level such study lacked even the most basic kinds of language analysis. Due to the absence of linguistic literacy from the national curriculum for so long, many teachers may lack the knowledge (or confidence in that knowledge) to teach aspects of language study at A-level.[10]

[9] Greg Myers, 'English Language, facilitating subjects, and the review of A Levels', *Use of English*, 65 (2013), 48–55 (p. 51).
[10] Andrea Macrae and Billy Clark, *Lang/Lit from A to BA: Integrating Language and Literature Study at School and University* (Higher Education Academy, 2014), p. 7.

With the 2015 GCSE English Language offering even less continuity with higher-level study than its predecessor, it is unlikely that this situation will improve any time soon. In this respect, transition initiatives such as the Integrating English project run by Billy Clark, Marcello Giovanelli and Andrea Macrae, provide a vital point of contact for those teaching 'Englishes' excluded from the 'facilitating' category.

Another imperative is to ensure that accountability measures in schools and colleges do not become the main drivers of teaching and learning. In an article that should be required reading for every English teacher in the land, Simon Gibbons sums up the realities of many teachers' lives today:

> If as a teacher one can convince oneself that the ministers and civil servants are right, or at least reconcile oneself to a belief that they are acting in the interests of all children, a career as an English teacher is bearable. To cling to any alternative view leads to frustration and probably to work outside the profession; there doesn't appear to be space any more for alternative – leave alone radical – thinking about the teaching of English. The thinking has been done, and if you're a successful teacher you take on the strategies and succeed; if you don't succeed you're probably not a very good teacher and the examination results will damn you to performance management hell.[11]

Mitigating this bleak state of affairs requires the concerted effort of those involved in teaching English at all levels. Subject associations and organizations such as the English and Media Centre do invaluable work in presenting inspiring alternatives to exam-focused teaching and learning; transition groups also have a key role to play, not least in keeping both sectors informed about key issues that might affect them: forewarned is forearmed. Academics need to know, for example, that the current GCSE English Literature is deterring some students from taking the subject through to A-Level, thus reducing the pool of potential applicants for English degree courses. Likewise, A-Level teachers need to be more informed about how English courses are organized, taught and assessed if they are to prepare their students for the step-up to higher-level study. Involving teachers more regularly in the stopping-off points between sixth-form and university (outreach events, university websites, open days, summer reading lists) would be just one way that this could be achieved. And those schools and colleges employing individuals with

---

[11] Simon Gibbons, 'W(h)ither the Radicals?', *English in Education*, 50:1 (2016), 35–43 (p. 36).

university teaching experience should do all they can to exploit their Janus-like perspective.

As we all manage ever-increasing workloads, there are bound to be times when finding time to liaise with colleagues in another sector will be way down the urgent list. But once channels of communication are firmly established, transition activities can be made to fit around the rhythms of the year. Less hectic periods might offer opportunities for exchange visits or conferences, while busy times might only allow for brief, though nonetheless purposeful, emailing. Social media, too, offers huge scope for transition initiatives to take shape or to be publicized. It was clear from the discussions that went on both formally and informally at the English: Shared Futures conference that there is much to be gained from cross-sector dialogue and that time devoted to sharing ideas around transition will always be time well spent.

English Outreach: Academics in the Classroom

CATHERINE REDFORD

English in Crisis: Can Outreach Help?

In the summer of 2017, as teachers, academics and other members of the wider English community met at the 'Shared Futures' conference, Year 11s across the country sat their examinations for the new reformed English GCSE. Graded with a numerical system of 9–1, the new course is designed to be more demanding and to stretch able students: coursework has been abolished, all examinations are closed-book, and there is an increased emphasis on the 'classics' of British literature. At the same time, the introduction of the new linear A-Level requires Key Stage 5 students to sit all of their examinations at the end of a two-year course, rather than in the stages facilitated by the previous AS system, and sees a reduction in coursework. Creative Writing did not survive the A-Level reforms. Critics of these changes have argued that they risk placing English studies in crisis and, indeed, there is already evidence to suggest that some students are being put off pursuing higher-level qualifications in English. A recent study conducted by John Gordon at the University of East Anglia's School of Education revealed that many pupils find the new literature GCSE off-putting and confusing, preventing them from having the kinds of discussions that allow them to enjoy the texts they are required to study.[1] This may well have a knock-on effect on the number of students choosing to study English at A-Level, with entries in 2017 already having dropped by 11.1% for English Language and Literature, 10.2% for English Language, and 4.7% for English Literature.[2] Bill Watkin, chief executive of the Sixth Form Colleges Association, fears that the 'love of the subject' that inspires students to continue English to A-Level is in 'danger of being

---

[1] Adi Bloom, 'New English GCSE "may be putting pupils off reading"', *Times Educational Supplement*, <https://www.tes.com/news/school-news/breaking-news/new-english-gcse-may-be-putting-pupils-reading> [accessed September 2017].
[2] Eleanor Busby, 'A-level results 2017: Politics entries surge by 12.8 per cent', *Times Educational Supplement*, <https://www.tes.com/news/school-news/breaking-news/a-level-results-2017-politics-entries-surge-128-cent> [accessed September 2017].

overshadowed' by the more rigid standards now expected.[3] Against this backdrop of educational reform, we also face an increased government-backed emphasis on the supposed superiority of STEM subjects and the accompanying perception that the study of English is only useful if it is skills-based and relevant to 'real life'.[4]

As many English departments in universities across the UK encounter a corresponding decline in applications, an increasing number of academics are considering how we can connect with younger students by offering educational outreach. Before seeking to build relationships with schools, though, it is vital that academics interrogate their reasons for reaching out beyond the academy, as these motivations will inevitably need to be taken into account when designing useful and engaging forms of outreach. Some English departments are seeking to work with students as a means by which to recruit for their programmes. For GCSE and A-Level students with little awareness of the richness and diversity of education offered by an English degree, this can be a useful way of sampling the opportunities offered by higher-level study. This form of outreach, however, has its limits, in that it will perhaps only be targeted at those who have been recognised as having the potential to progress to university and, in the case of programmes exclusively aimed at A-Level students, those who have already elected to study English beyond the level that is compulsory. It is worth our while considering how outreach programmes can be opened out to a wider range of students with the more general aim of promoting a life-long interest in English, with all of the benefits that this carries with it. In doing so, we seek to develop what Adrian Barlow, President of the English Association, has termed the 'community of English': a collection of readers – spanning school pupils, university students, teachers, and academics – reflecting upon what and how we read.[5]

It is vital to be open-minded and flexible when it comes to forming our understanding of how this community should function and flourish. It is certainly not a hierarchical grouping. Working with younger students can benefit academics by helping them to develop their pedagogical

[3] Billy Camden, 'English A-level applications drop 35% due to new "harder" GCSEs', *Schools Week*, <https://schoolsweek.co.uk/english-a-level-applications-drop-35-due-to-new-harder-gcses/> [accessed September 2017].

[4] Andrew Otty, 'The tyranny of "relevance" is razing English to the ground', *Times Educational Supplement*, <https://www.tes.com/news/further-education/breaking-views/tyranny-relevance-razing-english-ground> [accessed September 2017].

[5] Adrian Barlow, 'The Community of English', *Issues in English*, 12 (2017), 3–5 (p. 3).

skills, for example; it can prove surprisingly challenging to explain one's research to a less specialised – but often simultaneously less rigid and more creative – audience. Likewise, outreach need not involve academics working directly with school pupils at all; by focusing their attention on teachers, university lecturers can open up the latest developments in the field to colleagues in the wider English community who otherwise would find it very difficult to gain access to recent research. In turn, teachers can foster a mutually beneficial relationship by helping academics to understand the modern Key Stage 4 and 5 education system: this knowledge will not only aid academics when designing outreach programmes, but will also enable universities to support their first-year students in the transition from A-Level to degree-level study.

It is essential that academics should consider the backgrounds of the students with whom they are engaging during outreach work, whether that work is being carried out for recruitment purposes or to benefit and nourish the wider community of English. As Jane Rickard (University of Leeds) noted at 'Shared Futures', we should aim to work particularly with young people from disadvantaged backgrounds while being mindful of the challenges that these students may encounter, such as being unable to afford to buy books or fearing the debt associated with a non-vocational degree. If we fail to reach out to these students and draw their attention to the benefits of reading generally, and the advantages of pursuing the higher-level study of English more specifically, we risk losing diversity not only among our student body but also among our future teachers and academics of English.[6]

Planning Outreach: Obstacles and Opportunities

If this is a particularly opportune moment to be thinking about the ways in which the community of English can work more closely together, fostering relationships and engaging in dialogue, then it is also vital that the academics reaching out to schools do so in an appropriate and helpful way. It is important that they liaise directly with teachers when designing outreach sessions, taking into account the demands of the curriculum and the way in which the topic is to be assessed. Academics may well wish to introduce school students to texts and authors beyond the curriculum, but

[6] Jane Rickard, 'English Outreach and Widening Participation', paper given as part of the 'Academics in the Classroom: How Can Universities Deliver English Outreach for Schools?' panel at the 'English: Shared Futures' conference, 7 July 2017.

28 ENGLISH: SHARED FUTURES

they should be mindful of how they do this and be aware that – for students used to studying a single text over several weeks or months – it can be potentially intimidating to be asked to discuss new ideas out of context or with no preparation. This is not to say that we cannot take innovative approaches in outreach sessions; indeed, school students can really relish the challenge of looking at a text in a way that is new to them. In my own outreach work, for example, I often work with students who are studying Mary Shelley's *Frankenstein*; by showing these students pages from the manuscript and introducing them to the lively editorial process at work behind this novel, I try both to reinforce the ideas that they have already been forming in the classroom and help them to develop their thinking and consider the text from a new perspective.

For school students used to studying in a classroom setting with a figure of authority leading a teaching session, it can be intimidating to be catapulted into a university-style seminar with an academic who facilitates discussion rather than teaches. Lecturers who run outreach sessions may find that they need to provide younger students with more reassurance and guidance than they would for an undergraduate group, perhaps following what Jerome Bruner terms a 'spiral' path of learning,[7] whereby structuring concepts are, in the words of Trevor Hussey and Patrick Smith, 'encountered repeatedly in a spiral process involving the redefinition of fundamental ideas and concepts at evermore sophisticated levels of understanding and application'.[8] It can also be a very positive experience to run the session alongside the classroom teacher, with the two colleagues bringing together their different skills and areas of expertise in order to help the students get the most out of the session. However the session is structured, it is crucial that students are left with a sense of how they can follow up and continue to contemplate the issues covered. A detailed handout can be a useful revision aid, as can an annotated bibliography. Where possible, the potential secondary sources listed should be available freely and electronically, as many school and local libraries are facing closure or do not have the funds to stock expensive academic volumes.

While outreach programmes should ideally be sustained, this is not always possible: schools may simply not be able to release their students from the demands of the curriculum for anything more than a one-off interaction, and academics themselves are under a great deal of pressure in

---

[7] Jerome Bruner, *The Process of Education* (Cambridge, MA and London: Harvard University Press, 1960; 1999), p. 13.
[8] Trevor Hussey and Patrick Smith, 'The Uses of Learning Outcomes', *Teaching in Higher Education*, 8:3 (2003), 357–68 (p. 362).

terms of the amount of teaching, research and administration that they are expected to undertake. With some careful planning, however, one-off sessions can be successful. One of the key barriers to overcome is the fact that students can be nervous of working with someone unknown, especially if they believe that the academic is expecting them immediately to demonstrate evidence of thinking at a 'higher' level. In addition to working closely with our teacher colleagues in order to ensure that the session is pitched at the correct level and covers relevant ideas and material, it can also be very useful to listen carefully to the students with whom we work: what would they like to cover in the session? By engaging in genuine dialogue with students, we avoid inadvertently setting ourselves up as the arrogant 'experts' with all the answers. We consequently open up channels that enable students, teachers and academics alike to share different ideas and illuminate texts in new ways that are mutually beneficial for us all. When I first started to run my own outreach sessions, I was very rigid in my approach to what we should cover and what I wanted the students to gain from our discussions, even going so far as to replicate the lesson objectives that I knew students were used to working with at school. By ultimately dispensing with these restrictions, I found myself able to enjoy a freer and more flexible dialogue with school students; after all, one of the great joys of outreach is that it allows students, teachers and academics to come together as a group and consider texts that perhaps otherwise feel rather tired and familiar in a way that revitalises our thinking. It is helpful if students are given the opportunity to express their own opinions early on in a session in order to give them confidence and encourage them to talk, especially if the topic is likely to prompt different opinions across the group and lead to lively debate. When working with students on the *Frankenstein* manuscripts, for example, I always ask what the students make of the fact that the novel was edited by Percy Shelley: do they think that his changes were any good, but also do they think that he had the authority to alter the text in the first place? This has led to some very interesting and sophisticated discussions covering not only the dynamic between Mary and Percy Shelley, but also the idea of authorship and the concept of authority over a text's interpretation more widely.

The 'Academics in the Classroom' Project

Over the course of running my own small-scale outreach projects over several years, I realised that many academics were doing similar work but that there was little opportunity for us to share experiences and expertise. Crucially, I also felt frustrated that outreach sessions were often being designed and run without input from teachers themselves. For these reasons, in 2016 I launched 'Academics in the Classroom', a British Academy-funded project that aimed to bring early career researchers together with teachers of Key Stage 4 and 5 English in order to strengthen links between schools and universities, foster dialogue between the different members of the English community, and support students in their study of English.[9] 'Academics in the Classroom' commenced with a residential workshop for sixty teachers, early career academics, and other interested parties (including representatives from the English Association, the Globe Theatre, the British Library and the Brontë Parsonage Museum). Over the course of two days, the group heard about current outreach projects; the new GCSE and A-Level curricula; the latest pedagogical research; the transition from A-Level to university; public engagement with research; and working with external organisations such as libraries, theatres and museums.

The workshop was designed to provide multiple opportunities for networking and discussion, and two key conclusions were drawn by the group. The first of these was that, while it can be a very powerful thing for school students to work directly with academics (whether in a school setting or during a visit to a university), teachers and academics should also maintain a dialogue, sharing expertise and seeking to collaborate wherever possible. While the two groups currently have their own networks and opportunities for professional development, we rarely genuinely work together in order to improve the teaching of English across the secondary and tertiary sectors. An outcome of this discussion was the creation of the 'Academics in the Classroom' mailing list, which teachers and academics can use to build connections in their local area and beyond, design outreach projects in collaboration, and advertise opportunities.[10] The second conclusion reached was that – given that school students frequently turn to the internet as their first port of call when researching a text or author – we should be doing more in terms of online outreach. Many of the teachers at the conference expressed concern that their students were forced to use poor-quality free online resources in their work, and also explained that they themselves were often unable to access the

[9] I am grateful to the British Academy for the British Academy Rising Star Engagement Award that funded this project in full and for the support of Hertford College, Oxford, who hosted the conference. My thanks are also due to Adrian Barlow and Vincent Gillespie, both of whom gave generously of their time to advise on the project.
[10] Anyone wishing to join this mailing list should email catherine.redford@ hertford.ox.ac.uk.

latest research in their field, owing to paywall restrictions and the prohibitive cost of scholarly books. The group discussed the merits of projects such as the British Library's 'Discovering Literature' website – which provides open-access short articles written especially for school students by leading academics – and concluded that digital outreach is a particularly time-efficient and useful way for universities to engage students and their teachers with current research.

Over twenty individual projects – all of which saw teachers and academics collaborating to improve English outreach – developed from the conversations held at the 'Academics in the Classroom' workshop and in the following months. Velda Elliott (University of Oxford) organised a 'Texts and Teachers' event, which allowed teachers and early career academics to discuss the latest research on Key Stage 5 set texts and consider how this might inform the way in which we teach these texts to A-Level students. Alice Wood (De Montfort University) and Tom Mummery (Ashby School) organised an English enrichment day for Year 13 students that included research-led academic sessions and the opportunity for the students to work in De Montfort University's archives. Peter Auger (Queen Mary University of London) has not only worked with various teachers to deliver outreach sessions based on his research in schools, but has also set up an outreach component to his online 'Early Modern Boundaries' project; teacher Will McAdam (Lambeth Academy) has in turn used this network to build connections with academics that will help him to develop a further digital outreach project. Ushashi Dasgupta (University of Oxford), who had already carried out some innovative outreach work for schoolchildren with the Dickens Museum in Bloomsbury prior to the workshop, has continued to support schools in their promotion of Dickens by working with Annaliese Elphick (Westcliff High School for Boys) to provide an enrichment lecture for a study day. Other teachers and academics have created formal hubs and piloted collaborative projects that will benefit not only the students currently studying English at A-Level and GCSE, but will also support those who study the subject in future years.

Future Steps

From the online outreach project 'Peripeteia', which allows A-Level students to interact directly with academics, to the way in which the 'Definite Article' blog makes English language research freely available to those teaching the subject in schools, there are multiple ground-breaking projects that are currently working to bring school students, teachers, and academics together in our appreciation of English. The conversations held at 'Academics in the Classroom', 'Shared Futures' and beyond demonstrated that there is a drive from both schools and universities to strengthen this relationship further as we collectively work to promote the study of English and encourage school students to continue to read long after their formal education has ended. Teachers and academics should continue their dialogue and make space to exchange ideas, recognising that we are not aiming to instruct each other but rather to share our knowledge and discuss how it may be actively used by other members of the community. We need to be open-minded about new outreach opportunities by keeping ourselves updated about how the subject is taught and assessed at various levels, as this will inform the direction and methods of our collaborative outreach. How can universities support teachers in helping school students to develop the research skills that they need to complete the EPQ (Extended Project Qualification), for example? Are there innovative ways in which academics can develop free, high-quality resources for schools at a time when educational budgets are being slashed and the cutting-edge research being carried out at universities is often inaccessible to schoolchildren and their teachers? Can teachers help academics to better understand the way in which English is now taught in schools and encourage them to facilitate an easier transition from A-Level to degree-level for students? By working together – and understanding the challenges that our colleagues in other areas of the sector face – we can ensure that our community as a whole thrives in the future.

From Provider to Stager:
The Future of Teaching English in HE

BENJAMIN A. BRABON

Man's yesterday may ne'er be like his morrow;
Nought may endure but Mutability.[1]

With the rise of the gig economy, pop-up experiences and 'espresso learning', change has become a constant condition of life in 'liquid modernity'.[2]
Higher Education in the UK has experienced seismic shifts over the last
three decades that have had a significant impact on our understanding of
the Humanities more broadly and English specifically as a discipline. From
the now familiar narratives of crisis conceived in Widdowson's *Re-Reading
English* (1982), Guy and Small's *Politics and Values in English Studies:
A Discipline in Crisis?* (1993) and Scholes's *The Rise and Fall of English:
Reconstructing English as a Discipline* (1998), English has for some time
been enmeshed in a debate about the condition of the subject – literally
and figuratively – as the so-called 'theory wars' called into question not
only the purpose of the study of English, but also how it should be taught
in university and beyond.[3] English in all its forms, including English
Studies, English Language, English Literature or Literature in English
and Creative Writing, is defined conceivably as homogenous in its het-
erogeneity, as different institutions and courses prioritise diverse critical
and thematic inflections, genres, cultural contexts and historical periods.
At the same time, the demands of the skills economy in the UK have,
up to this point, deflected attention away from the Humanities towards
STEM and/or STEAM. These intrinsic and extrinsic forces in play have

---

[1] Percy Bysshe Shelley, 'Mutability', in *The Complete Poetical Works of Percy
Bysshe Shelley*, vol. III (John Slark, 1885), <https://www.poetryfoundation.
org/poems/54563/mutability-we-are-as-clouds-that-veil-the-midnight-moon>
[accessed 12 January 2018].
[2] See Zygmunt Bauman, *Liquid Modernity* (London: Polity Press, 2000).
[3] Peter Widdowson, *Re-Reading English* (London: Methuen, 1982); Josephine
Guy and Ian Small, *Politics and Values in English Studies: A Discipline in Crisis?*
(Cambridge: Cambridge University Press, 1993); Robert E. Scholes, *The Rise and
Fall of English: Reconstructing English as a Discipline* (New Haven and London:
Yale University Press, 1988).

exerted pressure on the subject to confront its historic limitations and to open up, not only the canon, but also the curriculum or syllabus – to use Raymond Williams's modulation of that term – to global interventions that have redefined English in a university setting.

As I contest in this essay, the war of words that defines the history of the study and teaching of English in HE is the lifeblood of innovation and adaptability that, in what only can be conceived as a metonymic twist of fate, does not just feed its future evolution, but also supports the graduate competencies and emotional intelligence that are so highly valued by employers. In other words, the interrogative stance of English as a discipline – the criticality that it fosters – is an asset to be celebrated in a 'post-truth' world, rather than the nub of an ongoing crisis that perennially tolls its death and the death of the Humanities more broadly. Fundamentally, English graduates have a role to play in fashioning societies where curiosity, creativity and questioning drive innovation and progress for all, so that humanity does not drift towards 'resigned compliance' in a neoliberal age.[4] Within this context, the study of English can still act as a tonic against the 'death of critical thought' identified by Giroux,[5] because it is the 'transactions between affect and knowledge, conscious and unconscious thought, that provide the subject with its transformative vigour, its edginess and danger'.[6] English as a discipline holds words to account in an age when there is, increasingly, a disingenuous disjunction between words and affect, an age in which 'fake news' have become 'real facts'.

Beyond this time-honoured relationship with words, English also speaks to an employability agenda that does not in itself value, for example, the study of the eighteenth-century novel, but rather so-called 'softer' skills that are being aligned by a number of UK HEIs with distinctive graduate competencies or attributes. At the same time, English as a subject needs to remain nimble and flexible in order to continue to adapt to ongoing and emerging debates about alternative degree structures and modes of delivery. The renewed interest in accelerated two-year degrees and degree apprenticeships should be seen as an opportunity for the Humanities, and for English specifically, to reimagine itself once again and innovate through curriculum design that speaks directly to the needs of the skills economy. In so doing, English as a discipline must put to one side criti-

[4] Jeremy Gilbert, 'What Kind of Thing is "Neoliberalism?"', *New Formations: A Journal of Culture, Theory & Politics*, 80–81 (2013), 7–22 (p. 13).
[5] Henry A. Giroux, *On Critical Pedagogy* (London: Continuum, 2011), p. 167.
[6] Ben Knights, ed., *Teaching Literature: Text and Dialogue in the English Classroom* (London: Palgrave, 2017), p. 7.

cism that aims to prioritise 'hard' subjects over 'soft' as an out-of-touch conception of the nature of employability in the twenty-first century, and connect the often perceived intangible set of skills developed, with a tangible range of competencies, emotional intelligence and behaviours that graduates of English degree programmes utilise in their careers. As Ian Diamond makes clear in the foreword to the British Academy's report on *The Right Skills: Celebrating Skills in the Arts, Humanities and Social Sciences*, this should not be understood solely in the context of economic need for the individual or the nation, and educational professionals should think again about how they develop and support students to make a valuable contribution to an inclusive society as engaged citizens. For Diamond, 'at a time when societies across the world are ever more diverse and where the need for inclusive social policies are paramount, the skills that come from graduates of the arts, humanities and social sciences become ever more critical to the creation of the sort of society to which we would all like to belong'.[7]

With over 50% of global leaders with arts, humanities and social science degrees and 62% of political candidates at the last UK general election with an AHSS background, there remains a significant opportunity for academics in these areas to shape future leaders through effective curriculum design and delivery that speaks not only to the needs of the UK's economy, but also society.[8] Alongside the leadership attributes that are evidently nurtured more broadly in AHSS degrees, enterprising and creative mindsets; a capacity to appropriately judge self-efficacy and to give and receive feedback effectively; intellectual curiosity; proficiency in finding, evaluating, analysing and applying data; international awareness and openness to the world, based on appreciation of social and cultural diversity, respect for human rights and dignity, to name but a few, are all cultivated in an unique way within English degree programmes. As far as the application of these abilities within a career context is concerned, the distinctive flavour of the discipline will not for most graduates who move beyond academia be defined by content, but rather in the ways in which these aptitudes connect with multiple career paths that reflect the real-world conditions of a portfolio career. For example, Luke Ramm's recent case study for the British Academy on a career in advertising accentuates how the bedrock of skills fostered throughout an English Literature degree are a firm foundation on which to build a career in advertising:

---

[7] *The Right Skills: Celebrating Skills in the Arts, Humanities and Social Sciences* (London: British Academy, 2017), p. 3.
[8] See *The Right Skills*, p. 11.

It's the ability to see art and culture 'turning a mirror on itself' which he believes to be a key skill in creating genuinely impactful and worthwhile advertising. The ability both to articulate and deconstruct a story proves essential when building an advertising campaign, something which relies on identifying a real-world insight, or cultural tension, and constructing an engaging narrative around it. Similarly, the way in which English Literature teaches us to reason, and sell our point with convincing, well-referenced arguments is a vital component of the creative pitch process, persuading clients and internal stakeholders, to buy work.[9]

The abilities of an English Literature graduate outlined by Ramm bring together the economic and social articulations of a set of aptitudes that hinge upon an a/effective quality that connects with individuals and transfigures them into consumers. Within the above context, an effective English Literature degree programme combines seamlessly the study of texts with the study of life, so that the affective qualities of 'real-world insight' and an understanding of the subject/people are commodified through the creative advertising process.

This 'affective turn' that has been witnessed more widely through the rise of the *experience economy* raises questions about curriculum design and approaches to learning and teaching.[10] If 'an experience occurs when a company intentionally uses services as the stage, and goods as props, to engage individual customers in a way that creates a memorable event', then HE providers will have to do more to reimagine curricula so that they speak to the economic and social conditions that underpin the experience of student success not just during their degrees, but also throughout their lives.[11] The affective qualities of the aptitudes nurtured in English degree programmes speak directly to the shifting terrain of the experience economy and its impact upon HE. There is an opportunity for English to frame its signature pedagogy – which still utilises the power of close reading, along with emotive and reasoned worldly insights into texts – within the context of the quest for memorable experiences and sensations that define economies of affect.

[9] *The Right Skills*, p. 31.
[10] For more on the experience economy, see B. Joseph Pine II and James H. Gilmore, 'Welcome to the Experience Economy', *Harvard Business Review*, July–August 1998, <https://hbr.org/1998/07/welcome-to-the-experience-economy> [accessed 12 January 2018].
[11] 'Welcome to the Experience Economy', <https://hbr.org/1998/07/welcome-to-the-experience-economy> [accessed 12 January 2018].

As one of the four realms of experience – along with entertainment, aesthetic and escapist – there is a need for more research into the role of education in the experience economy, particularly within an HE context. The altered relationships between the seller and the buyer, or the HE institution/individual tutor and the student, are readily conceivable. In this model, the language of educational provider metamorphoses into the concept of the 'stager', who presents an educational experience that continues to evolve and unfold well beyond graduation. Here, graduate skills are not static and contained by the assessment of intended learning outcomes, but instead, are 'staged' as attributes and behaviours that are more resilient to the shifting sands of economic whimsy and fickleness. The student too is no longer the customer understood in terms of a simple exchange of a service in return for a fee, but instead, a 'guest' who experiences the theatre of Higher Education. As Pine and Gilmore note:

> While prior economic offerings – commodities, goods, and service – are external to the buyer, experiences are inherently personal, existing only in the mind of an individual who has been engaged on an emotional, physical, intellectual, or even spiritual level. Thus, no two people can have the same experience, because each experience derives from the interaction between the staged event (like a theatrical play) and the individual's state of mind.[12]

Here the challenge for the 'stager' within the context of learning and teaching in HE is to design a programme that speaks to the individual's sense of self, as a memorable sensation that can be experienced at a personal level – a challenge that English as a discipline is well prepared to respond to, because 'the semantic and formal incompleteness of the text, its nigh-inexhaustible potential for multiple interpretations' becomes 'an exercise in the production of values'.[13] This is not simply to be understood as the performative quality of academic instruction, where content – if the separation can be made – is displaced in favour of engaging teaching methods that speak exclusively to orbiting agendas beyond the classroom. Equally, this is not about an instrumental approach to learning and teaching. The conception of 'staging' in curriculum design and the relationship between the 'stager' and the student as 'guest' must be rooted deeper in the teaching philosophy of the individual academic and team.

---

[12] 'Welcome to the Experience Economy', <https://hbr.org/1998/07/welcome-to-the-experience-economy> [accessed 12 January 2018].
[13] *Teaching Literature*, p. 5.

Within this context, the approach to curriculum design needs to focus on fully immersing the student as 'guest' into the educational experience of HE. The boundaries associated with an understanding of the curriculum within a 360-credit modular system become conceptually redundant in the experience economy, as it is not enough to sell a service for a fee. As a result, the lines between the visible and hidden curriculum, formal and informal learning, will ultimately dissolve into a unified lived experience.

As we look to the future of English in an HE setting, these possibilities and opportunities for English as a discipline will be best highlighted within the current system through the subject-level Teaching Excellence Framework (TEF). As I have written elsewhere, the subject-level TEF provides significant opportunities for Humanities subjects to disrupt the calcified strata of research-led excellence by showcasing innovative everyday teaching across mission groups.[14] Although the subject-level TEF pilot metrics may now look familiar to the institutional TEF, the importance of narrative – the domain of English as a discipline – will be increasingly important when it comes to articulating how English is 'staged' within a particular institutional setting. As English holds a mirror up to society and the systems that maintain it, questions are raised about how we measure successful outcomes in HE and society. An effective blend of high- and low-fidelity metrics that responds to the needs of individual disciplines is of paramount importance as we move further into the TEF cycle. Although the reliability of low-fidelity metrics can always be questioned, they speak more meaningfully to staff and students in a discipline context as they are local and rely upon intrinsic rather than extrinsic forces. For English, metrics that speak directly to the hidden curriculum and the affective transactions that support students on their career paths will be the most powerful indicators of success within the experience economy. For policy makers too, this will encourage differentiation within the sector that is advanced by teaching excellence within the disciplines; specialist areas of outstanding practice and centres for teaching excellence at a subject level.

The opportunity for English is to lead the way when it comes to expressing the value of Humanities degrees, by concretising the intangible transactions and exchanges that affect individual students on their learning journey and give them 'value' in a highly competitive job market. This can be achieved through curriculum design and approaches to learn-

---

[14]   See Ben Brabon, 'Beyond the Rubicon: Exploring the TEF in the Disciplines' (York: HEA,   2016),   <https://www.heacademy.ac.uk/blog/beyond-rubicon-exploring-tef-disciplines-dr-ben-brabon-hea> [accessed 12 January 2018].

ing and teaching that prioritise developing the graduate competencies and emotional intelligence valued so highly by employers.[15] Although perhaps conceptually undesirable within the context of traditional English degree programmes, this could be conceived as a more radical curriculum design process where graduate competencies – such as leadership – become the 'stage' upon which a textual exploration is played out across genres and critical perspectives. Such an approach would extend Biggs's conception of 'constructive alignment' beyond the ILOs, teaching methods and assessment strategy, to include graduate competencies aligned with employer needs.[16] In expanding Biggs's approach to constructive alignment, English as a discipline could play to its strengths by drawing out – as it does in its reading of texts – what is often latent and hidden within the curriculum. Evidently, there are possibilities and pitfalls in this approach, but the challenge remains for English programmes, and the Humanities more broadly, to 'cage' the affective quality of the educational minute 'within its nets of gold'.[17]

[15] See Maureen Tibby and Doug Cole, *Defining and Developing your Approach to Employability: A Framework for Higher Education Institutions* (York: HEA, 2013).
[16] See John Biggs, 'Enhancing Teaching through Constructive Alignment', *Higher Education*, 32:3 (1996), 347–64.
[17] See Louis MacNeice, 'The Sunlight on the Garden' (1907), <https://www.poemhunter.com/poem/the-sunlight-on-the-garden/> [accessed 12 January 2018].

Pedagogic Criticism: An Introduction*

BEN KNIGHTS

Pedagogic criticism involves reading texts through teaching, and teaching through texts. In so doing its aim is to bring into focus the transactions between the study and interpretation of texts and the social forms and rituals of pedagogy. It is a way of articulating a process through which an educational subject is talked into being. Literary studies is a form of cultural production, a collaborative process of making, carried out through a specialised form of dialogue: this form of conversation starts with what may look like confusion and moves towards a provisional order. Thus critical discourse – an intensified version of the meta-linguistic and interpretative conversations that constitute social living – is fashioned in the teaching relationship. Reciprocally, texts frequently prefigure the acts of pedagogy and politics of interpretation.

In exploring this interaction, pedagogic criticism borrows a leaf from New Historicism. Arguing that social energy is stored in literature not only in paper form, but in ongoing social exchange and transactions, Stephen Greenblatt proposes that 'we begin by taking seriously the collective production of literary pleasure and interest'.[1] In pedagogic criticism I attempt to re-submerge printed criticism in the oral pedagogic dialogues from which it has emerged, reading the history of the discipline as a history of practices as much as a history of ideas. While so much of pedagogy obeys invisible rules, this approach seeks to locate and listen to pedagogic voices within a discipline whose history can best be understood as being a history of practices as much as of the evolution of 'subject knowledge' arguing for a kind of isomorphism between the tropes of text and those of pedagogy.

* This is a specially adapted version of the introduction to Ben Knights's book, *Pedagogic Criticism: Reconfiguring University English Studies* (London: Palgrave Macmillan 2017), which was launched at English: Shared Futures. It is reprinted with permission from Palgrave Macmillan.
[1] Stephen Greenblatt, *Shakespearean Negotiations: The Circulation of Social Energy in Renaissance England* (Berkeley: University of California Press, 1988), p. 4.

The thick description of the discipline draws heavily on the work of the UK English Subject Centre between 2001 and 2011.[2] The subject 'English' (in both secondary and tertiary education), while subject to enormous and in many ways conflicting political and social pressures, may be at a moment of radical reformation from within. Pedagogic criticism seeks to contribute to that transformation by raising the level of visibility of largely unspoken assumptions about teaching and learning. Education is a formal process for enlarging the repertoire of individual and social choices: pedagogic criticism suggests that the study of literary and cultural texts is a potent stage for the development of ideas about learning – ideas that are frequently at odds with the 'evidence-based' shibboleths that dominate current educational policy. Forms of narrative prefigure and provide pointers to the management of cognitive and emotional energy in learning spaces – and how as teachers and as students we might occupy those spaces. The study of the relationship and shifts of the balance of power between author and narrator, text and reader parallels in important and instructive ways many of the debates over the last thirty years about the relative weighting of 'teaching' and 'learning'. Historically, the 'rise of the reader' parallels the rise of the student: Ference Marton, Roger Säljö and the influential Gothenburg school of educationists having performed in relation to the student an analogous role to that of Barthes and the reader response critics.[3] These related paradigms point towards a conceptualisation of learning spaces as sites of production for knowledge and culture. And more than that, they point towards education as 'becoming': a process of individual and group self-realisation and transformation.

An orientation for pedagogic criticism stems from my own background in adult education, in the Development of University English Teaching project, and subsequently at the English Subject Centre. These led me to urge the benefits of staging a conversation between literary and educational discourses.[4] Educational discourse is not something which,

[2] A flavour of the work of the English Centre can still be gained from the archived website: http://www.english.heacademy.ac.uk.
[3] See Ference Marton with Dai Hounsell, and Noel Entwistle, *The Experience of Learning* (Edinburgh: Scottish Academic Press, 1985).
[4] The Development of University English Teaching Project (DUET) was founded in 1979 at the University of East Anglia. Between 1980 and 1998 it ran a series of annual UK residential workshops, as well as shorter workshops in the UK and Continental Europe. The workshops drew extensively on the Tavistock School of group relations, creating frameworks in which colleagues could reflect upon their relationship to their discipline, their institution, their colleagues, and their students. Each comprised a weave of elements, known as 'events'. Typically

generally speaking, English academics find easy to accept or even tolerate. There are a number of reasons for this resistance, not least the formulaic vacuity and the erasure of disciplinary differences for which generic 'learning and teaching' programmes within universities have (with some justice) come to be renowned. Yet more fundamental status and boundary issues are involved. One element may be that assumption of the distinctiveness and superiority of one's own discipline. But there may be a deeper level, too. Deborah Britzman draws on Wilfred Bion, who sees the fear of development and change as deriving from the painful emotional experience of helplessness and frustration, and she shockingly proposes that teacher education 'is a hated field':

> Those in the university who may hate their own teaching hate it [teacher education] and those undergoing their teacher education hate it with their own hate. No teacher really loves her or his own teacher education. And university professors rarely identify their pedagogy as subject to their discontentment with having to learn.[5]

This may overstate the case, but my work with academics across many different kinds of institution persuades me that there is a good deal of truth in it. In the teeth of such blanket disdain one has to go on asserting the value (a value of estrangement, at the least) of importing educational discourse into the realm of disciplinary memory and folk tradition. One can, after all, discriminate between educational studies ('education' being no more homogeneous than 'geography' or 'English'), and the nutrients borne along on either stream of the dialogic tradition should be and could be common to both. In any case, some important studies oriented towards pedagogy take place within the discipline.[6] Pedagogic criticism constitutes an invitation to academics to analyse their own experience and to explore ways of complementing, questioning or developing perceptions, and so to contribute simultaneously to the study of pedagogy and of literary culture.

In this process, for pedagogic criticism, critical discourse (within the seminar or the virtual learning environment) is not a second-order or

---

these comprised an academic (text-based) event, a writing event and a group study event. The project carried on a vigorous life on the margins of the profession of English into the late 1990s.

[5] Deborah Britzman, *The Very Thought of Education: Psychoanalysis and the Impossible Professions* (Albany, NY: SUNY Press, 2009), p. 39.

[6] A conspectus of scholarship of teaching dedicated to HE English can be found in the *Arts and Humanities in Higher Education* virtual special issue, http://ahh.sagepub.com/site/includefiles/vsu2.xhtml.

instrumental language deployed to capture and illuminate the primary reality of the text. The self-reflexive examination of the processes of meaning-making is fundamental to both text and the envelope of discussion that surrounds it. (A discussion which, it is vital to note, is also carried on in and refreshed from countless sources beyond the institutional world of university or high school/secondary school English Studies.) In our own current context the pressures of commodity and modularisation tend towards packaged and streamlined knowledge (the metaphor of 'delivery' ubiquitous): to insist on devoting pedagogic time either to fragments or to ambiguous subject matter contrasts with the pervasive imperative of 'cutting to the chase', or going straight to the heart of the matter, homing in on some supposed informational or thematic core. Within neoliberal institutions, 'value for money', and its implied scaling between inputs and outputs, stands an admonitory presence over every educational activity. Yet, amid these instrumentalist assumptions, pedagogic criticism values obliqueness of approach as necessary and formative. So, here, as an anticipatory gesture in the direction of a more oblique approach, I'm going to reflect on a moment from Victorian fiction.

Philip Davis suggests that Victorian literature 'is a literature no longer of epic openings or great endings but of middles', a way of registering the way in which 'life in the present is constantly in thrall to its ever-ongoing outcomes'.[7] With this in mind, I shall focus on a passage from Trollope's late novel *The Duke's Children* (1880).[8] In chapter 66, Mrs Finn, a family friend, plucks up her courage to challenge the Duke's opposition to his daughter's marriage. 'How will it be with you ...?' she begins. The phrase occurs elsewhere in the novel. Trollope's novels are full of Shakespearean allusions, and it seems to me that this is an oblique memory of Hamlet's question to his mother 'How is it with you, Lady?' To that question, Gertrude (who apparently has not seen any ghost) replies:

Alas, how is't with you,
That you do bend your eye on vacancy,
And with th'incorporeal air do hold discourse? (3.4)

Apparitions frequently occur even in novels not usually categorised as uncanny: the ghosts of what might have been, or what might still be,

---

[7] Philip Davis, *Why Victorian Fiction Still Matters* (Oxford: Blackwell, 2008), pp. 98, 85.
[8] I have used the familiar version, as the discovery of Trollope's MS excisions occurred so recently.

proto-narratives akin to what D. H. Lawrence was later to call 'thought-adventures'.[9] Here, the floating pronoun 'it' seems like a sort of visitor in itself. Instead of asking 'how are you?', or 'how will you feel?' there is instead this detached 'it', a stray grammatical disembodiment, which is nevertheless – as so often in Henry James's late stories – indicative of a dissociated condition. Texts, I suggested above, commonly prefigure acts of interpretation and pedagogy. So this spectral visitation seems powerfully relevant to the enterprise of pedagogic criticism: the fragile, uncertain hope of speculating on the unseen. Which could be a semantic fragment, a ghost, a projection, or an alternative life: a detached bit of 'you'. For it is a ghost that Mrs Finn, gathering confidence and headway, actually wants the Duke to see:

> How will it be with you if she should live like a ghost beside you for the next twenty years, and you should then see her die, faded, and withered before her time …

In an analogous way, the subject of our pedagogy is not tangibly *there*; it cannot be identified with – and only obliquely rests upon – a body of authenticated, transmissible knowledge. The meaning of the text, like the identity of the learner, is summoned into being in conversation (hesitant, non-linear, tentative as that may be) between readers or between students and their teachers. And within that liminal conversation there are diverse latent interpretative roles. One model in-waiting is that of Hamlet, or of one of Henry James's more demented narrators: paranoid, obsessed, hyper-interpretative; another that associated with Gertrude herself or with Duke Theseus in *Midsummer Night's Dream* – rational, prosaic, aspiring to be symbolically in charge and perhaps apprehensive about the consequences of not being: 'aren't we reading too much in?' To that inclination of mind, the critic teacher holds discourse with 'th'incorporeal air': sketching allusions, alternative possibilities, oblique and far-fetched analogies. From this point of view the teacher attracts the accusation of indulging her elaborated interpretative skills as an act of self-aggrandisement and caste mystique.

This is a fairly exact fit with what Gerald Graff once luminously referred to as the 'problem problem' common to Humanities academics.

Nothing better exemplifies the apparently counter-intuitive nature of intellectual practices than their obsession with what often appear to

---

[9] For example, in *Kangaroo*. The idea is analysed by Robert Burden in *Radicalizing Lawrence: Critical Interventions in the Reading and Reception of D.H. Lawrence's Narrative Fiction* (Amsterdam: Rodopi, 2000).

be bogus 'problems'. Academic assignments ask students not only to become aggressive know-it-alls, but to cultivate problems to an extent that seems perverse or bizarre. I call this syndrome the 'problem problem'… In this penchant for problematizing, academic research scholars resemble avant-garde artists who 'defamiliarize' previously familiar subjects, using 'alienation effects' to make what seems obvious and unproblematic look strange.[10]

This intuition has particular implications for student discomfort within text-based disciplines. As Graff further notes, the

academic faith in the singular virtue of finding problems in subjects generally thought to be unproblematic seems especially bizarre and forced when the problems have to do with the meanings of texts.[11]

Nevertheless, from the standpoint of 'pedagogic criticism', we could put a more positive twist on this finding. The teacher's risk-taking role is to attempt to draw others into the discussion of precisely those symptomatic problems that fall below the radar of common sense: tactfully to fend off premature denotation while teasing out connotation. As teachers we have to license students to engage in quite peculiar activities – like taking 'precious' time to discuss things that common sense declares not to be worth wasting time over. Even, perhaps, to speculate on what the neurologist Antonio Damasio calls 'memories of the future'.[12] It's a role that carries its share of risks, and which marks the subject and its teachers as poised on borders, occupying an in-between space, one that cannot be authenticated by recourse to an armoury of authoritative scholarship. And – in the early days of literary criticism – this role carried the grave responsibility of systematically re-orientating reading behaviours away from comfort, escape or identification, and of weaning student writers from formula and cliché: marking, as it were, a boundary.

English literary studies has been from the beginning a border or boundary practice. One example is the conflicted border between academic subject and lay readers. Another, as we saw just now, the interdisciplinary border between academic subject and pedagogic studies. The pedagogic culture of English can be conceptualised as a border subject: a

[10] Gerald Graff, 'The problem problem and other oddities of academic discourse', *Arts and Humanites in Higher Education* 1:1 (2002), 27–42 (p. 29).
[11] 'The problem problem', p. 30.
[12] Antonio Damasio, *Descartes' Error: Emotion, Reason and the Human Brain* (London: Vintage, 2006), p. 262.

community of practice not frozen in time but constantly in the process of being crafted and argued into being, a site for the production of forms of knowing through interchange. Inside-ness and outside-ness may be culturally created, but the allegiances (and enmities) so inspired have nonetheless material effects. The pedagogic implications of this status resonate at several levels, and by way of a simple sketch map I shall speak tentatively of internal and external boundaries.

The forms of 'English' that took shape during the 1920s and went on to become dominant in universities have always exhibited contrary energies of openness and exclusion. The archaeology of the disciplinary landscape reveals ample traces of campaigns over what should count as core and what as margin – and what should be excluded altogether. The situation is especially complicated in the case of a discipline whose very name alludes at once, and confusingly, to a language, a nation and an educational subject. While there are radical differences with the history of English in schools, in higher education conflict between rival disciplinary subcultures continued, the literary critical tradition inheriting from the campaign against Philology (and, in the US and Scotland with Rhetoric) a radical – and ultimately damaging – distrust of Language Studies and subsequently of Linguistics. Yet even on the language front, the ongoing rivalries played out in very different ways in different institutional settings. While colleagues at universities as different as Glasgow, Edinburgh, Leeds, and Nottingham might dispute this, English Literature (strongly influenced by literary criticism in a wary armed alliance with Medieval Studies) widely laid claim to be the high status version of the discipline. This self-characterisation was subsequently reinforced by transatlantic alliances between colleagues in prestigious universities and colleges. It might be a more parochial effect, but it is nevertheless indicative that in England and Wales, a separate English Language A-Level only emerged at the end of the 1980s.[13]

Yet there is a common core of practice. While 'literary criticism' has widely morphed into 'critical practice', the patient study of representation, of the formation of meaning, of the complex layering of the written word (or visual sign), a commitment to the ambiguity – even ambivalence – of utterance has remained fundamental. Despite the discipline's lack of consensus revealed in the enthusiastic pursuit of competing paradigms, it's

---

[13] See summary in Angela Goddard and Adrian Beard, *As Simple as ABC? Issues of Transition for Students of English Language A Level Going on to Study English Language / Linguistics in Higher Education*, English Subject Centre Report Series, No. 14 (2007).

fair to say that representation and a dedication to the non-transparency of language, together with a zig-zagging movement between micro- and macro-focus have remained a common procedural core. This intellectual history is directly relevant to pedagogy precisely because the student experience – more accurately, the diverse experiences students collaborate in making – in some degree replicate and reproduce the process of negotiation and jostling for status of subject enquiry.

Obviously, the notion of boundaries internal or external is only a working and entirely provisional conceptualisation. But in pursuit of the argument that the negotiations across each shadow line have implications for pedagogy, I shall also note the external boundary, an imagined line between the professionalised 'subject' and two related communities: readers and students. Another attribute of a 'soft subject' may be its permeability, the leakiness of the membrane between everyday and specialised discourse. In promoting its own specialised value, 'English', like other Humanities subjects, occupies a position athwart commonsense understanding of language and representation. Since it promotes a principle of re-reading, the curricula it generates are spiral, involving the repeated return to familiar content at higher levels of sophistication and insight. This creates a dynamic field of energies, at once epistemological and pedagogic. The object of knowledge (whatever in fact critic, or group or student essay writer make out of the text or texts in front of them) is inherently unstable. While it might re-frame a text, it is highly unlikely that new knowledge will cause a reading to be completely superseded. This is not to claim that 'English' is an exceptional case in its lack of 'paradigm consensus': but any Humanities subject spends its life trying to regulate processes and materials that constantly escape its interpretative clutches. As McArthur points out, 'engagement with the type of knowledge that characterises a higher education directed at greater social justice ... is an inherently uncertain activity', and from no subject can we 'purge uncertainty'.[14] We would be betraying students and university by attempting to do so. But to the degree that all students pass through phases of managed bewilderment, the forms of bewilderment experienced by English students have their own specific and local habitations.

These forms of bewilderment draw both their richness and their puzzlement from the contrary gravitational fields of instrumental and metaphorical language. In the space of the seminar or the space of writing this tension produces unpredictable semantic energies – and may alternatively

[14] Jan MacArthur, 'Against standardised experience', *Teaching in Higher Education*, 17:4 (2012), 485–96 (p. 486).

result in defeated boredom or lethargy. Inasmuch as students find themselves longing for the dogmatic, they are perpetually teased with shape-changing complexities, theoretical cross-dressing, one conceptual overlay succeeding another. The whole thing can come to seem to students arbitrary, the safest recourse to lie low.

Yet the instability of the object of knowledge (what it is that you might *know* or be able to do as a result of this lecture, this seminar, this morning in the library) is common to all 'high' versions of the English discipline. It resides within a tension between linear, propositional knowledge (which favours accumulation and authority, and is reinforced by the recent explosion of research specialisation) and conversation. And it lends itself only very obliquely to calibration against the essentially behaviourist scheme of the 'intended learning outcome'.

In the history of literary studies the figure of what, on the analogy of the 'implied reader', I have come to think of as the 'implied student' plays a central role. Hence the ambiguity of the use I have been making of the idea of 'the subject'. The subject as the educational subject (the place where the discipline is activated) with its forms of knowledge, its rituals, its protocols for dialogue; but 'subject', too, as the identity in formation constructed through the learner's initiation into a set of practices. At each paradigm shift in literary studies the figure of the student has emerged not just as a neutral 'learner', but as the bearer of a cultural responsibility, as an agent of opposition to dominant cultures. Early literary criticism aspired to unfit students for their cultural environment:

As Denys Thompson has pointed out in these pages the aim of education today must be to turn out 'misfits' rather than spare parts. It is precisely by unfitting his pupils for the environment ... that the educator can hope to change it.[15]

More recently, as Bryan Vescio suggests, literary studies as a 'ministry of disturbance' has set itself to 'foster individual idiosyncrasy'.[16] The manner and degree to which the empirical reality of student experience aligns with or departs from these theoretical ideals constitutes a good deal of the history of the subject. And the curriculum itself has been constantly pulled in different directions. Thus, in its early years, literary criticism,

[15] L. C. Knights, 'Postscript on The Modern Universities', *Scrutiny*, VII (1938), 2–4.
[16] Brian Vescio, *Reconstruction Literary Studies* (New York: Palgrave Macmillan, 2014), p. 193.

still influenced by a Romantic inheritance that went back though Arnold to Coleridge and Wordsworth, charted a course for the maturing subject where the integration of the self was sought through the guided critical discussion of the organic unity, the ostensible self-harmonising, of the literary object. The critics contrasted the integrative process they advocated with the supposed dispersal of self and mind in consumerist abjection. The organic unity of the textual object prefigured and abetted a potential organisation of the mind.

In contrast, pedagogy is itself a boundary practice, entwined in a constant process of negotiation across borders. Where the object of early literary criticism was the integrated, mature self, its beacons the attributed wisdom of Shakespeare, Herbert, Yeats or Eliot, pedagogic criticism attends to the dispersed, role-playing identities of teacher and student. The curriculum and its teachers strive to produce a heteroglossic aesthetic space. If, as Stanley Fish argued, meaning is an event (rather than the extraction of embedded information) it is within that space that such events can occur.[17] This is a praxis that insists on re-complication, on pushing in the direction of hyper-lexicalisation and hyper-syntacticisation, advocating a joy in language that enables individual growth beyond the lazy relativism of opinion or the cursory dismissal 'whatever' and finding an aesthetic residually embedded in the practice of the subject. Thus the implied, ideal student was enlisted in the search for secular formalities, modes of speaking and thinking that would be sufficient for the re-making of culture. Students, in other words, were (and residually are) expected not only to identify and analyse the aesthetic qualities of texts but to internalise and re-enact, in however oblique and distant a way, the energetic linguistic procedures by which those qualities come into being.

In a context where funding imperatives have driven some of the most influential voices within English Studies to see the salvation of the discipline lying in specialised research, pedagogic criticism argues for a rebalancing towards teaching conceived as a fine mesh of networks, the mycelium of the subject. In doing so it treats as problematic the teacher's authority, an authority that stems quite as much from his or her courage and skills in eliciting dialogue as it does from scholarly knowledge. While I do not subscribe to the idealisation of literature of the early

---

[17] See, for example, 'Literature in the Reader: affective stylistics', reprinted in *Reader Response Criticism: From Formalism to Post-Structuralism*, ed. Jane Tompkins (Baltimore, MD: Johns Hopkins University Press, 1980). The argument was anticipated by Louise Rosenblatt in 'The poem as event', *College English*, 26 (1964), 123–8.

literary critics, I share enough with them to hold up literary reading as an activity that resists commodification. The practice of literature offers a public space, which – unlike the ostensibly common spaces of the new social media – is not the property of profit-seeking corporate behemoths. Underpinning this orientation towards habitats of learning is a sense of the importance of placing obstacles in the way of the relentless forward dynamic of the instrumentalised self. To seize a formulation that is more than ecological metaphor: in impeding this canalised flow, English literary pedagogy allows nutrients to settle and thus enables students to tap energies at once intellectual, emotional and social. The habitat of teaching will never be a utopia – the impossibility of such a utopia perhaps even its core working premise. But it could be a lot less dystopian than in the world of competing neoliberal institutions it is currently being compelled to become. Without major pedagogic re-thinking no amount of specialised scholarship will safeguard the continued existence of the discipline outside a handful of favoured enclaves.

Exquisite Tensions – Narrating the BAME ECA Experience

KEITH JARRETT

Recent events have initiated both a re-evaluation and, consequently, a re-write of what would otherwise have been a straightforward précis of an uplifting panel session where four academics – at very different stages of our careers – who fall under the BAME (Black and Minority Ethnic) category discussed our experiences. The thread binding us together was – despite our divergent journeys leading there – our work within British universities and, broadly speaking, within English departments. Aside from these commonalities, and the shared experiences and connections once inside the UK academy, we could arguably, present ourselves as a manifesto repudiating the idea of a monolithic BAME experience.

In fact, any conclusion from our initial presentations could be summarised thus:

(1) The BAME experience is not a monolithic one;
(2) The ECA experience is not a monolithic one;
(3) We're all interdisciplinarians now.[1]

To briefly address these points, it is salient to note that the panel was composed of four people, born in three different continents, from different ethnic backgrounds, educational backgrounds, genders, social classes, and, ultimately, different initial experiences of teaching within higher education institutions. If only more English departments were to boast such diversity in their employment practices![2]

---

[1] Here the author gives a wink to Lord Prescott, former Deputy Prime Minister, whose 1997 remark, 'We're all middle class, now' (1997), sparked a flurry of – initially hostile – articles and debates lasting over a decade. Perhaps, in a similar vein, this is intended as a provocation, a basis upon which to build an argument for re-thinking disciplines within the academy. 'Profile: John Prescott', 27 August 2007, <http://news.bbc.co.uk/1/hi/uk_politics/6636565.stm>.

[2] Richard Adams, 'British Universities Employ No Black Academics in Top Roles, Figures Show', *The Guardian*, 19 January 2017, <http://www.theguardian.com/education/2017/jan/19/british-universities-employ-no-black-academics-in-top-roles-figures-show>.

As loosely defined 'Early Career Academics', a range of previous employment, including teaching roles, had also preceded our presences on the faculty payroll. And on this note, our wealth of experience meant that we continued to cross disciplines once inside the academy. The idea of a permanent, secure job within academia is increasingly rare and, as such, expertise has widened. This phenomenon is not limited to BAME staff, of course, but it is also worth taking into account the large subset of BAME staff whose experience of living and being educated outside of the UK has enabled them to more easily reach beyond their immediate areas of expertise within English.

Here I shall divulge further my own peripatetic existence: as a British-educated PhD candidate, sat between the Creative Writing Department at one institution, on the one hand, and the Religions and Philosophies department at a neighbouring institution, on the other, my practice-led research comprising of fiction, Caribbean Pentecostalism and migration straddles disciplines in an atypical manner. I know no other academic in my position. Further compounding this peculiarity are the live tensions between Creative Writing and English departments, and the changing remit of the 'Study of Religion' – and even the definition of 'religion'. Both of these disciplines are relatively new to the rigour of academic exploration, and not without controversy. Consequently, it is easy to find oneself exploring new territory, while negotiating the frictions at the borders – both physical and metaphorical. How can quantitative measures be used to judge the merits of practice-led research? How comfortably can Creative Writing sit within the wider category of English? Where do Theology and Anthropology begin to push at the edges of the Study of Religion?

To further compound the situation, I find myself employed as an Associate Tutor on an English Literature module, encouraging undergraduate students in their critical approaches to text. Outside of the academy, most of my expertise and employment lays within live – or spoken word – poetry, in literature that is immediate and sometimes subversive. While successful academic writing requires narrow specialisation and encourages obtuse language, the spoken word poet and storyteller's success lies in her inviting a wide audience, in seeming accessible.

All of these tensions have been laid out on the line here to demonstrate a few of the considerations facing increasing numbers of academics within English; to then look at them through the lens of race and ethnic heritage requires further exploration still. Perhaps an essay is not the ideal format for unpacking these ideas; the continuation of a dialogue would better serve as a scaffold under which to build them. Under the scaffold is a broad church of BAME experience intersecting with ECA uncertainties. *Behold the cornices, the falling gargoyles, the crumbling Greek pillars!* Under the broad church is the author's recognition that confusing metaphors do not make for good poetry, nor do they best facilitate meditative prose on the current state of affairs. But herein lies the *true* metaphor: developing an academic career while black can be like early, first draft, poetic exploration: confusing, disorienting and yet full of exciting, creative possibilities and intrigue.

Exquisite Tension

Notwithstanding all the positive creative potential inherent within ECA experiences, one is reminded of the artist Sonia Boyce's 'Exquisite Tension' (2005),[3] a photograph in which a white man and a black woman have their hair entangled; the man appears to try to pull away from her, while she stares ahead with narrowed eyes. Neither look comfortable in their position, and the single, static capturing of their struggle keeps them in a perpetual state of tension, with no clues as to how they first came to have their hair entwined, nor to how they will eventually disentangle themselves. It does not require a huge imagination to project all of the racial tensions – both of the academy and elsewhere – onto this image.

Despite the wealth and breadth of our experiences, and the overwhelming positive effect we have within our disciplines, the very presence of BAME academics within largely uncontested traditions is sometimes perceived as threatening, something to push back against, or pull away from. Some of these traditions may manifest themselves through: a static literary canon; an assumed Western male gaze; a heteronormative approach to texts; the privileging of untranslated – and especially mainland English – works; an often-unquestioned lack of fellow non-white academic staff; increasing job insecurity for academics; an education system that leads to fewer BAME university places for those born in the UK, in proportion to A-Level attainment[4]; increased pressures due to Student Survey results and cuts to funding; a lack of communication between departments and disciplines – the list goes on. BAME staff risk being exposed to a hostile

---

[3] 'UAL Research Fortnight 2017 – Keynote Debate "Art in Polarised Times" – All Welcome', <http://events.arts.ac.uk/event/2017/3/6/UAL-Research-Fortnight-2017-Keynote-Debate-Art-in-Polarised-Times-/> [accessed 31 October 2017].

[4] Richard Adams, 'Black Students Still Struggle to Win Places at UK Universities', *The Guardian*, 26 January 2017, <http://www.theguardian.com/education/2017/jan/26/black-students-struggle-uk-university-places-ucas>.

climate, or may at times feel tokenised. Before we have even begun to write, or speak, or teach, we are political subjects, entangled in a polemic we did not necessarily seek out, and which we cannot be certain will unravel.

It is with all these factors in mind that we may consider the recent newspaper headlines at the time of writing. In both *The Telegraph* and the *Daily Mail*,[5] Lola Olufemi, an undergraduate student at Cambridge, was singled out as 'forcing' the university to 'drop white authors', after signing a co-drafted letter to her college department recommending ways – as part of an extensive list – in which they could 'decolonise' the English Literature curriculum. Despite *The Telegraph* apologising the following day for its multiple factual inaccuracies, this story speaks to the hyper-visibility of black students who question the status quo; a signature on a letter addressed to a college, asking for the inclusion of more texts by BAME authors, attracted national public attention, wilful misunderstanding and *ad hominem* violent threats. While what seem like reasonable demands may be up for debate within academic circles, the disproportionate response from the general public signals the wider tensions to be reckoned with, including a mainstream British culture that is violently sensitive to any reminders of its colonial exploits, or to any challenge of its subjectivity.

Olufemi, unfortunately, seems to be part of a growing trend, where BAME students who make any public statement about racism risk having their social media accounts intensely scrutinised and receiving death threats.[6] It is impossible to even attempt objectivity on this occasion, so here I declare my personal interests and discomforts: as one of too-few black *academics* in the UK, it is hard not to feel especially vulnerable in this climate, even with the most well-intentioned colleagues surrounding me. I would not dare question lightly any limitations of the curriculum I have been assigned to teach; and, were I to do so, I would need to feel I have not only the support of the immediate department, but also of the university's Communications Team, as well as all the various levels of management higher up the chain. In reality, I just want to teach!

---

[5] Camilla Turner, 'Cambridge to "Decolonise" English Literature', *The Telegraph*, 26 October 2017, <http://www.telegraph.co.uk/education/2017/10/24/cambridge-decolonise-english-literature/>.
[6] Oluwaseun, 'The Rise in Right-Wing Witch Hunts against Black Student Leaders Has Not Gone Unnoticed', *Gal-Dem* (blog), 31 July 2017, <http://www.gal-dem.com/rise-right-wing-witch-hunts-black-student-leaders-not-gone-unnoticed/>.

Expanding the Conversation

A panel consisting of BAME English academics is seated in a conference room. Guess the topic of conversation... *Are you thinking what I'm thinking?*[7] In this *particular* instance, our panel was mostly a summary of the paths that had led us to working at universities in the UK, and the various work we do outside of it, followed by a Q&A session, which had predictable moments, but also some refreshing ones.

While BAME academics gathering together often throws into relief the white space that many English conferences engender, and while it is necessary to address the inevitable challenges we face, we must also not let those challenges become our sole area of concern. *Diversity*™, the banner under which we sit, can often create its own homogeneity. As *diverse* contributors to academic knowledge and discourse, it is too easy to be led down the path of justifying our *own* space – and, of course, broadening it for others – so that, sooner or later, our work becomes, by proxy, about whiteness. Nevertheless, the idea of *objective* whiteness as default must be contested. English departments must address this – and BAME academics must feel empowered to do so too.

My introduction to Shakespeare's *The Tempest* and to the Caribbean poet Edward Kamau Brathwaite came not through reading English as an undergraduate, but Spanish. I opted for a module on postcolonial discourse, which meandered through Argentinian and Cuban re-imaginings of Ariel and Caliban, from Rodó to Retamar, respectively. Not only did it widen my reading and my critical skills, but it also taught me a permanent lesson on perspective: one person's *cannibal* can become another's *Carib*, and leave us with a 'Caribbean', and a 'Caliban', and a whole heap of literature in its wake. Caliban, as a character, speaks to the Western imagining of all that is uncivilised in the *other*, but Caliban can also be, and has been, reclaimed. He can be used as a metaphor for the limitations of the colonial gaze, which sees the *other* as monster and yet refuses to see itself in the mirror.

As a new academic, I long for more moments of reclamation and broadened perspectives within English departments. I also long for more

---

[7] Once again, the author wishes to make allusions to a political campaign through his italicising of this slogan. Perhaps conclusions could be drawn on ongoing dog-whistle politics and its links to the current climate in universities and beyond: Ben Baumberg Geiger, 'Immigration and the Politicisation of Everyday Experience', *Inequalities* (blog), 22 August 2012, <https://inequalitiesblog.word press.com/2012/08/22/immigration-politicisation-experience/>.

dialogue between departments, where it would be equally acceptable to pull the conversation in the opposite direction, studying *The Tempest* through the gaze of Retamar, Rodó and others, rather than regurgitating the uncontested gaze of their influencers. I also welcome a more wholesale embrace of Creative Writing within existing English Literature programmes as inevitable, and this is where my argument comes to land. There is a new generation of Calibans entering universities, and they seek to reconfigure their own history, to create the literature that doesn't always appear in their English modules, to see themselves reflected while also moving beyond that into the realm of new creative possibilities. This is an exciting and awkward time in which BAME Early Career Academics can inspire a new generation of thinkers and critics.

Postgraduate Futures: Voices and Views

CLARE A. LEES, LEWI MONDAL, HELEN SAUNDERS, EMILY ENNIS AND SUSAN BRUCE

Clare Lees, Introduction

Postgraduate researchers (PGRs), both collectively and individually, represent one of the most important cohorts in English Studies. It takes a considerable investment of time and intellectual energy to produce research commensurate with a PhD, and that work supports the future of English Studies. The award of the PhD is a remarkable individual achievement that we rarely celebrate collectively as a discipline. As a cohort, postgraduate researchers are supported by their supervisors, academic departments and institutions; they are offered training that is both discipline-specific and that cultivates professional development and wider skills necessary for their future careers. Yet, postgraduates are also precarious. Funding for research is highly competitive and increasingly rare; opportunities to teach, if available, are often provided via short-term contracts with few benefits and little or no support for research or professional development. That those who represent one significant future for English Studies in its broadest sense experience such precarity is increasingly recognised. The most recent example, perhaps, is the free membership extended by the University and College Union (UCU) to postgraduates on teaching contracts or working within teaching and support (see https://www.ucu.org.uk/free). Research councils such as the AHRC commit funding to postgraduates through a variety of routes such as Doctoral Training Partnerships (DTPs) and also provide opportunities, policy and support for career development. And subject organisations such as the EA and UE consider postgraduate support and development central to our work.

What of postgraduates themselves, however? In what sense are their voices heard whether as individuals or as a cohort similar to that of the ECA? English: Shared Futures (E:SF) provided an opportunity for postgraduates to present their work and for participants to engage with it. Aside from conference participation, however, the voice of the postgraduate researcher is most often heard within professional settings such as the department meeting, the Graduate Centre, College or School, or the research council. Listening to those who represent the various futures of our discipline outside these formal settings, however, is also vital. For this chapter, I invited three researchers, postgraduates or post-PhDs themselves, who had attended the E:SF conference to reflect on their experience in ways that they felt appropriate. I'm grateful to Emily Ennis, Lewi Mondal and Helen Saunders for their willingness to take up my invitation: their voices follow. This chapter concludes with a further reflection from Susan Bruce, who stepped down as Chair of UE in 2017; she has a particular interest in the future of the discipline and its ability to reach out into the wider community. Lewi, Helen and Emily remind us how much we have to learn from postgraduate and early career researchers as they research and engage with the discipline. That lesson is ongoing, as Susan and I are very much aware. Emily, Lewi and Helen speak for themselves, for their peers, their subject organisations, their students – and for our futures.

Lewi Mondal, postgraduate researcher, Teesside University, intern at E:SF

After having the apparent misfortune of being recruited as an intern at a seemingly mammoth cross-disciplinary conference, two things were clear when I arrived: my sense of misfortune was displaced, and the scale of the conference was, as anticipated, quite large. The conference was my chance to see many of the names I recognised from books and citations. As a PhD student who had hoped to attend the conference, 'working' it instead seemed to be at first a considerable setback, but interning at this conference was not entirely like work. Partnering with fellow PhDers presented an opportunity to both relay our own work and maintain sanity, and to hear about the many, differing and genuinely interesting projects other people were working on. Similarly, there was opportunity to attend panels that were correlative to our research interests. Needless to say, the scale of the conference presented many chances to abandon my interning partner and attend several panels on Neo-Victorianism and Mortality and the future of the nineteenth century, for example. However, it was Deborah Cameron's fascinating, informative and hilarious plenary on language and female authority that both interested me and voiced my experience of the conference.

While Cameron's plenary was on language and linguistics, it represented a number of things that are important for any PhD student to keep in mind. As scholars of language, the written word and the imagination, we need to think of the uses of our research as universal and transferrable. As a literature student, I had not considered the value of attending a language paper before. It was Cameron's effort to make relatable the content of her talk that has most stuck with me as a chief skill of our disciplines on display at E:SF.

As many PhD students would agree, there is a sense of nervousness and anxiety when potentially field-defining scholars might be milling around the same room. Meeting several eminent academics (often not realising who they were at first!) confirmed to me that the stereotype of the stuffy academic is scarce in reality. When informally chatting, it was obvious that even the most esteemed professors are susceptible to imposter syndrome, stage fright and anxieties. Similar worries were also addressed in conference panels and should be allowed more space for consideration by academia in general. Many people I spoke to were genuinely unlike the images I had of well-known academics. It was reassuring that such people existed in an outwardly quite formal and often very serious industry.

While it was a sobering experience in terms of finding my place in the field, attending the conference also promoted hope and determination. The importance of relatability and humility, and of maintaining broad horizons were very present to me after attending E:SF. As a potential future delegate of the conference – and of our disciplines as a whole – it's important to keep this message at the centre of all our work.

Helen Saunders, post-PhD King's College London, early career academic, E:SF presenter

Why do a PhD in Modernist Studies? I've been asking myself this question for around five years, which is to say the period prior to, during and immediately after completing a thesis dedicated to the work of James Joyce. I am sure I am not alone among junior modernist scholars in questioning often, and often vocally, why I do what I do, and how my chosen area of study might look in the future – both to myself and to my discipline.

Over the 2016–17 academic year, the British Association of Modernist Studies (BAMS) ran a survey of its postgraduate members, examining their views on their careers within or beyond Modernist Studies. This survey formed the basis of our panel at E:SF, taking into account the views of the 25 PGRs who provided responses (we'll be re-running it at our annual PGR conference and hope to increase the number and range of responses). We found that 20% of postgraduates in the field perceive Modernist Studies to be a unique field; others, again 20%, as simply an aspect of the Long Twentieth Century. No doubt partly due to our increasingly far-right US–UK political climate, a significant proportion of our postgraduates see the benefit of training in Modernist Studies for posts in Contemporary Literature, and its acute relevance in today's social world. Politics aside, many of our postgraduates did not consider themselves to have the transferable skills that humanities departments are so keen to establish among research students; possibly an attribute of postgraduate students of any literary period is the inability to recognise the transferable skills that a PhD generates for the non-academic job market, if desired or required. We found that single-author projects are largely on the way out (only two people recorded writing this kind of thesis), while multi-author, interdisciplinary and/or recovery projects dominate, which is probably consistent with other disciplines. The extent to which scholarship within Modernist Studies might be driven, and even accelerated, by the wishes and stipulations of funding bodies, and universities hoping to impress such organisations, was another issue that emerged within our survey.

This final point is a factor that shapes all study in the contemporary university, but it is an especially acute concern for Modernist Studies, which over the last few years and for the decade to come will be negotiating the fraught demands of anniversary culture. While this is an increasingly visible part of our scholarly landscape in the age of 'impact' and 'engagement', Modernist Studies more than any other field right now needs to understand and address its own relation to this as it comes to a complex and contestable fruition in 2022. While it can be intellectually validating to ride a wave, what might anniversary culture mean for the long future of research within the discipline, and for those scholars entering the field in this period? Will we look back on dusty centenaries and wonder what made Modernist Studies special or valorised as it currently is? This self-reflective, self-critical work has been under way ever since Douglas Mao and Rebecca L. Walkowitz's strident scholarly manifesto, 'The New Modernist Studies'; but, like modernist literature, modernist scholarship is quickly displaced, replaced and challenged.[1]

Something that emerged from E:SF very clearly was the role that scholarly societies can play in shaping and supporting their fields and researchers. Although founded to be interdisciplinary, BAMS is overwhelmingly a literary organisation (and is working to include a wider range of disciplines) and it provides an ideal intellectual home for modernist PhD students, for whom the issues raised here have tangible consequences on their research and career paths. This need not strike a note of panic: working in an area so willing to interrogate its own

[1] Douglas Mao and Rebecca L. Walkowitz, 'The New Modernist Studies', *PMLA*, 123 (2008), 737–48.

boundaries, practices and significance is daunting, but does certainly get postgraduates and early career researchers thinking explicitly about, and being able to articulate, their purpose within the academy today.

Emily Ennis, post-PhD, University of Leeds, early career academic, E:SF attendee

The futures for undergraduate students and postgraduate students of English are very different. For the former, literary studies has become about demonstrating transferable skills and how to apply them. There are now specific modules on employability, and there are work placements, opportunities in volunteering and extracurricular activities, as well as prizes and bursaries to be won, that complement rigorous academic literary studies. For undergraduate students, a degree in English is a route into the professional world. This approach embodies everything I believe students can take from literature. It proposes that English goes beyond consuming books. Instead English is a way of learning critical thinking, and of understanding the increasingly complex world around us. The movement towards environmental humanities provides English students with a way of coming to terms with the implications of our actions for the natural world; the medical humanities, too, provide a new, more holistic way of understanding disability and illness. Ultimately, it is understood that English studies provide access into and answers to complex political, scientific, and philosophical debates – a task that had always been at the core of my own interest in literary studies.

However, as a recently graduated PhD student, English has become less about answering life's great questions, and more about supplanting life altogether. Rather than allow literary studies to inform my life and my critical thinking, English literature has to become my focus if I am to achieve success in an academic discipline with limited career opportunities. During the initial few weeks of my PhD, members of senior staff informed me that the main aim for the next four years would be completing my thesis: all other pursuits were irrelevant. Yet while it is impossible to get a teaching post in English without a PhD, it is likewise seemingly impossible to get one *with* a PhD. While I was encouraged to pursue only the completion of my thesis, equally I was supposed to ensure that I *was* pursuing things alongside my PhD *as long as they served the higher purpose of benefiting my future career*. Moving away from a holistic model of English studies where literature unlocks the world around us, as researchers our time is spent ensuring that every activity in which we participate must contribute meaningfully to our CV, rather than our lives. Literature becomes a means of guaranteeing future funding, of promotion, of impressing a hiring committee, rather than becoming inherently meaningful for those who research it. This type of exclusive professionalism puts strain on those staff already in English departments worldwide, and makes it virtually impossible to enter this career without bringing with you your own form of funding: either self-funding or through grant capture. There is no understanding that literary studies are their own reward, or worthy of further investment.

As the future of English Studies lies with those who study it, those of us who teach English need to be able to capture the joy of finding meaning in what we read with our students, something that may become more difficult if we focus only on the profession of literary studies. As budgets become increasingly stretched in the Arts and Humanities, it seems obvious to me that literary studies must also demonstrate their value in understanding the world around us, in providing critical skills and not simply offering a career-path that might otherwise appear entirely closed off from that world.

Susan Bruce, Professor of English, Keele University, former Chair of University English, member of organising committee for E:SF

Back in November 2016, while Shared Futures organisers were poring over spreadsheets of speakers, panels and Civic Centre room numbers and discussing, among other things, the Early Career strand of our conference, an article appeared in *The Guardian* on the alarming growth of the UK HE precariat. Universities, the article noted, are accused of adopting 'Sports Direct' employment practices, especially with respect to more junior cohorts of staff, three quarters of whom experience low pay, zero-hours conditions or short-term contracts.[2]

Many of the universities named in the article protested vigorously about the validity of its statistics, but however questionable *The Guardian*'s figures may have been, there is no doubt that conditions for new entrants to our profession are extremely challenging. An AHRC report on *The Career Paths of AHRC funded PhD Students*, produced first in 2006 and re-visited in 2012, showed that although five to seven years post-PhD, 72% of AHRC-funded PhDs were employed in universities, only 61% of those had permanent academic positions, and of those, a

---

[2] <https://www.theguardian.com/uk-news/2016/nov/16/universities-accused-of-importing-sports-direct-model-for-lecturers-pay>.

smaller proportion still would be full-time.[3] The situation among the larger cohort of students who are not beneficiaries of AHRC funding is likely to be more challenging still. We don't know how many PhDs in English are produced across the country every year, but it is a fairly easy bet that their number will substantially outweigh the number of academic jobs – let alone of permanent, full-time academic jobs – into which that cohort might eventually progress.

So doing a PhD because one wants an academic job is, paradoxically, a rather bad reason to do a PhD. And because a PhD is a commodity with substantial hidden costs (most PhD students are not paying into pensions nor paying off mortgages; some may be deferring families; most will in some manner or form be sacrificing something), prospective postgraduates need to embark on their doctorates in the knowledge that, while their labour may well earn its costs back for them at some future date, for many, this will be in careers outside the academy, not within it.

Individuals and institutions would do well to keep this in mind, for if they do not, both individuals and institutions risk entrapment in the sunk-cost fallacy. There is an inverse relation between one's investment in something and the ease of abandoning it which can make it very difficult for those who have completed a PhD hoping to work in the academy to entertain other possibilities when academic jobs prove hard to get. But while a career within the academy can be a wonderful thing, those of us already within its walls should not fetishise the life of the mind. For a PhD in English is a fantastic training for many things, as is amply illustrated in the Storify account of an AHRC event that showcased for doctoral students the range of careers available to them outside the academy.[4] From journalism and radio, through publishing, museums, the civil service, policy and government, to the digital and creative industries: these are just some of the career paths for which a doctoral training in English is an excellent preparation.

So perhaps the final challenge for those of us already working in HE, and for those new entrants to it that we will welcome in future years, is to up our game in recognising – and fostering recognition of – the true depth and breadth of the skills inculcated by research in our disciplines. Let's seek to place our PhDs outside the academy as assiduously as we prepare them for a career inside it. Such a focus could only do good: to our students, to our institutions, to our discipline, and (most of all perhaps) to the worlds outside our own.

[3]   <http://www.ahrc.ac.uk/documents/project-reports-and-reviews/career-paths-of-ahrc-funded-phd-students-final-report/>.
[4]   <https://storify.com/ahrcpress/ahrc-postgraduate-careers-showcase>.

Shared Futures: Early Career Academics in English Studies

CLARA JONES, CLARE EGAN, ELIZABETH ENGLISH, ILSE A. RAS AND STEPHEN WATKINS

Clara Jones, Introducing the Early Career Strand at English: Shared Futures, 2017

In the early stages of the planning for English: Shared Futures my co-organisers and I decided to use the term Early Career Academic (ECA), rather than Early Career Researcher (ECR), to describe the colleagues our strand of sessions was designed for. It is easy to be cynical about the proliferation and high turnover of acronyms in Higher Education today. In our case, the shift in terminology, although slight, was a considered gesture. Funding bodies and universities have tended to define ECRs in terms of the length of time since the completion of a PhD – for the AHRC an ECR is an 'individual who is within eight years of the award of their PhD or equivalent professional training', or an 'individual who is within six years of their first academic appointment'.[1] Much of the diversity of early-career experiences gets lost in these definitions. One of the aims of the Shared Futures strand was to work with an expanded understanding of what it means to be an ECA in today's academy, including late-stage PhD students increasingly expected to face challenges formerly reserved for those in post, such as publication; precariously employed scholars in fractional or fixed-term work; or colleagues working as teaching fellows with no research duties in their contracts.

We were also keen for the strand to offer ECAs what they felt they needed, especially in terms of training. This included professionalisation staples, such Q&As with publishers and journal editors, a roundtable on demystifying the REF and 'Starting to Teach' workshops. The strand also sought to address barriers that prevent access to university English and think about how class, gender and race might define ECA experiences. A panel bringing together black and minority ethnic colleagues made an important and necessary intervention on the subject of BAME representation in English Departments. The 'Open Voices' session gave

---

[1] AHRC Early Career Eligibility, <http://www.ahrc.ac.uk/funding/research/researchfundingguide/eligibility/> [accessed 18 September 2017].

ECAs the chance to discuss the challenges I have already outlined. Four speakers from HE institutions across the country presented position papers on 'Publications', 'Precarious Contracts', 'Interdisciplinarity' and 'Class', speaking to their personal experiences of these issues and suggesting ways the academy as a whole and individual departments might work to improve the lot of ECAs. While each contributor comes to separate conclusions they are united by their sense of the need for more opportunities for intergenerational exchange and mentoring. My experiences at Shared Futures also convinced me of the need for strengthened ECA networks, to facilitate our ongoing support and mentoring of each other. ECAs often find outstanding mentors in senior colleagues, but the value of support from friends and colleagues who have been through the mill more recently and understand the very particular context in which ECAs operate in today cannot be underestimated.

Clare Egan, Early Career Academics and Precarious Employment

According to a *Times Higher Education* headline from April 2016, 'fixed-term [work is] now the norm for early career academics'.[2] This essay was written in light of the University and College Union's (UCU) report on the 'precarious' working conditions that are increasingly prevalent in UK Universities.[3] The report states that 54% of all academic staff and 49% of all academic teaching staff are on insecure contracts. Further, it evidences that staff below the level of senior lecturer and senior research fellow were much more likely to be on fixed-term contracts. 'Precarious' posts can range from hourly-paid work to zero hours, fixed-term (often below 12 months) and fractional (less than 1.0 FTE) contracts, but a significant part of the problem is that the exact scale of the issue across the sector is unknown. UCU used data from the Higher Education Statistical Agency (HESA), but supplemented this with their own research using Freedom of Information requests to Higher Education Institutions because it claimed that HESA's descriptive categories were flawed. However, the Universities

[2] Jack Grove, 'Fixed-term now the Norm for Early Career Academics, says UCU', *The Times Higher Education*, 14 April 2016, <https://www.timeshigher-education.com/news/fixed-term-now-the-norm-for-early-career-academics-says-university-and-college-union-ucu> [accessed 4 September 2017].

[3] University and College Union, 'Precarious Work in Higher Education: A Snapshot of Insecure Contracts and Institutional Attitudes', April 2016, <https://www.ucu.org.uk> [accessed 4 September 2017]; see also 'Precarious Work in Higher Education: November 2016 Update', November 2016, <https://www.ucu.org.uk> [accessed 4 September 2017].

and Colleges Employers Association (UCEA) disputed UCU's figures, saying that the HESA data shows that 75% of teaching staff are on 'open-ended ... contracts', rather than insecure ones. UCEA stated that what they describe as 'atypical workers' only accounted for 3.2% of the full-time equivalent academic workforce.[4]

Having held several fixed-term and fractional contracts as an ECA, I chose to speak about this topic for several reasons. Firstly, I believe that the variation of experience between institutions in terms of departmental support, the impacts of precarity, and provision for early career research need to be discussed in order to move towards more standardised and ethical ECA working conditions across HEIs; and, secondly, having experienced the immensely positive difference that effective mentoring can make to ECAs in these roles, I felt the need to advocate the benefits of this as the discipline moves forward. 'Precarious' working conditions can impact upon ECAs not just professionally, but also psychologically and financially.[5] One of UCU's most striking findings, though, was that precarious work 'geared research toward short-term results rather than long-term impact'.[6]

For ECAs navigating the current situation, then, bearing the longer-term nature of their own distinctive research plans in mind might be one way, however difficult, of negotiating the challenges of 'precarious' employment. Focusing on a personal research plan, as soon as possible post-PhD, across approximately five years (roughly in line with the Research Excellence Framework), instead of working to short-term, in-contract goals, has significantly helped me to develop my own research while integrating into wider department communities. However, this kind of approach to my research would simply not have been possible without the coaching and mentorship of senior colleagues. Looking to the future on this issue, English departments might increase mentorship of ECAs both in terms of their personal research and their employment situations in relation to the wider department. In a leading example of this, the English Association piloted their Welcome Scheme and mentoring

---

[4] Helen Fairfoul, 'UCEA Expresses Disappointment on Continued Misleading Use of Atypical Contracts Data', 21 November 2016, < http://www.ucea.ac.uk/ en/news/index.cfm/21nov16> [accessed 4 September 2017].

[5] See also the open letter signed by over 1,800 academics from UK Higher Education humanities departments calling for the ending of precarious and unethical contracts: 'Open Letter on Precarious and Unethical Short Term Contracts', by Emilie K. Murphy, <https://openletterhumanitiesukhe.wordpress. com> [accessed 4 September 2017].

[6] UCU, 'Precarious Work', p. 8.

sessions at 'English: Shared Futures'; English departments could follow this lead by implementing official mentoring schemes in their own institutions. Whilst the sector is under increasing pressure to move away from the widespread use of precarious working conditions where unethical, we can contribute an ECA voice to calls for change, support the creation of meaningful mentorship schemes, and look to foster longer-term research goals across the discipline.

Elizabeth English, Early Career Academics and Social Class

In July 2017, the Institute for Fiscal Studies reported that students from the poorest backgrounds in England could potentially graduate from university with a debt of £57k.[7] As this report demonstrates, while it is obvious that the policy of Widening Participation has made great strides over the last 15 years, resulting in a more diverse student demographic, this is only a small part of the picture. A recent research project entitled 'Paired Peers', conducted jointly by the University of Bristol and the University of the West of England, found that working-class students face a wide array of challenges.[8] If students from poorer backgrounds are receiving a distinctly different experience of education than middle-class students, and if they are likely to graduate with upwards of £57K of debt, how will they progress to PhD study and what will this mean for our community of scholars and educators in the long term?

Given that the first cohort to pay £9k annual fees graduated only in 2015, we are yet to fully understand the implications for entrance into academic careers. But it is fair to say that class already plays a significant, and often detrimental, part in the ECA experience. The most pressing issue is whether they have access to a financial safety net, which might ease the difficulty of the no-man's land that is the search for a permanent post. It is unlikely that ECAs from working-class backgrounds will have the luxury of financial security while trying to build their profile. This means that they often have to take jobs that may not be relevant to their career trajectory and which might require a substantial portion of their mental and physical energy. Notably, ECAs often feel compelled

---

[7]   Chris Belfield et al., 'Higher Education Funding in England: Past, Present and Options for the Future', *Institute for Fiscal Studies*, 5 July 2017, <https://www.ifs. org.uk/publications/9334> [accessed 15 September 2017].

[8]   'Paired Peers: Moving On Up. The Paired Peers Project Year 3 Report: A Degree Generation?', July 2013, <http://www.pairedpeers2.org.uk/pdfs/Year%20 3%20Report.pdf> [accessed 15 September 2017].

to obscure this work from potential employers, as if this might indicate compromised commitment to academia. In contrast, they might be fortunate enough to receive hourly-paid teaching, which is of course excellent for building a CV and networking, but the pitfalls of precarious zero-hours contracts are well-documented. This in turn impacts upon ECAs' ability to attend conferences, network, produce research and ultimately publications – the very things needed to exit this cycle of insecure and poorly paid employment.

There are also intangible, but no less significant, obstacles that ECAs from working-class backgrounds face. As Paula Black states, 'Education is a common source of both mobility and feelings of inadequacy. The ability to succeed in an unfamiliar world with a set of rules which remain alien, and are implicit until transgressed, depends upon learning to read, understand, and "pass" according to those rules.'[9] Black goes on to describe how this has given birth to a culture of self-surveillance and self-audit.[10] Class is undoubtedly a psychological state as well as a fiscal one, and this sense of alienation (as well as the pressure to assimilate) often leaves ECAs from working-class backgrounds on the margins within a system so competitive that they are immediately disadvantaged.

I've explored a few of the challenges faced by ECAs from working-class backgrounds, although much more needs to be said on this topic, in particular how this identity might intersect with other factors such as gender. I could have also easily commented on the strengths that a working-class background bestows on us – determination, for a start. It is also crucial that we approach this as an issue in which we have the power and responsibility to intervene. The solution begins with those of us already in post. We can make changes, however small, to departmental culture, to hiring practices, to the way we award funding, to the treatment and support of casual staff, and to the way that we interact with colleagues. In short, we can apply the same level of critique and analysis to our own environments and professional behaviour that we do to the texts we study.

Ilse A Ras, Early Career Academics and Interdisciplinarity

In a 2016 publication on 'the state of interdisciplinarity in the contemporary academy', The British Academy identifies five different forms of interdisciplinary research: research 'borrowing' knowledge from

---

[9] Paula Black, 'Class Matters in UK Higher Education', *Women's Studies International Forum*, 28 (2005), 127–38 (p. 131).

[10] 'Class Matters', p. 132.

another discipline and applying this in a primary discipline; 'exploratory collaborations between disciplines to find areas of common interest'; challenge-focused research that addresses particular issues using knowledge from various disciplines; 'emerging disciplines that bring together approaches from separate areas'; and established 'inherently' interdisciplinary fields, 'such as classics or geography'.[11] The same report recognizes that interdisciplinary ECAs are in need of particular kinds of support. It suggests that universities must work to enable them to do the following three things:

(1) Publish in recognised disciplinary journals, or books or monographs by high- status publishers;
(2) Build social-academic networks (reinforcing doctoral networks) via conferences or workshops;
(3) Secure research funding, hence demonstrating one's capacity to get further research grants – in particular disciplines at least.[12]

Work is currently being done by research councils and funding bodies to address points (1) and (3). The Higher Education Funding Council for England recently announced their plan to investigate the REF's approach to interdisciplinary research – their results will be announced in 2018.[13] Funders also increasingly issue challenge-based funding calls, and this interdisciplinary funding also goes some way to addressing point (2). I recently completed a stint as a research assistant on one of these challenge-based projects, examining representations of human trafficking. It brought together a criminologist, two English Literature scholars, two English Language scholars and a policing specialist. This project was funded by the Partnership for Conflict, Crime & Security Research (PaCCS), an initiative of RCUK of which the AHRC, Economic and Social Research Council, and Engineering and Physical Sciences Research Council are core members. As a scholar researching news reporting of serious crime and working between English Language and Criminology, this was an invaluable experience. Being immersed in the conventions of Criminology, English literature and

[11] *Crossing Paths: Interdisciplinary institutions, careers, education and applications*, July 2016, p. 5 and p. 8, <https://www.britac.ac.uk/sites/default/files/Crossing%20 Paths%20-%20Full%20Report_2.pdf> [accessed 4 September 2017].
[12] *Crossing Paths*, p. 29.
[13] *Interdisciplinary Research Advisory Panel Announced*, 10 April 2017, <http:// www.hefce.ac.uk/news/newsarchive/2017/Name,113331,en.html> [accessed 4 September 2017].

English language simultaneously clarified my sense of my own interdisciplinarity, while our project's symposium and publications have helped me build my profile in both Criminology and English Language.

Many ECAs are not so fortunate in their employment during and immediately after their PhDs. As Clare Egan points out in her contribution to this chapter, ECAs, interdisciplinary or not, often work in hourly-paid positions across various institutions. These 'portfolio careers' are time-consuming and financially insecure, and hourly-paid employees miss out on the benefits awarded to permanent members of staff. This set of circumstances has a particular impact on interdisciplinary ECAs. For one thing, it is often difficult for them to secure teaching and research that is spread across various departments in a single institution. A way of addressing this would be to create the administrative function of 'interdisciplinary support', whose remit would be to engage with interdisciplinary scholars across the institution, to address administrative problems raised by these scholars and to help with navigating the administration of different departments. Interdisciplinary support officers would also be responsible for helping potential PhD students to secure cross-departmental supervision.

The interdisciplinary portfolio career nevertheless offers the interdisciplinary ECA one particular benefit: the opportunity to teach in different fields at the same time. Hiring committees should recognise the value and versatility of interdisciplinary ECAs: their ability to work across disciplinary boundaries makes them uniquely well placed to negotiate the pressures and challenges of today's academic landscape, and offer students an alternative perspective on their field(s).

Stephen Watkins, Early Career Academics and Publication

It is no secret that publishing is an important aspect of academic life: this chapter itself is a testament to that fact. For ECAs it is a prerequisite for securing that first, highly coveted post and, in the longer term, for establishing one's reputation as a scholar in the field. Few, if any, research-active jobs are offered by British universities today to those without at least one publication to their name, and highly competitive postdoctoral fellowships often expect (demand?) evidence of a track record of publication for success.[14]

---

[14]   See, for example, the rubric offered to ECAs by the British Academy (<https://www.britac.ac.uk/british-academy-postdoctoral-fellowships>) and the Leverhulme Trust (<https://www.leverhulme.ac.uk/funding/grant-schemes/early-career-fellow

The imperative to publish is not confined to those ECAs seeking a permanent position in the academy, of course: the REF, impact agenda, and countless other factors have caused even the most experienced members of the professoriate to reflect on their publication strategies and research practices across the academy. No wonder, then, that many ECAs feel acutely anxious about that bogeyman 'Publication', whether that be because they have begun to embark on what is an often unfamiliar and complex process, or because they categorically have not.

What might be done to improve the situation for ECAs in light of all this? I believe we need to radically re-think the provision we offer PhD students and those in the early years of their postdoctoral career. We are indisputably at the point where the little leverage ECAs have on the academic job market comes from their publications and book contracts. The ECA provision that we offer should then reflect this, and build in time and space for publication of, say, one substantial journal article, submitted to a high-profile, peer-reviewed journal into the life cycle of the studentship. Rather than three or four years dedicated solely to the production of a thesis, this new model would offer all ECAs the opportunity to publish an academic research output under the guidance of their supervisor or research mentor. We know that ECAs are already publishing, but they are doing so when already overburdened with competing pressures: to teach, attend conferences, and develop professional and intellectual skills. Often, they write publications without adequate institutional and financial support. By formalising this extra labour, departments and, where relevant, funders would be properly supporting and monitoring their ECAs in a responsible and sustainable manner. It would also see ECAs developing research strategies and plans that they can then carry forward beyond the ECA stage.

Recently, there have been moves in the sciences to alleviate the pressures ECAs face in terms of publication. In June 2017, a group of Cambridge ECAs composed an open letter calling on institutions and funding bodies to reassess their publication priorities, to focus more on online, open-access platforms rather than traditional print journals with limited readerships that favour established academics.[15] My proposal is

ships>) for their respective Postdoctoral and Early Career Fellowships [accessed 1 September 2017].

[15] See Anna McKie, 'Researchers Push for Publishing Reform', *Research Professional*, 9 June 2017, <https://www.researchprofessional.com/0/rr/news/uk/careers/2017/6/Researchers-push-for-publishing-reform.html> [accessed 20 August 2017].

somewhat different. I do not deny there is a larger issue regarding academic publishing (I am very sympathetic to the scientists' concerns), but from the point of view of what English can achieve as a discipline in that larger structure, it seems to me that we should be more modest in our ambitions. My proposal is that publication should be recognised as a key milestone of the PhD process, and should, therefore, be given the proper resourcing such activity requires. This milestone might fall somewhere between the transition from MPhil to full PhD student and thesis submission.

The pressure to publish is not going to disappear for ECAs anytime soon. With that in mind, it is crucial that we accept the implications this has on our ECAs' time and energies. If we are to be a fully supportive discipline, then we must help our ECAs to achieve their full potential by offering them the opportunity to be as competitive as they can be.

Some Reflections on the Funding of English Departments

RICK RYLANCE

Why should academics in English take an interest in the funding of their discipline? The answer may be obvious. But in practice, even at quite senior level, I've observed, few follow matters to any depth. This is perhaps understandable as little effort is generally made to make this sort of information widely or accessibly known while, as a whole, we make little effort to follow it. As a result, headline issues such as student fees, or limited postgraduate funding, or 'marketised' higher education, consume our attention, sometimes separating them from broader patterns. The deep political and ethical resonance of such issues is naturally more interesting than quotidian income and expenditure. I have strongly held views about some of these high-level issues, which I will come to, but with the encouragement of the editors I want first to consider the bare bones of HE funding in a discipline like English.[1]

Though different disciplines have them in different ratios, and some (such as medicine) have supplementary sources, university departments have essentially three sources of funding: from teaching, research and other. I will reflect on each. The first is generally called 'T'-stream funding. This derives from undergraduate and postgraduate teaching for which a fee is charged. The UK and EU undergraduate fee is notionally variable, and universities could discount it from the capped maximum (currently £9,250 in England) to reflect actual costs or gain market advantage by competing on price. In reality, however, fees cluster in thunderous numbers at the maximum. Past attempts by a small number of publicly funded universities to offer courses at a lower fee to attract more students (thus offsetting lower unit price by larger volume) failed.

Committed to 'driving value' (so-called) into the provision, recent administrations have been keen to introduce 'private' (for-profit) providers

---

[1] What follows focuses on the situation in England; there are variants (some significant) in Northern Ireland, Scotland and Wales. Equally, there can be large variants in the situations of different English departments owing to organisational structures, teaching volume and research intensity. The analysis that follows will not be equally true for all.

into competition with 'public' (not for profit) institutions, hence establishing the market that didn't materialise voluntarily for reasons I will give below. The argument is that this will disrupt what is in effect a cartel at £9,250, thereby lowering costs for students and forcing universities to 'drive up' quality to compete.

Things are often 'driven' in this theory, but, so far, journey times are slow with little impact except as a theoretical (and ideological) challenge. Though some pressure is put on courses in, for example, professional-vocational areas such as accountancy, business studies, or some aspects of law, the actual impact of the private providers is negligible except as a challenge to the principles of public provision. So, there are two aspects to consider: has the introduction of 'alternative' providers had effects commensurate with the aim? (there seems little evidence it has); and, second, on what terms have the principles of public provision been challenged by 'marketisation'?

The truth is that what marketeers like to call 'level playing fields', when they are not calling them 'free markets', are no such thing. Private providers provide privately; they do not (except indirectly) provide the public goods and benefits expected of publicly funded institutions, all of which are a significant but legitimate cost on all parts of the system, English departments included. They include: research, support for public-benefit facilities (such as hospitals), technology transfer and innovation, business services, social and cultural facilities such as theatres, concert halls, museums and galleries, regional rallying points, international reach and influence, and extensive (and expensive) libraries for the storage and transmission of knowledge across generations and populations.

Nor are 'private' institutions extensive local employers, unlike public universities, which individually or clustered are often among the largest. Foreshortened in civic obligation, social responsibility and local connection, private providers are not, as the jargon has it, 'anchor institutions' in their communities. Nor do they do much to further the body of knowledge they teach. They do not offer extensive and expensive coverage across the disciplines and largely confine themselves to cheap-to-run, high-demand, high-return areas. You find little or no provision for high-cost medicine, engineering, or natural science, and private providers make little contribution to public bodies such as the NHS. This cost is (rightly) carried by the public sector. Amid all the theoretical driving that goes on in this line of thought, public universities are like the motorway system; 'alternative' providers are like the short private drive leading to some mansion. For all the talk about 'open markets' and 'price sensitivity', the theoretical focus on 'the customer' rather than the value of the provision means that what is 'priced' is highly selective and partial; in the public sector, fee income inevitably cross-subsidises multifarious activity.

Research (the so-called 'R'-stream) is the second source of departmental income. This includes both the QR ('Quality Related') money that comes from the Research Excellence Framework (REF) and that derived from research grants from public funders like the Research Councils, charities such as Leverhulme or Wellcome, European funders (for now), or business, industry or similar. The difference between QR income and income derived from grants is that the former is 'unhypothecated', a long word to indicate that no explicit stipulation is made as to what it might be spent on; whereas grant income is won for a specific project (Research Council postgraduate support, for example), and cannot be 'vired' (i.e. transferred) to anything else. This difference carries an important, structuring consequence for English departments, which I will come to.

The 'R' system is usually known in the UK as 'dual support'. It has many advantages. The theory is that QR money supports infrastructure (staff salaries, general facilities, R-related part of the bills, etc.). Project funding supports the specific projects enabled by the infrastructure, including a portion of general expense known as 'indirect costs' or 'the overhead'. It is a sensible dualism enabling departments to ride out income fluctuations, support young talent without compromising immediate income, and sustain a long-term strategy. Humanities disciplines benefit particularly from QR, as they spend proportionally more on longer-term commitments (mainly staff), and the gearing of QR income to grant income is much higher, a theme resumed below.

The third kind of income is 'anything else'. It can be: endowments, donations, intellectual property, money for events, conferences, summer schools, professional development courses, consultancy, etcetera. This tends to be a minority portion of a department's revenue, but is increasingly important. Some characterise it as wilful profit-seeking. But in fact it chases lost funding or escalating real-terms costs. Research rarely pays its way, as the funding councils' Transparent Approach to Costing (TRAC) exercises repeatedly demonstrate, and, as we shall see, 'T' funds are variably distributed. There used to be government money for capital projects like buildings or renovation, but this is much reduced. Universities now need to raise revenue internally or by borrowing, which naturally increases the amount collected from departmental income for central purposes. Increasing openness, and welcome changes in the way universities display their budgets, calls attention to this. Instead of departments receiving unexplained allocations (a not too distant practice), more detail of departmental income and expenditure is now provided, using explicit cost-allocation models to divulge institutional deductions. Though not always easy to understand, and with models that can be contestable, they reveal not inappropriate purloining by 'the centre', but actual costs and needs, and how difficult it can be to balance these off.

What are these costs? The largest cost is people: you, me, and our administrative colleagues. Across the sector, staffing amounts to 51.1% of expenditure just now,[2] and staffing is a larger cost in the Humanities as a proportion of overall expenditure than in the sciences. Then there are costs relating to many things organised centrally but consumed by all: utilities, offices and classrooms, recruitment/admissions, key shared facilities (computing, the library, and so on) the general estate (e.g. the campus, halls of residence), and services (cleaning, catering, porterage, HR, finance, student accommodation, inward goods, the Vice Chancellor, etc.). Then there are day-to-day operational costs: photocopying, new computers, external examiners, research support (including research leave), travel.... Finally, in most cases, a sometimes-significant portion of income is levied for general use by the university for investment. These might be new buildings or enhanced facilities; supporting academic areas under-funded relative to cost, or troubled by low recruitment or other causes; or expansion of existing areas or stimulation of new fields.

Most (but by no means all) universities accrue surpluses and significant 'unrestricted reserves' (i.e. disposable cash). A few of these are historically large, though increasingly concentrated in a low number of HEIs (14 hold half the total for the sector[3]). They accrue in the context of fine and somewhat vulnerable financial margins below 2% sector-wide.[4] Surpluses are used to guard against emergency or bad times, or for investment as above. Universities also have debts, usually on loans taken out for capital projects (such as new student residences). They also have assets that are theoretically disposable (mainly real estate but also art collections, technical equipment, etc.). But these are mainly dormant because they cannot be cashed-in without damaging core functions.

[2] Higher Education Funding Council for England, *Financial Health of the Higher Education Sector: 2015–16 to 2018–19 Forecasts* (2016), p. 25.
[3] Simon Baker, 'Future Prospects?', *Times Higher Education*, 17 August 2017, pp. 33–43; *Financial Health*, p. 11.
[4] Higher Education Funding Council for England, *Financial Health of the Higher Education Sector: 2016–17 to 2019–20 Forecasts* (2017). The 2017 estimate is reduced to take account of uncertainties about fee income, Brexit and other factors as compared to 2016 (*Financial Health* (2016), pp. 4, 7, 35.)

A macro-level trend is worth observing. In 2017, 75% of capital pro-jects were funded from HEIs' own resources or borrowing; this figure was 31% as recently as 2014–15.[5] Meanwhile, capital spending in 2015–16 was up 51% over the previous four-year average.[6] The reasons for this are increased student numbers, institutional expansion, demands for expen-sive fit-for-purpose facilities (e.g. libraries), and backlogs of repair and renovation accumulated over decades. HEFCE estimates this to amount to £3.6bn on non-residential estate alone.[7] Most of the sector there-fore faces falling liquidity (basically: 'cash') and increased borrowing. As noted, this makes additional demands on departmental budgets, and exposes HEIs to market risk. (In summer 2017 the credit ratings agency Moody's downgraded several UK universities, including Liverpool, Leeds, Southampton, Cardiff and Manchester.) What public universities don't of course have are shareholders or similar claimants on resource outside core function.

What is the significance of all this? The first and most obvious point is that departmental finances are unavoidably enmeshed with institutional finances. An English department cannot stand alone apart from the facili-ties and services that support it. Though it is not uncommon to hear colleagues complain, for example, about the amount levied for central charges or provisions, or that 'our' money is being used to support 'their' science, the latter is foolish in my view. It is reasonable to protest about over-charging, but it seems to me short-sighted to fail to recognise that universities are communities – or in the current jargon 'ecosystems' – in which interdependency is essential and fruitful.

This is a particularly interesting matter for disciplines such as English where there are frequently high levels of recruitment and a major gap between real cost and fee income. If each undergraduate in English brings in £9k+ in fees, the cost of educating her/him is only around two-thirds of this. A piece in *Times Higher Education* provided cautious comparative calculations.[8] It estimated that English was the fourth cheap-est subject (only psychology and behavioural science, law, sociology, and sports science and leisure studies lie beneath), and average costs are below £6,000. As the article acknowledges, making such calculations is difficult.

[5] Universities UK, *Patterns and Trends in UK Higher Education 2017* (2017), p. 44.

[6] *Financial Health* (2016), pp. 9–10.

[7] *Financial Health* (2016), p. 4.

[8] Simon Baker, 'Costs of subjects reopens debate over variable fees', *Times Higher Education*, 5 October 2017, pp. 24–5.

Good data are hard to get and, in any case, it depends on what one includes.

Nonetheless, a team at the Institute for Fiscal Studies (IFS) calculated that income from 'Band D' disciplines (largely those taught, like English, in classrooms) has risen by 47% since 2012, while that of 'Band A' by only 6%.[9] It is therefore reasonable to assume that money earned in English is distributed across a university and not spent 'at home'. Is this transfer of resource from low-cost/high-yield disciplines like English a good thing or a bad thing? It is likely to have helped sustain the growth in STEM disciplines of recent years, protecting these disciplines against real costs not covered under a capped-fee system. It is also said that it may distort investment, because 'rates of return' in the Humanities are higher, and initial costs lower, than elsewhere. I am sceptical about this (I see little evidence of short-termist growth on any scale). But it remains true that the actual contribution of the Humanities to institutional financial life is generally underestimated and often under-recognised.

There is a different perspective to consider. Communities are of different kinds, negative and positive, as George Eliot's novels, for example, explore so intelligently. There are communities of narrow, local interest, and these can be defensive, inward- and backward-looking, small-minded and ungenerous. 'Little England' chauvinism, newspaper hatred of the European Union, so-called 'gated communities', or various NIMBY (Not in My Back Yard) movements might be examples. Other communities can be welcoming, supportive of 'the other' as well as the included, and focused on the common good. Popular sentiment that welcomes migrants is exemplary. Which is the discipline of English to be? If English retreated into itself (as though it could), a university in the way I understand it – a community of intelligent minds brought together by common interest in exploring the world – would be supplanted by mindsets which say, always and first, 'this is mine'. A university without science (ludicrously under-priced in relation to cost at £9,250 despite 'top-up' support from funding councils[10]) would not conform to this vision, nor would expan-

---

[9] Chris Belfield, Jack Britton, Lorraine Dearden and Laura van der Erve, *Higher Education Funding in England: past, present and options for the future* (Institute for Fiscal Studies, July 2017), p. 3. These are aggregate figures. In citing them, I do not mean to make light of the predicaments of some English departments struggling with student recruitment, nor the systemic plight of, say, Modern Languages or Archaeology.

[10] This top-up in fact amounts to just 4% of overall 'T' income (*Higher Education Funding*, p. 11).

sion of investigation at the borders of enquiry be possible. It would in fact be a vision of that private driveway to the isolated mansion. Nobody wants appropriation, or unfair workloads consequent on revenue transfer, but we need to think bigger and wider, and not be grumpy.

The second point to observe is that, financially, teaching is more important than research in English. This has rather far-reaching consequences and is a touch sobering from a point of view that thinks the opposite; nor is it entirely compatible with, for instance, some university promotion criteria or career advice. Commentators sometimes distinguish between 'hard' and 'soft' money. 'Soft' money is that which is time-limited or otherwise circumscribed in use, for instance a fixed-term research grant. It cannot be factored into longer-term planning, even humanly crucial questions such as whether to give someone a permanent contract. 'Hard' money is that on which one can reasonably rely (i.e. recurrently predict), such as money from the serial recruitment of students.

Ten years ago, I did some rough-and-ready calculations on the balance of 'T' and 'R' income in notionally typical English departments (i.e. ones of moderate-to-large size with both UG and PG teaching and research). The picture may have changed but not, I suspect, crucially. The ratio of 'T' to 'R' was 80/20.[11] 'T' is more secure as well as larger than 'R', and, within 'R', grant money is more exposed than QR (see above). I also did work on notionally typical Physics departments: the ratio was the other way around. Physics is heavily dependent on the serial acquisition of 'R', especially 'soft' money from research grants and contracts. As a result, far more short-term staff are employed; and there is a greater emphasis on central facilities ('the lab'). This defines a department's relationships.

English departments (despite increasing employment of cheap 'adjuncts' to underwrite research as well as cope with increasing student numbers) have greater core staffing, which persists over time. I think it is easy to see a connection between this and, for good or ill, greater stability and durability in departmental identities and careers. Less anchored to 'the lab', the culture, perhaps a touch paradoxically, values dispersed, off-site working habits *and* proprietorial (or is it dedicated?) attitudes to 'my course' or (especially in PhD supervision) 'my' student. A biologist friend jokes that the real differences between humanists and natural scientists aren't intellectual ones, but the fact that the latter tend to attend the workplace from 9.00 in the morning, and humanists don't. In English,

---

[11] In the sector as a whole, 55% of income derives from 'T'; 23% from research; and 22% from other sources (endowments, investments, etc.). (UUK, *Patterns and Trends*, p. 40.)

the source of funding, which is not so grant- and facility-dependent, supports a more disaggregated group, a more personalised outlook, and sometimes a nebulous self-image as 'the departmental community'. Its less utilitarian work routines would not be supported in 'the lab'. It is always contrastively interesting to talk to science colleagues about how they approach matters such as the distribution of workloads or undergraduate teaching, for example.

My third point may be more provoking. My recent book *Literature and the Public Good* described English's customary disregard of the economic side of literature and lack of engagement with the literary economy. It also described a long-entrenched hostility to money and finance *per se* within the literary community.[12] Being rather estranged from these matters can lead to some basic economic ignorance, or a lofty feeling that it is someone else's business, or silly ideas. (How often have you heard it said that 'my research doesn't cost anything' for instance? If that were true, most should take a 20% pay cut as the 20% of income deriving from 'R' would be removed.)

However, it is also true that HE finance takes some understanding, and often finance professionals who work there are not conspicuously gifted with skills of non-specialist or even clear communication. This, paired with our matching lack of curiosity, means we have a regrettable and sometimes harmful pair of parallel lines between which complacency, prejudice and other awful assumptions grow at compound interest. I think we in English should take a more engaged interest in these matters, and that finance colleagues (as some do) should commit to explanation. We all have a duty to understand our situations and each explain endeavours that are not readily apparent to those outside. It takes effort.

Then there is the vexed question of student fees and loans, which needs more than technical understanding to have a coherent position, but some technical awareness to make that position significant. The following seems to me true: first, there is now large-scale dependency in UK HE on fees (42% of universities are dependent upon them for two-thirds of their income[13]); second, the money from fees has brought much-needed supplementary revenue to a stressed system (funding per student is currently the highest in 30 years[14]); third, there is a manifest need for the UK to provide adequate funding because it invests in future

---

[12] Rick Rylance, *Literature and the Public Good* (Oxford: Oxford University Press, 2016), chapters 3 and 4.
[13] 'Future Prospects?', p. 35.
[14] *Higher Education Funding*, p. 28.

social benefits including prosperity (worldwide, HE investment is corre-
lated with economic growth). So, eliminating fee income without viable
replacement is idiotic. And fees without loans is nuts.

The introduction of loans is said to have removed the HE portion of
the government's overall deficit, previously estimated at 10%. This is not
because actual, up-front expenditure has been reduced – cash for loans
has still to be found – but because loans, unlike grants, do not count on
the balance sheet for 30 years when repayment is due or they are written
off. In accounting terms, loans are notionally repaid so remain an asset;
whereas grants are dead-weight, unrecoverable costs. The flaw in this is
that most commentators predict mass default on student loans. The latest
projection from the IFS, following modifications in 2017 to the loan
system made under political pressure, is that the changes (which reduce
interest rates and thresholds for repayment) will result in no less than 88%
of those receiving loans not repaying them in their entirety. This is a rise
from the previous estimate of 73%. The government's own calculation –
generally regarded as conservative – is that 45% of the money paid out
in loans will not be returned. (This is the mysterious RAB – Resource,
Accounting and Budgeting – charge, which estimates the 'impairment'
on the loans – that is, folks not paying it back.[15]) Over 30 years, the
long-run cost to the taxpayer of loans over providing grants does not seem
discernibly different to me. The upfront spend (accruing to just under
£90bn in England alone) is not very different from the amounts needed
to fund grants.[16]

So, we have the nutty situation whereby the money is needed and paid
out, but a bit of accountancy pretends we're not paying it and keeps it off
the balance sheet for now, while trouble is stored for later public finances.
At the same time, an ideological drive to introduce a notional competitive market has minimal impacts and difficult-to-discern benefits. The
outcome is that in England we have the highest level of predicted graduate debt in the developed world,[17] paradoxically aligned with increasing
numbers going to university. Perhaps these 'informed customers', and
theoretical 'rational agents', simply know a good thing when they see it.

---

[15] Chris Belfield, Jack Britton and Laura van der Erve, *Higher Education Finance Reform: Raising the repayment threshold to £25,000 and freezing the fee cap at £9,250*, IFS Briefing Note BN217 (Institute for Fiscal Studies, 3 October 2017).
[16] Jack Britton, Karl Emmerson and Laura van der Erve, 'How much would it really cost to write off student debt?' (Institute for Fiscal Studies Observations, 14 September 2017).
[17] *Higher Education Funding*, p. 2.

The point is that cost, pricing and the rest of the theoretical bundle are poor measures of why HE exists and what it does.

Meanwhile, the system is non-progressive in being unable to deliver discernible advantage to those less well-off and in fact cements existing privilege.[18] As the IFS's *October Briefing Note* points out, the lifting of the repayment threshold only really helps higher earners because they will pay off less and later, while the majority are not anticipated to pay anyway, magnifying the problem for the public 30 years hence. In addition, there appears to be some evidence that students from prosperous backgrounds avoid loans and seek support from their families. 'Twas always so perhaps. But as there is a link between such backgrounds and subsequent high earnings, the 12% pool of those who will pay back their loans reduces further, increasing the amount not collected. And we haven't yet got to objections in principle (which I support) concerning rights to free education, issues of unequal social access to HE, and the ways in which the public benefits of HE are 'accounted for' in policy makers' minds.[19] In policy terms, politically, and as a matter of social responsibility – let alone as a way to run one of the UK's most productive and valuable economic sectors – the current fees-and-loans system is a dog's dinner.

The IFS report on the 2017 tinkering with the loans system justly remarks that: 'higher education funding per pupil has consistently been characterised by gradual real terms falls over a number of years punctuated periodically by relatively sharp increases following large-scale reforms. This is not a sensible path for university funding …'.[20] Indeed. And we haven't even got to the self-harming impacts of Brexit.

[18] *Higher Education Funding*, pp. 20–21.
[19] Martin Wolf, the *Financial Times'* chief economics commentator, is excellent on this: 'Why universities are not supermarkets', *Times Higher Education*, 16 February 2017, pp. 44–49.
[20] *Higher Education Finance Reform*, p. 7.

English: The Future of Publishing

KATHERINE ISOBEL BAXTER, MARTIN PAUL EVE AND LINDA BREE

Katherine Baxter, Journal Publishing

When it comes to editing journals, the advice available is plentiful. A quick search for recent reports on the experience of journal editing discovers a striking similarity in the experiences they discuss. Editors of academic journals in disciplines ranging from medical science to geography tend to refer to and reflect on the same basic challenges and rewards. These follow directly from the main activities of the journal editor. For most editors, the primary remit of a journal is to publish excellent, timely and original research that is relevant and accessible to its audience. Many journals also include commentary on recent published research in the form of review essays and state-of-the-field surveys, and some include other kinds of material such as editorials, roundtables, original creative work (whether visual or verbal), obituaries, and so on. Nonetheless, the main purpose of most academic journals is to provide a venue for supporting and showcasing new scholarship. In what follows I consider some of the common issues noted by journal editors, before exploring the impact and potential of Open Access and digital media for the landscape of journal publishing.

To publish scholarship one must receive it first, and many editors reflect on the challenges of encouraging plentiful, high-quality submissions.[1] Once material comes in the next step is to find willing and competent reviewers. As the competing pressures on academics' time increase, many scholars can struggle to find the time or the will to undertake what is usually uncompensated and invisible work. And this leads to the final shared woe among academic editors the world over: institutional support. Although universities are usually happy to provide a nominal home for a scholarly journal, the realities of institutional support are frequently meagre unless the journal in question comes with a major stipend or reputational kudos. Ian Hay sums up this situation concisely:

---

[1] See, for example, Charles O. Jones, 'On Being an Editor Twice', *Journal of Public Policy*, 6:1 (1986), 113–15.

Given the key role of editing in the maintenance of academic standards, it is deeply ironic that as the need for astute and erudite editors
grows, so have some of the institutional barriers to participation intensified, depriving aspirants from some of the fulfilling personal and
professional opportunities editing offers.[2]

To address this problem the Council of Editors of Learned Journals
(CELJ) have published a statement that outlines a list of recommendations for support and recognition: 'The Contributions of Journals
and Editors to the Scholarly Community and the Responsibility of
Universities to Foster Academic Communication through Scholarly and
Creative Journals'.[3] As Hay and the CELJ both emphasise, the benefits
that journals provide to the academy, through rigorous peer-review and
the timely publication of original research, vastly exceed the expenditure
required in terms of adequate workload allowances, use of facilities and
technical support.

As general editor of *English* I have been fortunate to have received
encouraging support from my institution, from my editorial team and
from our publisher, Oxford Journals. The digital systems that Oxford
Journals have in place are comparable to those used by many other major
journal publishers (ScholarOne Manuscripts is commonly used for literary publications, while Editorial Manager and Elsevier's Evise are representative of other equivalent systems). These systems limit our need as
an editorial team for extensive on-site technical support and facilities.
Nonetheless, numerous smaller journals do not have the systems and
support structures that major publishers can provide, and when 'camera-
ready' copy is required from journal editors, the time and technical expertise necessary for production are demanding.

The significance of journal publishing as a marker of quality has also
led to other pressures that come from within and beyond the academy.
Whether for tenure dossiers in North America or for national programmes
of research assessment (such as the REF in the UK, RAE in Hong Kong,
ERA in Australia), the journal article is a key piece of evidence for scholars
who are required to demonstrate the quality, importance and influence of
their academic work. As Hay affirms, anxieties about prestige and 'reach'
can lead to high-profile journals becoming overwhelmed with submissions

[2] Ian Hay, 'Why Edit a Journal? Academic Irony and Paradox', *The Professional Geographer*, 68:1 (2015), 159–65 (p. 159).
[3] Council of Editors of Learned Journals, <http://www.celj.org/resources/Documents/celj_letter-of-support.pdf> [accessed 11 July 2017].

of varying quality, while others with lower or narrower profiles can find themselves hunting for enough material.[4] Moreover the deadlines for both tenure dossiers and research assessment exercises can create pressures around review and production times, particularly where print copy rather than advanced access is necessary.

These requirements sit alongside an increasing demand for Open Access publication. Publishers who manage large stables of journals, such as Oxford Journals and Taylor & Francis, have been able to build Open Access and 'Free Access' systems into their production structures, albeit at a cost to authors and/or their institutions. For many independent journals, however, the demand for Open Access has been problematic. This is especially the case for journals published by smaller learned societies that rely on membership subscriptions. These journals have had to negotiate ways for Open Access requirements to be met without compromising their financial security by undermining the very service for which their members pay subscription fees.

It goes without saying, however, that though the challenges of editing a journal are multiple and varied, the rewards in doing so are also plentiful. Once again, the reflections that journal editors have shared about this aspect of their experiences are broadly similar. Christa van Kraayenoord, among others, notes the opportunity for collaboration that editing a journal offers.[5] This can be particularly rewarding for scholars who tend to perform their research independently. Journals are almost invariably edited by a team but, in addition to that team, editors also work with the members of advisory and/or editorial boards, as well as with the reviewers on whom they call, with the publishers who produce the journal, and – crucially – with the scholars from whom they commission or receive contributions.

This last relationship can be particularly rewarding, enabling the editor to support an author in producing the best possible version of their work and in bringing that work to new audiences. It is always a delight to receive a contribution that has been carefully researched, written and formatted, and which is evidently ready for publication with just a little fine-tuning. There can be another pleasure, however, in working with an author to bring out the potential in a submission that requires further development, nuancing or focusing. In both cases, seeing the final version

---

[4] 'Why Edit a Journal?', p. 160.
[5] Christa van Kraayenoord, 'The Importance and Pleasure of Editing and Publishing Research', *International Journal of Disability, Development and Education*, 58:4 (December 2011), 335–39.

in print, following the collaborative work of authors, editors, reviewers and publishers, is always very satisfying.

Jennifer Hochschild notes that '[o]ne pleasure of editing a journal [...] is that sometimes a manuscript will answer a question that I had only vaguely formulated, but nonetheless knew was intriguing and important'.[6] This is certainly my experience with *English*, and I would venture to add that with a journal whose remit is as broad as *English*'s one also learns a great deal about subjects that otherwise fall outside one's own specialism. A good manuscript will always get me thinking and formulating new questions, and will, consequently, broaden and deepen my understanding of the discipline.

The process of digital (and advanced) access means, of course, that the shape of an issue, as a collection of works, is not always visible to the reader, especially those who find articles through database searches. This manifests in a number of ways, including in the difficulty that some students experience with understanding the protocols of journal referencing. For some, the article is a purely digital object: one found, accessed and consulted solely through digital media. The situatedness of an article within a particular journal, volume and issue, alongside other possibly related material, is often obscured by the process through which that article is discovered and read.[7] One consequence of this is definitely positive. Readers who search for journal articles via institutional or global databases using keyword searches are no doubt finding relevant material in a far wider range of journals than if they had consulted printed indexes of likely titles, as was common practice in the past. As my own search for editors' reflections on their work demonstrated, a keyword search does not recognise disciplinary boundaries, unless you add in relevant parameters, and so the inquisitive researcher might find the insight they seek in an unlikely journal otherwise outside their discipline. The difference is both quantitative and qualitative: multidisciplinary databases do not simply make *more* available; they make a *wider variety* of material available. Although much of what one finds may not be pertinent to his or her particular needs (one reason behind our students' concern sometimes that they 'can't find anything relevant'), tactical searching can lead to surprising, even serendipitous discoveries. Seen in the most optimistic light this fact suggests that there is greater possibility for, and likelihood

---

    [6] Jennifer L. Hochschild, 'Introduction and Comments', *Perspectives on Politics*, 2:3 (September 2004), 437–38 (p. 437).
    [7] James Mussel reflects on this at some length in 'Moving on by Staying the Same', *Journal of Victorian Culture*, Digital Forum, 21:1 (2016), 95–101.

of, interdisciplinary research and mutual cross-disciplinary understanding than ever before.

What the digital search often obscures, however, is the care that goes into, and the value of, the issue and/or volume as a collection *per se*. The editor of the specialist journal might convincingly argue that careful reading of its pages can give the researcher all they need. Likewise the editor of the generalist journal might rightly point to the interdisciplinary range of that journal's contents. Titles such as *Journal of Victorian Culture* encompass a striking range of disciplinary interests within the parameters of 'nineteenth-century society, culture, and the material world'.[8] The nineteenth-century scholar, the editors might argue, need look no further. Moreover, the journal format allows the editor to select and arrange material on the reader's behalf, and to use editorials and other apparatus to help readers navigate their way through that material. In fact, journal editors frequently make use of digital formats to gather together material beyond the print pages of their journal in ways that mirror the practice of selection and arrangement that govern the editing of print-based issues. At *English* we have compiled virtual issues to coincide with particular conferences, for example, providing a tailored editorial to introduce the collection, and making all the articles within the virtual issue free to access for a given period.

Thus, whether collected digitally or bound, the value of the issue as an intellectual form should not be missed. Richard Rose sums up the underlying point when he explains that the 'art of editing a journal is to combine disparate authors and interests in ways that are intellectually satisfying'.[9] Indeed, some of the most satisfying reading that journals can provide is to be found in that combination of disparate interests. Journals like *Notes & Queries* are a rich source for this sort of intellectual epicureanism, gathering together the answers to a wide range of questions that, like Hochschild, we had otherwise only vaguely formulated. Even the most specialist of publications, however, can provide something of that satisfaction. The special issue, for example, might attend to a single author, text or theme, and yet the editor will nonetheless be looking to ensure that the issue's contributions reflect a diversity of thinking and approaches. In this sense the issue, and particularly the special issue, might be compared to

---

[8] 'Aims and Scope', *Journal of Victorian Culture*, <http://www.tandfonline.com/action/journalInformation?show=aimsScope&journalCode=rjvc20> [accessed 13 July 2017].

[9] Richard Rose, 'Editing an International Interdisciplinary Journal', *Journal of Public Policy*, 6:1 (1986), 117–19 (p. 117).

the rhetorical situation of the classical symposium, with each contributor offering a different perspective on a topic in the light of evolving scholarly discussions.

Certainly for us at *English*, one of the opportunities that editing a modern journal offers, one less available to the ancient symposiasts, is that of diversifying the voices in the conversation. Professors and graduate students alike receive the same review process and care in ensuring the best version of their work is published. Digital processes of submission, review and publication make it possible for us to work with scholars around the world both as contributors and reviewers so that good work can be published no matter where it is produced. Moreover, although cost can still create barriers to access for some international readerships, Oxford Journals operate sliding scales for subscription in order to reduce those barriers where they appear.

Engaging with Anglophone literary production, wherever it is found and wherever scholarship of it emerges, is one of the core ideals of our work at *English*. That ideal, however, is not self-fulfilling. Material and perceptual barriers exist to engaging authors and readers in Anglophone communities beyond Europe and North America, particularly, and overcoming these barriers is not straightforward. To raise awareness of our interest in global Anglophone literary culture we have instituted an occasional 'View from Here' feature, in which contributors from around the world reflect on the state of the discipline in their region. Another practical step we have taken is to ensure that authors are clear about the journal's remit: what kind of material we welcome, and what lies beyond our interests in terms of both quality and subject. Assembling an international editorial board whose varied expertise and experiences reflect the full range of the journal's interests has been essential. Such actions take time to bear fruit, and another skill the journal editor must develop is patience.

The future of journal editing is not wholly certain. Open Access debates are ongoing and continue to pose varied challenges.[10] These challenges are not uniform, and different kinds of journals will feel their effects in different ways. Moreover, although questions of Open Access are often driven by localised pressures, such as national policy (for example HEFCE's prerequisites for funding distribution) or institutional directives (such as the 'Harvard' prior license), journal contributors are not all equally subject to these policies and directives by virtue of their diverse situations and geographical locations. Those journals that wish to draw contributions

---

[10] See, for example, the current debates around the proposed UK Scholarly Communications License.

from a broad and international constituency are likely to find themselves having to be increasingly alert and responsive to the various localised requirements of their contributors. As I have suggested, another challenge to the tradition of journal editing is the impact of advanced access and digital searching on the cultivation of conversation within the pages of any given issue. Again institutional and policy pressures upon contributors that prioritise the article as a singular 'output' can sometimes obscure the collective value of that 'output' in relation to the issue in which it appears. Interestingly, digital formats have also provided some of the most rewarding answers to these challenges to the traditional print format of the journal. Stanford's *Arcade* website, for example, experiments with a variety of forms to bring together scholarship in thematic ways, notably in their 'Colloquies'.[11]

As might be expected, there are no straightforward answers to these challenges, and journals will respond to them according to their particular needs, priorities and communities. As a consequence, and this is surely a good thing, the diversity that journal publishing has always reflected is unlikely to diminish and the opportunities for experimentation and invention are likely, in fact, to increase.

Martin Paul Eve, The Future of Open Access

'Open access' (OA) refers to peer-reviewed scholarly material that is disseminated freely online (with no charges to readers) that also grants some additional permissions to readers (such as the right to re-distribute the work and to create derivatives).[12] Open access clearly has benefits for readers since academic journals and books are often priced well above a level that is affordable for individuals. It also has benefits for authors since sales runs on books have narrowed considerably over the past thirty years, and online digital availability, without a paywall, can increase one's readership substantially.

This is not to say that open access is easy to achieve, particularly in the humanities disciplines. The labour of publishing still must be remunerated, even if more technologically orientated thinkers believe that much

---

[11] 'Colloquies', *Arcade: Literature, Humanities and the World*, <http://arcade. stanford.edu/colloquies> [accessed 22 July 2017].

[12] Peter Suber, *Open Access*, Essential Knowledge Series (Cambridge, MA: MIT Press, 2012), p. 8, <http://bit.ly/oa-book>; Martin Paul Eve, *Open Access and the Humanities: Contexts, Controversies and the Future* (Cambridge: Cambridge University Press, 2014), pp. 1–3, <http://dx.doi.org/10.1017/CBO9781316161012>.

of this work could be taken on by authors to lower costs (just as the role of 'typist' was absorbed into 'author' with the advent of the word processor).[13] Institutional accreditation procedures can also motivate academics to publish in toll-access venues for purposes of appraisal and career accreditation, thereby slowing the rate of uptake of OA.[14]

I will discuss here 'the future of open access'. This is no easy task; for everything is easy to forecast, except the future. Those who would like more information about open access in general should see my book on the subject.[15] In this section, though, I will now discuss three areas of potential future open-access expansion and evaluate the challenges and opportunities that each presents. These areas are: monographs, preprints, and humanities data.

Monographs

Annex C of the UK's Consultation on the Second Research Excellence Framework (REF) notes that the Higher Education Funding Council for England (HEFCE)/Research England 'intend[s] to move towards an open-access requirement for monographs in the exercise that follows the next REF (expected in the mid-2020s)'.[16] While monographs have heretofore been excluded from OA mandates, this signal shows that research funders are interested in harnessing open, digital dissemination for research books. Such a move will likely cause alarm in the disciplinary space of English, but there are some reassurances. Any mandate at present stresses the co-production of print editions; the codex looks set to remain. HEFCE's document also follows Geoffrey Crossick's sensible report by hinting at liberal exemptions in areas with challenges of third-party copyright; creative writing; and trade-crossover books.[17]

[13] For more on the absorption of the labour of typing into authorship, see Matthew G. Kirschenbaum, *Track Changes: A Literary History of Word Processing* (Cambridge, MA: The Belknap Press of Harvard University Press, 2016), pp. 139–65.

[14] See Peter Suber, 'Thinking about Prestige, Quality, and Open Access', 2008, <http://dash.harvard.edu/handle/1/4322577> [accessed 21 April 2014].

[15] Eve, *Open Access and the Humanities*.

[16] HEFCE, 'Consultation on the Second Research Excellence Framework', *Higher Education Funding Council for England*, 2016, sec. Annex C, <http://www.hefce.ac.uk/pubs/year/2016/201636/> [accessed 2 May 2017].

[17] Geoffrey Crossick, 'Monographs and Open Access: A Report for the Higher Education Funding Council for England', *Higher Education Funding Council for England*, 2015, <http://www.hefce.ac.uk/pubs/rereports/year/2015/monographs/> [accessed 24 May 2015].

However, as a member of the UUK/HEFCE Open Access Monographs Working Group, I undertook some economic analysis of the costs of such a mandate. There were 28,628 outputs across categories A (authored books), B (edited books), C (chapters in books), and R (scholarly editions) in REF 2014. Taking a rough measure of eight book chapters to be equal to a single book, this yields 17,032 outputs (with no de-duplication for entire edited books being double-counted via all their individual chapters). Assuming HEFCE wanted a 75% compliance rate, this would be 12,795 outputs. In early 2017, a market average of open-access publication charges between Open Book Publishers (a small, new, but prominent and high-quality OA press), Manchester University Press, Cambridge University Press and Palgrave Macmillan came to £6,725 per book. Rounding this up to £7,500 for mathematical convenience means that the mandate would cost approximately £96m to move the UK's monographic REF outputs to a gold open-access mode over the next census period, or roughly £19m per year in a five-year cycle.[18]

There are many complexities and nuances to these headline figures that I am unable to discuss here for reasons of space. Readers may be interested to know, though, that despite the fact that UK academic library budgets could not bear these costs, since the UK is moving faster on OA books than other nations and we must still purchase books from abroad, there are funding budgets that are large enough. The funds are, for instance, just 1.2% of the total QR allocation, 19.2% of the AHRC budget, or 9.6% of the ESRC budget. A combination of funding sources, then, could make this possible, were it not politically impossible to top-slice these budgets. It is also important to note, though, that it is not necessarily the case that a single business model (book-processing charges) will be used to achieve OA, just as it is not in the field of journal publication.[19] That is to say that consortial funding mechanisms such as Knowledge Unlatched could also have a part to play in distributing costs worldwide.

In reality, this expense makes it likely that the proposed mandate will be scaled back, albeit not removed entirely; the first of my future-spotting predictions. Certainly this is not to say that OA books will be forever impossible; the internet is not going away, and other funders are

---

[18] Figures derived from Martin Paul Eve and others, *Report of the Budget Transition Sub-Group* (Open Access Monographs Working Group, 2017).
[19] For an example of a journal model that has no author-facing charges but maintains peer-review and high production quality, see the Open Library of Humanities, which I run with my colleague Dr Caroline Edwards.

vigorously pursuing OA monographs.[20] It is also not to detract from any enthusiasm about the possibility of widespread digital dissemination of otherwise under-read humanities books. It is just to note that a smaller-scale pilot probably holds more potential over a decadal timeframe.

Preprints

In high-energy physics and other mathematical disciplines it is common to post working papers online on a site called *arχiv* (pronounced 'archive' with the chi character). For authors this establishes priority over a claim, allows others to investigate their findings far more quickly, and creates a permanent record of the work. A recent initiative under Kathleen Fitzpatrick's stewardship at the Modern Language Association – Humanities Commons – is helping to pioneer the practice in our subject area.

Of course, there are humanities disciplines that have a long history of sharing working papers. Philosophy, for instance, has a robust culture of sharing work in progress, even if these are not called 'preprints'. (Although note, of course, the anachronistic nomenclature of 'pre-print' implying the digital object's originary status but defined teleology towards print.) Those working in various social sciences, which can cross-over into the study of English, also have the *SocArχiv*; an *arχiv* for their disciplinary space.[21] My own crossover work in the social sciences greatly benefited from preprint exposure, gaining national media attention and invaluable peer feedback before undergoing formal review and publication.[22]

MLA Commons and its underlying platform, CORE, though, form both a subject repository and a preprint server.[23] In the first of these functions, the MLA Commons asks users to deposit their accepted manu-

---

[20] 'AAU, ARL, AAUP to Launch Open Access Monograph Publishing Initiative', *AAUP*, 2017, <http://www.aaupnet.org/news-a-publications/news/1561-aau-arl-aaup-to-launch-open-access-monograph-publishing-initiative> [accessed 24 April 2017].

[21] SocOpen, 'SocArXiv', *SocOpen: Home of SocArXiv*, 2017, <https://socopen.org/>.

[22] Samuel Moore *et al.*, 'Excellence R Us: University Research and the Fetishisation of Excellence', 2016, <https://doi.org/10.6084/m9.figshare.3413821.v1>; Samuel Moore *et al.*, 'Excellence R Us: University Research and the Fetishisation of Excellence', *Palgrave Communications*, 3 (2017), <https://doi.org/10.1057/pal-comms.2016.105>.

[23] Modern Language Association of America, 'CORE', 2016, <https://mla.hcommons.org/core/> [accessed 13 July 2017].

script versions after publication – a procedure that will be familiar to most UK academic authors who work under REF conditions. Although this is hardly drastic news for those already subject to green OA mandates in the UK, it is likely to increase awareness of green deposit substantially in the United States, where centralised government policies have a far lesser effect on scholars' behaviours. Of the most interesting statements from MLA Commons's website, though, is the assertion that the site is 'not just [for] articles and monographs', exhorting users to 'upload your course materials, white papers, conference papers, code, [and] digital projects'. Aside from the pedagogical angle here, that white papers and conference papers could be shared in a preserved digital environment is a relatively new development for English Studies. That said, there are always the pioneers who have led the way before such matters were formalised. For instance, Steven Connor, now the Grace 2 Professor of English at Cambridge, has shared the full texts of his conference papers in the open on his personal website for many years.[24]

Here, then, is the second of my reckless predictions: formalised, open digital sharing of informal pre-documents will become the norm in the spaces of English Studies. This will have many advantages for our disciplines in an era of globalised communication, but one in which air travel becomes less and less tenable in the face of global warming. On the other hand, it will also open cans of worms around our double-blind peer-review processes. While I remain sceptical of such processes anyway (how often, in small literary sub-communities, is such reading actually blind?), in a time when pre-copies can be easily identified online and attributed to authors, will this model remain viable?

Humanities Data

For some, the term 'humanities data' will be an oxymoron, antithetical to the study of culture and bringing an overwhelming quantifying bias that distorts the very purpose of the humanities. If, however, we change the term 'data' to 'evidence', would the reaction be so strong? While 'open data' comes from the natural sciences, we could bolster the rigour of the work we conduct in English Studies through the availability of 'open evidence'. For we all draw upon source texts and artefacts as evidence that, often, could be made more accessible to reading publics than they are currently.

[24] Steven Connor, 'Complete Listing', 2017, <http://stevenconnor.com/listing.html> [accessed 13 July 2017].

There are some difficulties. Often, it isn't possible for our sources/ evidence/data to be open access. Sometimes they are under copyright. Other times, source material is neither digital nor even has a digital-correlate object. Yet, sometimes we are referring to digital texts for hermeneutic projects – working on editions from Project Gutenberg, for example. Sometimes we have consulted digital manuscripts online. Sometimes people write about openly licensed works of e-literature. In these cases the possibility arises that, alongside other research outputs, copies of the underlying 'data' could be stored and preserved, making it viable for others to check and verify findings and arguments.

All this, of course, is not even to mention the rise of digital methods in the study of literature that do produce quantitative datasets. While these methods are far from prevalent and it is unclear how far they will spread, the same arguments from the natural sciences about replication, reproducibility and verification hold here.[25] In making underlying data openly available, the degree of confidence we can hold of such work is increased. Further, this also comes with the possibility that others will further our work, using the same datasets to re-evaluate and interpret the work.

Should the digital humanities continue to grow, there is also the question of software availability and preservation. Certainly, given the moves to open access in other areas, it would be disappointing were such work to fall back on closed software that was inaccessible to most people. Such arguments most likely have limited potential in this current moment but they could loom large for us, as they have in other fields of endeavour.

This, then, is my third prediction: ideas of open evidence, open data, or open software will eventually come to prominence in the field of English Studies. This is the most speculative of my predictions.

Conclusions

Open access is here to stay; the questions that remain pertain to scale and delivery routes. In my closing words, though, I do want to address one challenge that could be mounted against my thinking here. A frequently used argument is to suggest that the humanities should 'not just follow the sciences' and to claim that open access is being 'forced upon us' because of its progress in science.

---

[25] See, for example, Martin Paul Eve, 'JSON-Encoded Textual Variance Between the Published Versions of David Mitchell's *Cloud Atlas* in "an Orison of Sonmi ~451"', *Journal of Open Humanities Data*, 2 (2016), <https://doi.org/10.5334/johd.6>.

I disagree profoundly. To resist practices that could bring so many benefits to our discipline simply to avoid change is a terrible loss for education, a loss for culture and a loss for university study of human-made artefacts such as literature. Certainly, we can continue to debate how and at what pace we move to the open circulation of articles, books, ideas, data, conference papers, and software. We can discuss the implications of various open licenses. We must also not neglect economic realities and the need to remunerate labour, alongside concerns for the futures of our learned societies. But to argue that it would be better that interested people should pay to read research material becomes, to my ears, less convincing every day.

Linda Bree, Monograph Publishing

As every academic – and every academic publisher – knows, a monograph is a specialist piece of research, written at book length (broadly speaking, usually somewhere between 60,000 words and 160,000 words, or 150 and 400 pages), by specialists for specialists in their field, and disseminated by means of a formal publishing process. For more than half a century, in most humanities subjects, the monograph has maintained a pre-eminent position for both scholars and their institutions. For scholars it has been the main means by which they circulate the fruits of their research, so that the success of a monograph – success being measured by sales, visibility and the number of other scholars taking note of it – can make a reputation and a career, and can change the way a whole area of academic research is regarded. For academic institutions it offers an external measure of the scholar's achievement, and so feeds directly into the structures of academic recruitment and promotion, and into the reputation of the department and the institution itself.

Academic publishers have willingly accepted the pre-eminence of the monograph, tailoring their own role to complement the requirements of authors and institutions. Within this tripartite endeavour the publisher has responsibility for selecting which monographs to publish, managing the peer-review process, working with the author on shaping the material into final form, managing the full range of practical matters surrounding the project, and guiding the author and the monograph through the production process. Once the monograph is published it is the task of the publisher to publicise, market, distribute and sell it, while at the same time protecting the author's intellectual property interests according to the law and the specific contractual terms agreed.

Around the late 1990s external factors began seriously to challenge this well-established, perhaps even complacent, process. The major expansion in higher education on both sides of the Atlantic over the previous decade meant that more academics than ever before were wanting – or needing – to publish monographs. At the same time increased financial pressures on institutions of higher education meant that the acquisition budgets of academic libraries – where most monographs would expect to find a home – were being capped or reduced, while demands on their funds were increasingly dominated by the spiralling costs of subscribing to the major scientific journals, and the expense of new on-line resources. The wider ramifications of these changes have multiplied their effects: technological advances have transformed the way that most academics carry out their research, while also in many cases reducing the time they have for reading because of the many other responsibilities connected with providing and conserving data; ever-increasing budgetary constraints have had an adverse effect on the purchase of monographs, to the extent that many universities no longer have an 'acquisitions policy' beyond responding as best they can to requests from faculty to purchase individual titles.

In the face of these changes, sales of individual monographs began to atrophy, publishers began to be very nervous about their profitability, and 'The death of the monograph' began to be widely forecast. It is a matter of surprise in many quarters that this forecast has not only failed to be fulfilled, but that the monograph itself – in a form that would be instantly recognisable to any academic from the 1950s – is still proving more robust than most people imagined.

In fact to some extent technological change has given the monograph a new lease of life. Digital printing techniques mean that the monograph is no longer reliant on a formal print run – with the accompanying risk of lower than expected sales resulting in surplus stock, or higher than expected sales resulting in the volume becoming prematurely out of print – for its existence; various forms of print on demand mean that monographs can be produced more flexibly and (in many cases) need never go formally out of print. Moreover, printing can now take place near where the books are to be sold, with a great increase in speed and efficiency of supply, a reduced risk of damage in transit, and a very welcome diminution of the cost, risk and carbon footprint involved in ferrying books around the world by sea in pallets. Of course, for the increasing number of books distributed in digital formats the costs of delivery, as well as production, are even lower (though the heady expectations, in the early days of digital publishing, of huge cost reductions have largely been replaced by increasing concerns about the costs of ongoing curation of the material).

In the light of all this, far from monographs withering on the publishing vine, the number of publishing routes for monographs is larger than it has ever been. If all else fails there is the self-publishing route, through Google or some other facilitator, though while that may satisfy a very basic requirement of getting the content of the monograph out to others in the field it is not much help with the 'career profile' purposes of the monograph. But the number of more formal publishing routes is also expanding. A report by Michael Jubb for the Academic Book of the Future Project[26] records that the 2014 UK Research Excellence Framework contained submissions from academics in the arts and humanities published through no fewer than 1,200 publishing sources. Some of these represent articles in journals, but a large proportion are monographs published by book publishers. The publishers range from small specialist presses publishing a few titles a year in select fields, through large university presses covering a relatively comprehensive span of subjects and kinds of books, to major commercial publishers with big lists in their chosen areas. They might be based in the UK, North America or Australia or Asia, as a single publishing community, all in their different ways negotiating a workable balance between the twin priorities of commercial viability and academic value. The great majority will be publishing monographs, primarily in the traditional print format, though increasingly in digital too, for sale; and a growing minority might be publishing in the first instance only or mainly in digital and/or Open Access formats. According to Jubb's investigations, there are in fact more monographs being published each year than ever before: and there is no reason to believe that this trend is likely to reverse any time soon.

But Jubb also pointed out in his report that while the number of individual academic titles published in the humanities increased by nearly 50% between 2005 and 2014 the average sale per title in print fell sharply over the period (p. 49), with average print runs now around 200 copies (and some falling well below that); though there are an increasing number of sales in electronic format the aggregate sale still shows a sharp fall. Of course some academics are only really interested in their book being visible to a very few people (either because it's on a highly specialised subject, or because it is needed primarily for a tenure or promotion committee to examine). And others are either enthusiastic about, or are being strongly encouraged to accept, their book being freely available in

[26] Michael Jubb, *Academic Books and their Future: A Report to the AHRC and the British Library* (London: Arts and Humanities Research Council/British Library, 2017).

Open Access format, where the number of sales in a traditional sense can be an irrelevant statistic. In these circumstances other factors will come into play. But most want to make sure that the publisher who agrees to publish their book is able to produce, present, market and distribute it as effectively as possible, and give it some kind of imprimatur of quality, in terms of the reputation of the publisher, the rigour of the peer-review process the publisher manages, and the appearance of the actual book in print form. And inevitably current sales expectations raise questions, for many publishers, about the resources necessary to sustain viability, where a couple of decades ago more than twice the number of sales of each title might have been expected.

The Research Excellence Framework must itself take some responsibility for the increase in the number of monographs published, at least in the UK, since its requirements strongly encourage the monograph as a unit of submission. It may be future REFs that exercise the most influence on the future course of the monograph – not so much in its form and content, but in the method of its dissemination. It was at one point suggested that in order to be eligible for the 2021 REF monographs would need to be published in Open Access format. That requirement has now been deferred on the valid grounds that the structures for OA monograph publishing are not yet in place, but the Government's intention to impose OA on REF submissions in the longer term is clear.

Publishers are responding to these changing requirements by experimenting with various OA models. However, the OA format poses huge challenges for the traditional system of monographic publishing, which has been based until now largely on a print model, and the general principle that the costs of producing a monograph, reflected fairly precisely in the price, are met by those who wish to own or read it. Shifting the responsibility for meeting the costs of publishing research on to private grant-awarding bodies, public institutions (i.e. eventually the taxpayer), or the author himself or herself, will bring different priorities and more radical changes. The initial impulse towards OA came from the sciences. There, significantly, research findings are mostly disseminated at article length. Commercial organisations, seeing potential for profits, charge large sums for subscriptions to journals containing the fruits of research often obtained with government, or other outside, funding, and this situation was felt to be intolerable. As a result, a system is developing whereby the article is paid for in advance either by the university department or another sponsoring body, or alternatively is, by agreement, made available free after a certain period of time during which charges can be made.

Applying the same principles to humanities monographs brings new challenges. The sum required to cover the cost of a monograph up-front (not to mention making a contribution towards the costs of administering the much larger number of monograph projects that don't pass the hurdle of peer review) is substantially more than would be needed for an article. At the same time grants are more sparse in the humanities than in the sciences, where the capacity of most research outcomes to cover their costs commercially is much lower. It seems unlikely that money will be available within university departments to fund all the applications for monographs from their members. Ironically this may lead to the kind of internal assessment/prioritising that the arms'-length academic publishing system was designed to avoid, and which inevitably risks disadvantaging those without secure institutional support, including part-time and non-tenured faculty, and early-career, retired and independent scholars, and which could be at odds with the principles of external peer review. Green OA, whereby the material is sold for a period and then made freely available, also raises questions for publishers who have until now depended on income on a title earned over a lengthy period of time. Already publishers are having to work out how to respond to first books where the dissertations from which they derive are likely to be freely available on the university's website. Increasingly they need also to take into account institutional requirements for posting some version of later research, and individuals' own moves to circulate their work on-line. An expansion of the requirement for OA in all these ways is going to require a major rethink on the part of publishers as to what their role, and – equally importantly, their financial structures – are going to be going forward.

The other major factor likely to usher in change is any shift in the way in which the universities come to regard the monograph in the humanities. Should universities start valuing journal articles, or web projects, equally with or more highly than monographs then one main impetus for monograph publishing will disappear. But so far there is little sign of this, partly because web-based projects – though the number of them is expanding fast – are very difficult to evaluate in academic (as distinct from technical) terms.

All in all, while the monograph may still be facing ultimate demise, so far it seems to be hanging on, perhaps increasingly outdated in some of its expectations and in the publishing structures that underpin it, but holding its position through the sheer usefulness of the form both to the academics who continue to feel comfortable disseminating their research that way, and to their institutions who continue to regard it as an appropriate means of assessing the quality of those whose careers are in their care.

Digital Futures

ANN HEWINGS AND LYNDA PRESCOTT

A casual observer on any university or college campus watching under-graduates on English courses heading into their classrooms may well conclude that the digital future is already with us. These students are now less likely to be arriving with bundles of books under their arms and much more likely to be carrying a lightweight laptop or tablet. They will not merely be word-processing assessment tasks for their coursework or reading texts online, but diving into digital databases and archives, and taking part in virtual discussions with other students. Although as an academic discipline English is still strongly identified with terms, concepts and formats from the era of print, it is increasingly infused with the potentialities of digital technology and digital culture. If, as seems likely for the foreseeable future, both technologies continue to co-exist, how will this influence our teaching, research and scholarship?

Some aspects of English's digital future provide researchers and students with opportunities to extend and develop established academic enquiries, using the power of digital technology to do things differently and at scale. Other aspects tap into the way that the digital culture of the twenty-first century is changing the way we read, write and interact with each other; these still-fluid developments include the impact of contemporary higher education's technology-rich environments on pedagogy. In some areas, continuities overlap with new developments, most markedly in English Language Studies. Perhaps the most obvious example is corpus linguistics, whose development runs in tandem with the increasing sophistication and decreasing size of mainframe computers. In the 1960s Brown University created the million-word Standard Corpus of Every-day American English, and this has been followed by both increasingly larger corpora and smaller, more specialized, corpora. Such digitized collections allow investigations of language features across corpora designed to represent particular genres or to represent, as far as possible, the language as a whole. Specialized corpora relating to a particular writer, text-type or genre allow easy searching, comparison and, where relevant, quantification. Corpora based on geographical or historical sources support investigation of English in particular places, at particular periods and through change over time. In relation to contemporary English, Ronald Carter and

Michael McCarthy's work on spoken and written corpora has enhanced our understanding of the difference in the rules of grammar that differentiate the two.[1] The fast pace of unplanned conversation requires different communication strategies to that of writing, and corpus analysis has enabled these differences to be systematically and quantifiably investigated, providing evidence that speech is not ill-formed and ungrammatical: rather, the traditional grammatical rules that hold for sentence-based writing cannot be transferred wholesale to speech, and indeed the meta-language of grammatical description needs to evolve. Importantly, thanks to the computing power of most laptops and readily available software, corpus compilation and analysis is now available to student researchers as well as academics.

When we turn from writing and speech to reading, one of the most visible ways in which university English courses have been transformed is through the availability of e-books, especially free e-books. Many students will be familiar with Michael Hart's Project Gutenberg, which provides an electronic library of well over 50,000 books. Hart created his first electronic text at the University of Illinois in 1971, and almost from the outset Project Gutenberg has relied on the efforts of volunteers, aiming to provide 'as many e-books in as many formats as possible for the entire world to read in as many languages as possible'.[2] Although Hart's initiative pre-dated the internet by two decades, it is a prime example of the internet's democratizing tendency. Another prominent advocate of world-wide accessibility is Brewster Kahle, whose free, open-access Internet Archive, founded in 1996, hosts one of the largest book digitization projects in the world.[3] Other initiatives, such as Google Books, straddle the divide between free e-books and commercial enterprise, but the downside of the drive towards greater accessibility is that sometimes quality and accuracy of texts is a secondary concern.

However, scholarly approaches to developing online collections have arguably had an even more profound effect on teaching and learning than the rise of the e-book. Many of the collaborations between libraries and private technology companies that have led to the creation of major

[1]   Ronald Carter and Michael McCarthy, 'Spoken Grammar: Where Are We and Where Are We Going?, *Applied Linguistics*, 38 (2017), 1–20.
[2]   Michael Hart, 'Project Gutenberg Mission Statement' (2007), <https://www. gutenberg. org/ wiki/ Gutenberg: Project_ Gutenberg_ Mission_ Statement_ by_ Michael_Hart> [accessed 8 October 2017].
[3]   Brewster Kahle, *Internet Archive*, < https://archive.org/> [accessed 18 December 2017].

online collections are distinguished by their concern for textual integrity and quality. One of the best-known products of such collaboration is Early English Books Online (EEBO), a digital collection of over 125,000 works printed in England before 1700. This enrichment of early modern scholarship was the joint product of ProQuest, a Michigan-based technology company, the University of Michigan and the University of Oxford, but the drive to digitize is by no means confined to the English-speaking world. A later ProQuest project, Early European Books, draws on the resources of libraries in France, Italy, Denmark and the Netherlands, as well as the UK, to bring together thousands of texts from the time of Gutenberg to the beginning of the eighteenth century. The chronological successor to EEBO and Early European Books is Eighteenth Century Collections Online (ECCO), another digital project linked to the University of Michigan Library's Text Creation Partnership, the partner in this case being the US educational publishing company, Gale. ECCO's two parts make available 180,000 titles, mostly in English, but also including works in French, German, Dutch, Italian, Latin and Dutch, and although more than a quarter of the titles fall under the heading of Literature and Language, the collection covers a wide range of subjects, from Religion to Law to Medicine. When it comes to online collections of nineteenth-century materials, there is an ever-increasing flow of digitized archives – no longer simply or mostly books – from numerous organizations, both public and commercial. The impact of digital collections on research and teaching can be gauged from the 2015 study commissioned by JISC, in co-operation with ProQuest, focusing on two relatively mature digital collections, EEBO and House of Commons Parliamentary Papers. Although there was more diversity than expected in the range of disciplines making use of these resources, it is no surprise that EEBO features strongly in publications related to English, so the report's finding that 'digital collections have become fundamental to modern scholarship' can be conclusively applied to English Studies.[4]

Just as physical libraries continue to play a key role in facilitating a digital future, so too do publishers of print books for whom quality is a key criterion. Marilyn Deegan and Matthew Hayler suggest that '[p]robably the most important online initiative for the study of English being undertaken by publishers is the Oxford University Press initiative Oxford Scholarly Editions Online', which began as digital republishing

---

[4] Eric T. Meyer and Kathryn Eccles, *The Impacts of Digital Collections: Early English Books Online & House of Commons Parliamentary Papers* (1 March 2016), <https://ssrn.com/abstract=2740299> [accessed 13 October 2017].

of OUP's own titles but has grown to encompass scholarly editions from other publishers.[5] Reflecting on the difficult editorial decisions involved in reproducing original print editions leads to some questioning of popular assumptions about textual stability in the era of print. There is, in fact, scope for nuance when contrasting the apparently 'fixed' nature of printed texts with the potential fluidity of electronic ones. Taking a wider perspective on overlap and continuity between different media, the cultural historian Robert Darnton notes:

> In the history of communication ... one medium does not displace another, at least not in the short run. Manuscript publishing continued for centuries after the invention of printing by movable type, and ... [t]he sustainability of the codex in a world of computers, iPads and smart phones should not come as a surprise. Reading has become more complex and varied, not shallower and shorter ... The digital is not the enemy of the analog. They live together in an environment where new possibilities constantly open up without closing off old ones.[6]

One rather paradoxical instance of 'living together' is the significance of the internet for the in-depth study of the history of books. The study of print cultures has become an expanding area of twenty-first-century English Studies, and Leslie Howsam suggests that both so-called 'digital natives' and 'digital immigrants' find the history of the book attractive 'because it puts the digital communications and "new media" with which they are familiar into juxtaposition with "old" media and their development over centuries'.[7]

These 'old' media include manuscript as well as print, and digital facsimile software such as the British Library's 'Turning the Pages' has made rare and fragile manuscript materials widely accessible.[8] 'Virtual books' created from the British Library's own archives include unique items such as Jane Austen's *History of England*, 'in the hand of the author, aged 13',

[5] Marilyn Deegan and Matthew Hayler, 'Digital Humanities and the Future of the Book', in *Futures for English Studies*, ed. Ann Hewings, Lynda Prescott and Philip Seargeant (Basingstoke: Palgrave Macmillan, 2016), pp. 161–78 (p. 170).

[6] Robert Darnton, 'First Steps Toward a History of Reading' (Preface), *The Australian Journal of French Studies*, 51 (2014), 152–77 (p. 153).

[7] Leslie Howsam, 'Book History in the Classroom', in *The Cambridge Companion to the History of the Book*, ed. Leslie Howsam (Cambridge: Cambridge University Press, 2015), pp. 253–67.

[8] British Library, <http://www.bl.uk/turning-the-pages/> [accessed 13 October 2017].

Charles Dodgson's 90-page manuscript of *Alice's Adventures Underground*, complete with 37 illustrations and an illuminated title-page, and William Blake's *Notebook* with sketches and annotated drafts of his poems. Ease of access to virtual (not simply e-) books brings into focus the interplay between print and visual cultures, including aspects of books as material artefacts, such as bindings, paper types and fonts. The experience of reading a virtual book from a period more distant than that encompassed within personal memory also adds another dimension to awareness of historical context, and brings the reading experience of twenty-first-century readers closer to those of a text's original readers.

'The reading experience' is another aspect of book history that has benefited enormously from digital technology. The Reading Experience Database, 1450–1945 (RED), began life in 1996 as a collaboration between the Open University and the Institute of English Studies, University of London, supported by the Centre for the Book in the British Library, with the aim of gathering as much historical evidence as possible about past reading practices and the actual experience of readers in earlier periods. The original database, which currently has over 40,000 entries, is now renamed UK RED, as there are fast-growing partner projects in Australia, Canada, New Zealand and the Netherlands.

The growth and easy availability of such resources (RED is open-access, and volunteers have contributed many of the entries) supports a shift of emphasis in learning and teaching towards the reader's perspective. Although the so-called Theory Wars of the later twentieth century have, arguably, subsided into assimilation, so that terms such as 'reader-response criticism' and 'reception studies' along with other once-prominent 'isms' are less likely to feature as stand-alone components in a university or college English syllabus, reading processes and practices form a prominent focus for investigation. Rob Pope suggests that 'reading as an opaque and contentious activity' can, like other central issues in contemporary literary study, be inflected with 'a wide range of emphases and orientations'.[9] Reading as a focus for literary investigation links easily with questions about the category 'Literature' itself: in *The Intellectual Life of the British Working Classes*, Jonathan Rose argues for a 'history of audiences' that focuses on readers, incorporating their responses not only to literature but to other elements of their cultural diet.[10] Here again digitization plays a

[9] Rob Pope, *Studying English Literature and Language*, 3rd edn (London and New York: Routledge, 2012), p. 10.
[10] Jonathan Rose, *The Intellectual Life of the British Working Classes* (New Haven and London: Yale University Press, 2002), p. 3.

part. For example, study of the responses of Dickens's original readers to his serially published novels can be cross-referenced to their reading of related texts, such as his weekly magazines, *Household Words* and *All the Year Round*, available and searchable in their entirety via *Dickens Journals Online*.[11] Awareness of the cultural context within which Victorian readers encountered literary works is further enhanced by digitized collections of ephemera such as posters, playbills, advertisements, etc., which are just one click away from the 'Charles Dickens' page in the British Library's 'Discovering Literature' online resource.[12]

Digitally derived enrichments to English Studies of the kind described here are often interdisciplinary, and could equally well be discussed under the heading of 'Digital Humanities'. But through its fundamental concerns with language, reading and writing, English is also at the forefront of discussions about linguistic, social and educational shifts that will influence the shape of our digital future. One prominent area of investigation is the way that digital communication has disrupted what Deborah Tannen in the 1980s[13] described as the spoken–written continuum from spontaneous speech through planned speech to carefully drafted writing, which has given rise both to concerns about literacy levels and also to celebrations of new ways in which to read and be creative with language and other means of visual communication. The newspaper headline in the Mail Online, 'Facebook and Twitter "harm pupils [sic] literacy"'[14] precedes a report that cites a headmaster as claiming that excessive use leads to a deterioration in spelling and grammar and a reliance on computer spellcheckers. In contrast, Gunther Kress in a study entitled *Literacy in the New Media Age* argues that

> the increasingly and insistently more multimodal forms of contemporary texts make it essential to rethink our notions of what reading is [...] [M]any contemporary texts make use of image and of writing at

---

[11] *Dickens Journals Online*, <http://www.djo.org.uk/> [accessed 16 October 2017].

[12] British Library, *Discovering Literature: Romantics and Victorians*, <https://www.bl.uk/people/charles-dickens> [accessed 16 October 2017].

[13] Deborah Tannen, 'Spoken/Written Language and the Oral/Literate Continuum', Annual Meeting of the Berkeley Linguistics Society, 207–18 (1980), <https://journals.linguisticsociety.org/proceedings/index.php/BLS/article/view/2133> [accessed 25 September 2017].

[14] Mail Online, 15 November 2015, <http://www.dailymail.co.uk/news/article-2507642/Facebook-Twitter-harm-pupils-literacy-claim-headmasters.html> [accessed 25 September 2017].

the same time, using both to carry meaning in specific ways. In that context, a theory of reading which relates to the graphic material of 'letters' alone is no longer able to explain how we derive meaning from texts.[15]

The emphasis on multimodal meaning-making is not new, but the variety of digital platforms and their widespread use has increased the visibility of communicating in ways that disrupt and augment the 'graphic material of "letters" alone'.

Our understanding of the production and reception of digital texts (where 'texts' here encompasses traditional letters but also symbols and numbers, colour, font and images) is still in its infancy and also, because of the speed at which digital texts are evolving, in a constant state of becoming. A case in point is the use of emoji. Text chat is more spoken-like than, for example, traditional letters between friends, but has fewer means of conveying affect through voice and gesture or expanded phrases. Emoji, therefore, provide a means of supplementing the communication through the written word. Philip Seargeant suggests emoji offer a way of compensating for aspects that are missing in text-based communication,[16] and Katherine Bourzac, writing in *Nature*, reports on the development of specific emoji for scientists including the desire by one academic to have a frowny-faced scientist to show that his experiment went wrong.[17] Playful uses of emoji and other symbolic language are now making the journey from the digital to traditional print media, further complicating the evolving relationship between different media.

Critical digital literacy is a current concern for those researching social digital media, and arguably this is an area where English Studies is able to contribute to wider public civic education. The concerns over so-called filter bubbles on Facebook, which result in users seeing all or mostly content that reinforces their own views, married with fake or false news, has led to calls for greater emphasis on the teaching of critical digital literacy skills at school and university level. Following extensive analysis of Facebook posts, Caroline Tagg and Philip Seargeant advocate a shift

[15] Gunther Kress, *Literacy in the New Media Age* (Oxford: Routledge, 2003), p. 140.
[16] Philip Seargeant, 'What can emoji teach us about human civilization' (2017), <http://www.open.edu/openlearn/languages/linguistics/what-can-emoji-teach-us-about-human-civilization> [accessed 16 October 2017].
[17] Katherine Bourzac, 'I can haz more science emoji? Host of nerd icons proposed', *Nature*, 539 (2016), 341, <http://www.nature.com/news/i-can-haz-more-science-emoji-host-of-nerd-icons-proposed-1.20960> [accessed 16 October 2017].

towards 'raising awareness of how the flow of information in society as a whole is managed in the era of social media, and the implications this can have for the maintenance of an effective society'.[18] The breadth of the English curriculum across language, literature and creative writing offers rich opportunities for citizens of the future to interrogate the media they consume.

The pervasiveness of social media is also impinging on digitally related pedagogy, although at present the relationships between social networking, informal learning and more formal educational structures still appear to be fluid. Discussions around the positive advantages and potential problems are taking place within wider debates about the kind of knowledge that we value and the respective roles of teachers and learners. Like other academic disciplines, English Studies has seized on opportunities to enrich teaching and learning through the use of digital resources, and online forums or conferences are facilitating exchanges between tutors and students. These developments have had an especially marked impact on Creative Writing, where the long-dominant pedagogic model of the workshop now sits alongside a variety of online approaches. The UK pioneer of Creative Writing courses, the University of East Anglia, currently presents short Creative Writing Online courses in collaboration with the Writers' Centre Norwich, and many other higher education institutions offer distance learning qualifications in Creative Writing, mostly at Master's level. In some cases one-to-one student-tutor interaction by email is a key component, while in courses such as those at Lancaster University and the Open University student–student interaction via online forums or conferences is a major component in the teaching model. The 'virtual workshop' thus favours co-operation and collaboration, and facilitates peer review as a means of developing skills and self-awareness. The potentialities of online group learning are not confined to Creative Writing, and teachers such as Rosie Miles at the University of Wolverhampton, a specialist in Victorian literature, have helped to influence the development of digital pedagogy in other areas of English, with an emphasis on student participation and interactivity.[19]

All academic disciplines are being re-shaped by the impact of digital

---

[18] Caroline Tagg and Philip Seargeant, 'Critical digital literacy education in the "fake news" era', in *Digital Literacy Unpacked*, ed. Jo Parker and Katherine Reedy (London: Facet Publishing, forthcoming).

[19] Rosie Miles, 'Research, Reflection and Response: Creating and Assessing Online Discussion Forums in English Studies', *English Subject Centre Newsletter*, 12 (2007), 32–35.

technologies, but English occupies a special place in this process of fundamental change. Cyberspace is not only a crucible for linguistic change but
it is also a place where new social practices lead to the emergence of new
genres – the blog being a prominent example. And the very way that we
read online is a topic of pressing relevance across and beyond academia.
English Studies, with its multiple focus on language, writing, and reading,
has a crucial role to play in exploring and analyzing what the digital future
involves, both for the humanities and in relation to society as a whole.

A View from the United States: The Crisis in the Humanities; the Liberal Arts; and English in the Military Academy

MARION THAIN

This short essay offers a few frames of reference from my current perspective within the US. I am a professor at New York University, but worked in UK universities for over fifteen years before that, and while the essay will raise more questions than answers I hope it might offer new perspectives for thinking about the future of English within the UK.

The most pressing context for English in the US right now is the 'crisis in the humanities'. That anything of the sort exists has been disputed by Peter Mandler,[1] but it remains the case that many major English departments in the US have suffered forty to fifty percent losses in English majors over the space of a few recent years.[2] Whether it's fifty percent over five years or forty percent over three years, the story is much the same in many places: recruitment of majors has fallen off a cliff. This has been reported and analyzed in a number of articles in *New York Times* and *Inside Higher Ed*.[3] Many are wondering what the future of English in the US might look like.

Numbers are falling in the UK, I believe, but at present nothing like they are in US. When we think of a crisis in the humanities in the UK we might think of the lack of government support in a STEM-driven vision of the future, but students are still opting to study English in relatively large numbers. So, what is going on in the US, and might the trend spread to the UK? It is worth pointing out that in the US English does not seem to be losing out to the sciences as much as to disciplines that are perceived to lead more directly to sectors in which the number of jobs

---

[1] Peter Mandler, 'Rise of the Humanities' (17 December 2015), <https://aeon. co/essays/the-humanities-are-booming-only-the-professors-can-t-see-it> [accessed 7 September 2017].

[2] Colleen Flaherty, 'Major Exodus' (26 January 2015), <https://www.inside-highered.com/news/2015/01/26/where-have-all-english-majors-gone> [accessed 7 September 2017].

[3] See, particularly, Verlyn Klinkenborg, 'The Decline and Fall of the English Major' (22 June 2013), <http://www.nytimes.com/2013/06/23/opinion/sunday/the-decline-and-fall-of-the-english-major.html > [accessed 7 September 2017].

is growing. The 2008 financial crisis – and a resultant sense of income instability and a fast-changing economic landscape – contribute (as the commentaries already cited point out): the steady rise of computer science and business studies suggest students are opting for disciplines that they expect (rightly or wrongly) will deliver them to sectors in which jobs are perceived to be plentiful and in which wages are relatively high.

Yet such pressures are at work in the UK too. Does that mean Britain is on the verge of the same exodus? There are, of course, additional features at work in the US that one might point to as responsible for this crisis. Often the university fees are higher and the resulting debts might make students think differently about their career plans post-study. A greater sense of insecurity around state-provided healthcare, for example, might also affect students' choices. Whatever the reasons for the difference in recruitment between the two countries, it might be helpful to outline some of the successful responses US universities are developing to this situation.

I work in the Global Liberal Studies program at NYU, an interdisciplinary program that reconfigures the liberal arts for the twenty-first century, which has a humanistic and global outlook.[4] The program is designed particularly to use the possibilities offered by NYU's network of campuses that stretch around the globe, to Buenos Aires, to Shanghai, to Florence, to Abu Dhabi, to London, to Paris, and elsewhere. The students spend at least one year abroad. The remit the program offers for crossing disciplinary lines and national boundaries is an exciting one, and we have a rapidly growing cohort of well-qualified students. The success of the program might be seen not only in its healthy recruitment but also in the achievements of its most recently graduating class, which produced a Rhodes scholar, a Gilman Scholar, as well as students with places in some of the top-ranking graduate programs and law schools.

What of teaching English literature in this context? I work in an interdisciplinary arts and literatures group, where literature is taught in dialogue with the visual arts, as well as other media. To teach, for example, late-Victorian British poetry, might be to do so in relation to impressionism in the visual arts and the aesthetic influences from France and from Japan. My experience is that there is a keen interest among the students in the intersection of issues of identity with aesthetics, material culture, and other topics that we consider central to the practice of English studies and the humanities. The interdisciplinary environment gives students the

---

[4] Liberal Studies, New York University, 'Global Liberal Studies' (n.d.), <http://liberalstudies.nyu.edu/about/about-the-global-liberal-studies-ba.html> [accessed 7 September 2017].

opportunity to study art objects (whether, for example, books, paintings or new media), in conjunction with the social sciences – and the possibility for interdisciplinary, or co-taught, courses allows for a topic-driven approach that can put English in closer dialogue with other disciplines. The introduction of liberal arts programs in the UK in recent years has, I understand, been driven in part by the same desire to reconfigure a humanities education for the twenty-first century.

For the faculty, such an approach to pedagogy can help represent and develop interdisciplinary research interests. We all know that research by scholars of 'English literature' is often intensely interdisciplinary – in relation to other cultures and issues of transnationalism, and in relation to other artistic media, let alone in relation to, for example, science, philosophy, or the social sciences. The concept of the interdisciplinary liberal arts can provide an institutional structure to match the rhetoric of interdisciplinarity that is so valued and encouraged by the research councils but so often not reflected in the realities of academic positions and working environments that enshrine traditional disciplinary divisions.

Many English departments in the US are themselves, of course, also working hard to rethink how they present the discipline. One renowned for its reinvention is the English department at Florida State University. They offer a variety of tracks and programs that enable students to specialize in 'Editing, Writing, and Media', 'History of Text Technologies', or 'Publishing and Editing' as well as in the more expected fields of 'Literature', and 'Creative Writing'. It is an enticing list of options, and, moreover, it doesn't include much that is not already an expertise that can be found in most large departments. It is a clever way of making the work of scholars in English departments accessible to and appealing to today's students. After all, many faculty members are editors, many do write for the media – why not share those skills with our students if those are the things they want to learn? Changing an English department's offering might be not so much about changing what we, as scholars, do, as creating programs that reflect more of what we actually do. Often our work is much more engaged with culture industries, much more interdisciplinary, and more varied, than our syllabuses suggest.

The 'History of Text Technologies' graduate program is something for which FSU has become particularly known – and with good reason. It is an innovative program that combines studies in the history of the book and media cultures.[5] It includes courses on, for example, 'History of

5 Florida State University, 'History of Text Technologies' (n.d.), <http://hott. fsu.edu/> [accessed 7 September 2017].

Illustrated Texts', 'Visual Rhetoric in the Digital Age', 'What is a Text', 'The Book as a Material Object' and 'History of Reading in Everyday Life'. It is taught by faculty from a number of different departments, and is interdisciplinary in its range but very focused in its concerns. It provides an exciting way to think afresh about literary studies, and it also provides an interesting twist on the turn to technology – and particularly digital humanities – as a response to the crisis in the humanities.

Digital humanities itself is a field that has frequently flourished in English departments of late, offering another area of potential development for the discipline, yet there is currently a good deal of ambivalence surrounding it. For some its new-found prominence is in danger of compounding rather than opposing the crisis in the humanities by suggesting a turn to STEM even from within the humanities, and an apparent acquiescence in the empirical and instrumentalist agendas that many see as responsible for devaluing the humanities in the first place. Yet there are many ways of bringing the humanities in touch with the digital world that connect with and exploit much more directly what we might think of as the strengths of humanities methods. However much we need workers who can code, arguably the greater deficit we will shortly be facing is for people who can engage with that technology ethically and creatively, and who can bring new perspectives and ideas. Who better placed for that work than humanities students who have learnt to engage with technology? At NYU I have designed an undergraduate course exploring digital cultures that aims to introduce liberal arts students to the big issues in thinking about the digital world (for example, freedom versus regulation, privacy, anonymity versus accountability), and both literary fiction and the type of cultural theory regularly taught in English departments are central to this course. Moreover, the value of literature can be clearly seen in this context in its ability to provide a vision of the possible consequences (utopian or dystopian) of the choices that currently face our society. In this course I don't teach the students to use any computer languages (although I do introduce them to some), but I do give them knowledge that will enable them to lead in the digital age. The growth of a technologically engaged humanities is an area of huge potential (not least for employment: several students who went for job and internship interviews told me how interested their potential employers in the tech sector were in the Digital Cultures course).

If the above gives some examples of responses to the plummeting recruitment of English majors in the US, I want now to turn to the one place in the US I have found where English seems less immediately troubled by the crisis in the humanities. A few months ago, I was eating inside a vast dining hall in the middle of the US Military Academy (USMA) campus at West Point. All four thousand cadets at the academy were also there, sharing the daily communal lunch. This visit offered a context very different from any other in which I have spoken as a literature professor. USMA at West Point is a large campus situated on the top of some cliffs along the Hudson Valley about fifty miles north of Manhattan, with breath-taking views down the river and the valley. Everything about it is impressive, and a little intimidating. I was curious to know what English as a discipline looked like in this, for me at least, rather novel context. USMA has specialized in the past above all in engineering: at one time all cadets graduated with an engineering degree. Yet times have changed and skills that once had an obvious role in the life of a soldier are now no longer considered so central (they now have three core courses for all cadets but are considering reducing further). But English? What of poetry and the literary arts in this context?

Some of the cadets I spoke to said they were English majors against the advice of parents – but they had all chosen a path that put them in a small (relative to engineering) but not apparently embattled group of students in the English program. English at the West Point campus feels perhaps relatively distant from the crisis of the humanities for several reasons. First within the environment of the military academy it was probably never central, so the faculty have always had to make a strong case for it. The case was already made before 2008. As one of the English professors at USMA suggested to me: before the crisis in the humanities, English was perhaps much stronger outside the military academy; since the crisis in the humanities, literary study is embattled outside of military academy but holds a relatively secure position within it. The general officers who lead the institution champion the liberal arts, sometimes by way of an appeal to the quotation by British general Sir William Francis Butler: 'The nation that will insist on drawing a broad line of demarcation between the fighting man and the thinking man is liable to find its fighting done by fools and its thinking by cowards.'[6] Literature has been on the West Point USMA curriculum since the mid-nineteenth century, and a department of English and History was formed in the early twentieth century.[7] English is now in a department of English and Philosophy, with a major in each discipline. The fate and character of the discipline within the military academy rests, in part, on the different factors structuring student choice:

[6] Elizabeth D. Samet, *Soldier's Heart* (New York: Farrar, Straus and Giroux, 2007), pp. 75–76.
[7] *Soldier's Heart*, p. 80.

they don't pay fees and are guaranteed a job in the army at the end of it. This structure takes away some of the pressure that is driving students into computer science and business studies, and they are perhaps freer to follow their interests.

The English majors I taught at West Point were highly motivated, bright and engaged – and a pleasure to work with. But what had drawn them to the subject? The cadets' time is divided between the physical program, the military program and the academic program: how does the study of poetry dovetail with push-ups and military drills? They stressed the need for good communication skills in a military setting. We talked of the absolute importance for officers not just to be understood but to not be misunderstood. They also talked about the role of literature in fostering an appreciation of the perspective of others, and for understanding cultural difference. It is interesting to see how strongly USMA emphasizes the importance of studying literature for developing empathy, gaining an appreciation of the points of view of others, and also for helping thinking through moral or ethical dilemmas. One English professor who has taught there for many years has written, for example, of the importance of imaginative literature in helping cadets to anticipate various eventualities, and the value of fiction for imagining circumstances for which history offers insufficient plots.[8] She also wrote about her experience of cadets going to fight in Afghanistan and finding their knowledge of the poet Rumi a crucial source of connection with Afghan colonel allies, for whom poetry is a far more important cultural touchstone than for the average American.[9]

These ways of thinking about the value of studying literature are deeply engrained in West Point culture, as can be seen from their advertising brochure for the English major. Under the heading 'Why Major in English' one can read the following:

> With a true appreciation of our diverse world, English majors are prepared to negotiate the problems facing twenty-first century leaders. The study of literature moves beyond simple awareness of other perspectives and equips students with the skills they need to engage with other cultures. The resulting understanding of humanity and culture is a vital contributor to success in the military profession. The study of literature fosters essential leadership skills including critical thought, clear and persuasive communication, creativity, and ethical awareness. By engag-

[8] *Soldier's Heart*, pp. 67–68.
[9] *Soldier's Heart*, p. 80.

ing with the diversity that characterizes the human condition, English majors are ready to solve problems creatively and also to communicate their ideas and solutions clearly and persuasively – talents essential to a meaningful life of service.[10]

Under the heading 'Literature Matters':

> From issues of civic responsibility to the lasting impact of colonial rule to current race relations, the range of topics in English is boundless. Armed with a variety of critical lenses through which to examine literature, English majors not only solve problems but do so creatively. Not only do majors gain an ability to interpret a variety of texts, but they engage with vital cultural, sociological, and political issues represented in literature.[11]

They make a strong case for the skills learned from studying English as useful in professional life of the twenty-first century. The points they make about leadership, dealing with other cultures, creative problem-solving and ethical awareness might be relevant to many fields. They also quote military personnel who note the powerful connection between officership and the liberal arts. Former Army Chief of Staff, and former faculty member of the Department of English and Philosophy, Eric Shinseki notes:

> It is to the skills and lessons I acquired in the study of art, philosophy, and literature that I turned most frequently and used each and every day to understand, to communicate, to educate, and to motivate others in helping me accomplish my military responsibilities.[12]

Such testimony is powerful, particularly in relation to what might be seen by some as an unlikely combination of military training and the humanities.

These are all good reasons to study literature, but not necessarily reasons that English departments in the UK typically appeal to these days. A substantial but by no means exhaustive trawl through websites of English programs in a variety of types of UK university found little of

[10] United States Military Academy West Point, New York, 'The Major in English' (n.d.), <westpoint.edu/dep/Documents/Draft EnglishTrifold 1.pdf> [accessed 7 September 2017]

[11] 'The Major in English'.

[12] 'The Major in English'.

this type of argument for the discipline. Seeing how USMA articulated the value of studying English made me wonder whether we might think more about what brings students to the academy to study literature, what they are looking for from it, and how it might connect for them with their future career plans. USMA at West Point is an institution with a rather specific purpose and context, so their particular pitch may or may not feel relevant to our own contexts, but it might prompt us to think more about what our students need. Do UK students share a desire for literature to forge points of cultural understanding, models of engagement with the other, and a development in empathy and moral understanding? Could we be using this and other models as a prompt to think more broadly about how we can best engage students with literature? Similarly, what might an interdisciplinary liberal arts school (like that at NYU) offer to scholars and students of English? Teaching the humanities in an interdisciplinary environment in dialogue with other disciplines around topics of current concern might enable us to engage new audiences for our work, but what would this mean for our disciplinary communities and how might it be possible to preserve a strong disciplinary foundation while also building institutional structures that enable more opportunity for cross-disciplinary work? The answers to these questions will depend a great deal on individual UK contexts and the particular opportunities and challenges they present, but we don't need to wait for a crisis in recruitment to make them worth asking.[13]

[13] Acknowledgements: many thanks to Prof. Justin Sider for inviting me to USMA, and to Prof. Patrick Query for discussion about English at USMA.

The Future of Borders

DANIEL O'GORMAN

In May 2014, the then-Education Secretary Michael Gove sparked controversy by proposing to effectively restrict the 'Post-1914' section of the GCSE English curriculum to 'fiction or drama written in the British Isles'. The decision was met with anger from English teachers and literary scholars around the country. As Anna Hartnell argued, the policy – which would result in the cutting of texts such as Harper Lee's *To Kill a Mockingbird*, Arthur Miller's *The Crucible* and John Steinbeck's *Of Mice and Men* – is 'not just parochial and regressive', but

> also fails to recognise the dynamics that make up modern Britain. It fails to understand that a large part of the value of reading literature lies precisely in the kind of empathic leap Scout makes at the end of Lee's novel, one that enables her to see herself through the eyes of an 'other' and so more fully comprehend her own identity.[1]

The ferocity of the debate surrounding Gove's decision brought to the fore something quite singular about English as a core subject at GCSE level: namely, its centrality to collective feelings about British national identity. In contrast to Science and Maths (and, at least until 2015, when English Literature was made an optional GCSE, more intensely than other Arts and Humanities subjects), the debates that take place in the English Literature GCSE classroom are debates that actively and substantively contribute towards the construction of our national imaginary; or, in Bendict Anderson's often-cited phrase, our 'imagined community'.[2] What's more, three years on, this political row has taken on an extra degree of significance: in the wake of his stint in the Department for Education, Gove has proceeded to become one of Brexit's most outspoken champions. This development, of course, reveals an unnerving warning

---

[1] Anna Hartnell, 'Michael Gove Should Not Kill the Mockingbird', *Guardian*, 26 May 2014, <https://www.theguardian.com/commentisfree/2014/may/26/michael-gove-to-kill-a-mockingbird-harper-lee-gcse-syllabus>.

[2] Benedict Anderson, *Imagined Communities: Reflections on the Origins and Spread of Nationalism* (London and New York: Verso, 2006).

of things to come in his earlier GCSE English policy change, but, more importantly than this, it also reflects how crucial a role the subject of English plays in the way we conceptualise our national borders: not just in terms of immigration and the economy, but also, on a deeper, more paradigmatic level, in terms of how we demarcate Britishness itself and the values we perceive it to contain.

It is for this reason that English, and the decisions taken about the study of texts on school syllabi, occupy an important place in today's climate of uncertainty over the future of Britain's borders. As a subject concerned with language, English is never completely disconnected from politics, and debates in the classroom inevitably form a key part of the process by which pupils' views about the world are both challenged and developed. To borrow bell hooks' memorable words:

> Like desire, language disrupts, refuses to be contained within bounda-
> ries. It speaks itself against our will, in words and thoughts that intrude,
> even violate the most private spaces of mind and body.[3]

Literature is language, and it is impossible to read it and remain unchanged in some subtle way. Nonetheless, while English does, for this reason, maintain a 'disruptive' pedagogical potential, by restricting the pool of texts to those that are perceived to be British-authored, as well as quietly dropping the Literature component from what is now solely a core English Language GCSE, the Government *has* effectively acted to police the subject's borders. At the very least, these decisions will have an impact on the number of students who will go on to study it at university in coming years. As a result of these policies, clearly not just political but actively *politicised* and ideological, English's ability to inspire an intellectual transgression of borders at GCSE level is undoubtedly now more limited than it was before: looking back, we can see that the subject experienced a small-scale Brexit of its own in the lead-up to the national EU referendum.

One need look no further than the transnational turn in literary studies over the past two decades to see that Gove and the Conservative Government's recent changes to the English GCSE are out of step with the direction in which the subject is going at the level of research. These are reactionary measures clearly designed to protect a deeply traditionalist understanding of what the study of English is for, enforcing arbitrary boundaries around it at a time when the subject's leading experts are

---

³ bell hooks, *Teaching to Transgress* (New York and London: Routledge, 1994), p. 167.

repeatedly calling such boundaries into question. Postcolonialism, trauma theory and ecocriticism are just three strands of contemporary literary studies that do not only encourage a consideration of texts in a context that transcends national borders, but that also push against and frequently subvert the borders of the discipline itself. The English Literature GCSE is being forced into a restrictive, long-outdated mould at a time when English in universities has never been more multifaceted or open to interdisciplinarity.

This border-crossing impulse was palpable throughout the inaugural English: Shared Futures conference in Newcastle in June 2017. The panel that I organised, for instance, was named for the prefix 'trans-', a term that denotes, variously, the following: 'across', 'beyond', 'through', 'changing thoroughly', 'on the other side of'. The transgression of borders, whether national, personal, or disciplinary, is frequently among English's central concerns, and recent years have seen the emergence of entire sub-categories of literary and theoretical analysis reliant upon the prefix: transgender studies, transnationalism and transmediality to name just three. These were all examined in four diverse presentations that actively worked to foreground the capacity of the subject to encourage radical border-crossings. Kirstian Shaw began by outlining the political import of transnational fictions in the post-Brexit moment; next, Dorothy Butchard explored the exciting interfaces between transatlanticism and transmediality in contemporary fiction; Emily Rose then went on to discuss the complications that arise in the translation of transgender narratives into English; and, finally, Oliver Paynel closed the session by explaining the continued relevance to the discipline of philosopher Jean Baudrillard's concept of transaesthetics. The presentations drew out the intersections between these diverse literary and theoretical sub-fields, and in doing so, productively called attention to an ongoing ideological preoccupation in the discipline with this border-crossing prefix, which we in the discipline so frequently employ.

A glance at panel titles from throughout the conference reveals that a similar drive to challenge borders was at play across its entire three days. For a start, five panels, all from what might at first appear to be quite disparate branches of the discipline, included the word 'border' in their titles:

- **'Migration and Borders'**, a creative writing panel, which also hosted a poetry reading session;
- **'B/Orders of Standard English: Registering Linguistic Difference in the Academic Writing Classroom'**, which spanned linguistics and pedagogy;

- **'The Borders of Irish Studies'**, the official panel of the British Association of Irish Studies;
- **'At the Borders of Globalisation'**, organised by the Manchester Metropolitan and Nottingham Trent joint 'Troubling Globalisation' research network; and
- **'Crossing Borders in the Nineteenth Century: Genre and Time'**, a nineteenth-century literature panel.

These were in addition to the numerous panel titles in which border crossings of one sort or another were heavily implied. To mention only a handful: 'Shared Responsibility: Auto/Biography and the Ethics of Representation'; 'Global Futures'; 'After Brexit: Life Without Erasmus'; '"Between and Across Languages": Scottish Literary Studies in the Twenty-first Century'; 'Romanticism and the Stigmatised: Transnationalism, Migration and Trauma'; 'Divided by a Common Language: Creative Writing Discourse in the US, UK and Australia'; 'The Environmental Humanities: The Interdependent Present'; 'Beyond the East/West Divide'; 'Multi-cultural Textualities'; 'Transnational Scholarship and the Digital Edition'; 'Music as Literature, Literature as Music'; and 'Across the Great Divide: the Scientific Humanities and the Future of the Discipline'. These border-crossing sessions collectively underscored the shared disciplinary futures of the conference's title.

There were two strands of the conference in particular in which the border-crossings of contemporary English Studies were interrogated with an extra degree of nuance. These were the strand of sessions on contemporary literature, and also that on postcolonial literature. In the former, what might better be described as a kind of disciplinary border-*dissolving*, was clearly at play in the panel 'Awake and Present: A Roundtable on Why Contemporary Literature Matters', sponsored by the British Association for Contemporary Literary Studies. Its premise began with an acknowledgement of the increasingly blurred borderline between fiction as experienced in literature, and in the increasing virtuality of twenty-first-century culture in which we are all immersed, whether as readers, writers or critics:

> In the age of speculative finance, employment by smartphone app, globalised production chains, and nano-imaging technologies the experience of "contemporary fiction" far exceeds reading contemporary literature. ... As literary critics of and in the contemporary, we need to acknowledge our immersion in this emerging scene, not feign some critical distance.

Rather than to suggest that criticism in this immersive contemporary environment is somehow anachronistic, the session called to acknowledge the twenty-first-century critic's inescapable situatedness in the contemporary moment. Additionally, it underscored a need to recognise that astute, politically conscious contemporary literary criticism necessarily entails an understanding that what both publishers and academics both tend to automatically delineate as 'fiction', perhaps through an over-eagerness for taxonomy, is actually impossible to contain within traditional disciplinary boundaries.

A similar disciplinary self-questioning was evident in the conference's sessions on postcolonial literature. With Brexit and Donald Trump forming a repeated touchstone for speakers across the conference, particularly among those for whom borders were a primary concern, the postcolonial sessions had a sense of recognition about them. Borders have been central to postcolonial studies for as long as the field has existed, and while contemporary events have necessarily pushed them centre-stage in current affairs (whether in the form of the refugee crisis, or in that of Trump's proposed US–Mexico border wall), these panels reminded their audiences of borders that have been persistent for certain groups and communities for decades. There was a particular focus, for instance, on the borders that have been faced by Muslim communities in Britain and the United States since 9/11, in both of the event's 'Multi-cultural Textualities' panels.

Importantly, a number of postcolonial scholars, either implicitly or explicitly, also warned against an indiscriminate celebration of literary border-crossing, drawing attention to instances in which borders might be better left respected. Anshuman Mondal's discussion of Michel Houellebecq's novel about Islamism, *Submission* (2015), for example, examined the ethics of a prominent fiction writer's claim to transgressing a border perceived to have been imposed by politically correct liberals, when those who might be maligned as a result of this kind of border-crossing are always most likely to be those in Paris' highly marginalised Muslim communities. Meanwhile, as part a session on 'The Past, Present and Future of Postcolonial Studies', Shital Pravinchandra warned against the potential depoliticisation that can sometimes accompany contemporary impulses to 'move beyond' the postcolonial. The border crossings implied in categorisations such as transnational, global Anglophone or 'world' literature must not, she reminded, lose sight of the material iniquities, injustices and neocolonialisms inherent to a contemporary world in which we, as critics, are ourselves once again immersed, and to which postcolonialism continues to be particularly well attuned.

English crosses borders, draws attention to borders, and can also defend borders. As Gayatri Chakravorty Spivak has recently argued, 'Radical teachers and thinkers must keep thinking and teaching a border-less world,' but this conception of borderlessness demands nuancing in recognition of the kinds of borders that protect civil rights, whether in the form of social norms or actual legislation.[4] Pointing, as an example, to 'the seemingly permeable female body', she writes: 'In a symmetri-cal world, "bordered" and "borderless" would be substitutable. But all situations are marked by the asymmetry of interest and power.'[5] Many of the sessions at English: Shared Futures demonstrated precisely this kind of nuance, exploring the ways in which the discipline contributes to the 'thinking and teaching' of a borderless world, while simultaneously helping support the kinds of socially and legally agreed-upon borders that protect the vulnerable from discrimination and abuse (through feminism, antiracism, and other kinds of diversity work).

What the contemporary literature and the postcolonial panels drew particular attention to was the question of where, exactly, the borders of English in the twenty-first century lie: one that could hardly be further removed from recent decision-making about English as a subject by the Department for Education. The questioning of English's borders is always inherently political, whichever side of the argument one chooses to sub-scribe to. One of the reasons it is political is that it is closely tied to ques-tions about other kinds of borders, as is evident from recent front-page news stories about the fury sparked by debates about 'decolonising' the curriculum at Cambridge and other universities. As Priyamvada Gopal put it in the *Guardian*, 'English Literature ... involves learning about the lives of others', and '[a] decolonised curriculum would bring questions of class, caste, race, gender, ability and sexuality into dialogue with each other, instead of pretending that there is some kind of generic identity we all share.'[6] Indeed, such self-questioning is also evident in debates about the surreptitious borders that are still in place at an institutional level, despite English's relative disciplinary progressiveness, by the continued lack of diversity within many of the university departments at which it is

---

[4] Gayatri Chakravorty Spivak, 'A Borderless World?', in *Conflicting Humanities*, ed. Rosi Braidotti and Paul Gilroy (London and New York: Bloomsbury), p. 48.

[5] Spivak, 'A Borderless World?', pp. 48–49.

[6] Priyamvada Gopal, 'Yes, We Must Decolonise. Our Teaching Has to Go Beyond Elite White Men', *Guardian*, 27 October 2017, ‹https://www.theguardian.com/commentisfree/2017/oct/27/decolonise-elite-white-men-decolonising-cambridge-university-english-curriculum-literature›.

studied. In Sara Ahmed's words: 'Histories come in with who comes in. *You can be stopped from using a space by how others are using that space.*'[7]

However, despite its persistent diversity problems at an institutional level, as a subject, English remains well equipped for challenging these kinds of borders: it is a discipline in which issues of difference and diversity have been increasingly debated over the past three decades, and it has done so on a platform that is both large and relatively prominent (English is offered as a degree at almost every British university, with thousands of undergraduates passing though departments around the country each year). It is the sort of discipline that is poised to produce, through an increasingly diversified and decolonised curriculum, the next generation of diversity activists, working both inside and outside of the academy: those whom Ahmed memorably terms 'institutional plumbers', as 'they have to work out not only where something is blocked but how it is blocked'.[8]

What English offers in this regard, perhaps more effectively than other subjects, is an ability to make visible these blockages, or institutionalised borders, that continue to exist across contemporary society, and which those unaffected by them might prefer to leave unacknowledged. This is because, as trauma theorists know well, literature can often offer a way of bearing witness to marginalised experience (and this is true even where such bearing witness is not necessarily intentional, as Said's 'contrapuntal reading' of such classics as Austen's *Mansfield Park* attests).[9] It is no coincidence, for example, that Ta-Nehisi Coates turned to literature to make his recent scathing critique of the cultural and institutional borders that continue to inhibit life chances in many black communities in the United States, drawing on Richard Wright's 1935 poem 'Between the World and Me' in his book of the same title.[10] Likewise, it is telling about literature's ability to bear witness that pop star Beyoncé sampled Chimamanda Ngozi Adichie in a hit song, with the aim of conveying

[7] Sara Ahmed, 'Institutional as Usual', <feministkilljoys.com>, 24 October 2017 (italics in original), <https://feministkilljoys.com/2017/10/24/institutional-as-usual/>.

[8] Ahmed, 'Institutional as Usual'. See also Sara Ahmed, *On Being Included: Racism and Diversity in Institutional Life* (Durham, NC: Duke University Press, 2012).

[9] Edward Said, *Culture and Imperialism* (New York: Vintage, 1994), p. 66 and pp. 80–97.

[10] Ta-Nehisi Coates, *Between the World and Me* (Melbourne: Text Publishing, 2015).

feminism to millions of young female fans around the world.[11] In both cases, literature helped enable a challenging of borders.

It is for this reason that Conservatives such as those in charge of the Department for Education are right to be fearful of English's diversification: it is a process that contributes to an unblocking of the systems of privilege that maintain the status quo. The Government's recent changes to English at GCSE level are an assault on the subject as a whole, and will have a damaging impact on its future provision well beyond Key Stage 4. With fewer pupils potentially taking the subject at GCSE, and the version of the subject that they take becoming narrower and more provincial, university intake in coming years may be smaller, and students less well-equipped for the challenging questions about identity and culture that they will be faced with in their degrees. What's more, the changes are out of step even with the increasingly global outlook of the book industry: one need look no further than the Booker Prize, which, since it began further internationalising its shortlists, has been won two out of the past three years by authors from the United States (a prospect for which the *Daily Telegraph* expressed distaste in 2015).[12] Indeed, the 2017 shortlist contained a novel explicitly *about* the future of borders: Mohsin Hamid's *Exit West*. In reference to the kind of reactionary anti-globalism that has underpinned both Brexit and Trump (and of which the changes to GCSE English are also a part), his narrator perceptively notes: 'it seemed that as everyone was coming together everyone was also moving apart. Without borders nations appeared to be becoming somewhat illusory, and people were questioning what role they had to play.'[13]

In a response to Spivak's 'A Borderless World?', Ankhi Mukherjee points out that 'While not every reading of a text is the moral equivalent of a war or political crisis, it is possible to say after Edward Said that "works of literature are not merely texts".'[14] As the controversies over changes to GCSE English, decolonising the curriculum, and the opening up of the Booker Prize all attest, literature is not, and never has been, outside of politics. On the contrary, like us, its critics and teachers, lit-

[11]   Beyoncé, '***Flawless', *Beyoncé* (Columbia Records, 2013).
[12]   Victoria Ward, 'American Dominance of Man Booker Prize Longlist "confirms worst fears"', *Daily Telegraph*, 29 July 2015, <http://www.telegraph.co.uk/culture/books/booker-prize/11771096/American-dominance-of-Man-Booker-Prize-longlist-confirms-worst-fears.html>.
[13]   Mohsin Hamid *Exit West* (London: Hamish Hamilton, 2017), p. 155.
[14]   Ankhi Mukherjee, 'Borderless Worlds?', in Rosi Braidotti and Paul Gilroy, eds, *Conflicting Humanities* (London and New York: Bloomsbury, 2016), p. 73.

erature is immersed in it, and the attempt to enforce its borders along reactionary nationalist lines is an attack on literature itself. Defending the transgressive, border-crossing character of English today is a necessary step towards challenging governmental attempts to interfere, under the nefarious guise of political neutrality, with the subject's outward-looking future direction.

'Between and Across Languages':
Writing in Scotland and Wales

KIRSTI BOHATA AND ALISON LUMSDEN

Robert Crawford writes that in Scotland we live 'between and across languages'.[1] In doing so he draws attention to the fact that Scotland is, and has long been, a multilingual nation where English, Scots and Gaelic are both spoken and literary languages, and where many people slide between these languages in their daily lives. This multilingualism is something that Scotland shares with Wales, where a fifth of the population speak Welsh and there is a vibrant Welsh-language literary culture. This essay will explore how such diversity has manifested itself in different (and similar) ways in Anglophone literature from Scotland and Wales, and how this potentially opens up a space to consider what writing in 'English' may mean today.

The histories of the two Celtic languages of Scotland and Wales are rather different. The decline of Gaelic and its near eradication in the wake of the defeat of Jacobitism in 1746 and in the light of mass emigration from the Highlands in the eighteenth and nineteenth centuries has been well documented. Welsh remained the majority language (though with no institutional status) until the late nineteenth century, when a combination of economic, educational and cultural pressures ensured a rapid decline, which was halted only by concerted activism and political change in the second half of the twentieth century. While the pressures on both language communities remain intense, writing in Gaelic, as in Welsh, continues to develop and evolve in creative ways.[2] In Wales it is the (sometimes uneasy) coexistence of Welsh and English that contrib-

---

[1] Robert Crawford, *Identifying Poets: Self and Territory in Twentieth-Century Poetry* (Edinburgh: Edinburgh University Press, 1993), p. 161.

[2] For introductory discussions in English of Gaelic and Welsh-language literature, see Máire Ní Annracháin, 'Shifting Boundaries: Scottish Gaelic Literature after Devolution', in *The Edinburgh Companion to Contemporary Scottish Literature*, ed. Berthold Shoene (Edinburgh: Edinburgh University Press, 2007), pp. 88–96; Moray Watson, *An Introduction to Gaelic Fiction* (Edinburgh: Edinburgh University Press, 2011); Dafydd Johnston, *The Literature of Wales*, 2nd edn (Cardiff: University of Wales Press, 2017); *A Guide to Welsh Literature, Vol. 6: 1900–1996*, ed. Dafydd Johnston (Cardiff: University of Wales Press, 1998).

utes to the linguistic hybridity of Welsh writing in English. In Scotland, the influence of Gaelic on English-language literature, including recent Anglophone fiction by Gaelic writers such as Alasdair Campbell (Alasdair Caimbeul), shares some of the features of Anglophone Welsh literature.[3] In the wider Scottish, context, however, what is perhaps more immediately pertinent to a discussion of linguistic hybridity is the presence of Scots as a language and its persistence in both spoken and literary forms.

Scots was historically the language of both court and law in Scotland, but the departure of the court in 1603 had a severe effect on its status. The introduction of the King James Bible in 1611 and the Union of the Parliaments in 1707 placed it under further pressure. As James Robertson has pointed out, Scots is a close relative of English but with far greater connections to Norse, French and northern dialects.[4] Described as 'oor Inglis', Scots had a long literary tradition, and in the medieval period poets such as William Dunbar and Robert Henryson employed it as part of a complex poetic medium. Yet the term 'Inglis' and the labelling of these poets as 'Scottish Chaucerians' acknowledges a hybridity that was to become a feature of writing in Scots. By the eighteenth century, Scots (as least as a written language) was in demise, and the literati of the Scottish Enlightenment went to considerable lengths to eradicate Scots from their discourse. At Edinburgh University, for example, Hugh Blair sought to teach his students a new form of English appropriate to the status of Scotland as part of a British nation.[5]

However, while Scots may have disappeared in one sense its close relationship to English also ensured that it was never entirely eradicated as a spoken language since many Scots are adept 'code-switchers', or perhaps more accurately 'code-gliders', moving freely between various levels of Scots and 'standard' English in their everyday speech. Moreover, Scots, which seems particularly adept at reinvention, almost immediately reasserted itself as a literary language in the eighteenth century with writers such as Alan Ramsay, Robert Fergusson and, most famously, Robert Burns writing poetry in both English and Scots. While in his paper at the conference Gerard Carruthers rightly noted that these poets did not write

---

[3] See Michelle Macleod 'Gaelic Prose in English', in *The Edinburgh Companion*, pp. 149–56 (pp. 150–51).

[4] James Robertson, 'Writers negotiating between Scots and English: voice, text and translation', a conference paper delivered at the English: Shared Futures conference, Newcastle-upon-Tyne, 6 July 2017.

[5] See Janet Sorensen, *The Grammar of Empire in Eighteenth-Century British Writing* (Cambridge: Cambridge University Press, 2000), p. 97.

only in Scots (and that we cannot assume that their best poetry was in Scots), nevertheless such writers set a pattern that continues to the present day by which Scots undergoes a series of 'revivals' as a literary language. In the early nineteenth century poetic Scots expanded to include the use of Scots in prose, with John Galt, James Hogg and Walter Scott all demonstrating how it could certainly be used to capture the speech of the common people, but, particularly in the case of Galt and Hogg, was also robust enough to be employed in narrative. While the received wisdom is that in the later nineteenth century Scots entered a low period as Scotland consolidated its place in the British Empire, being employed only in the couthy narratives of 'kailyard' literature, this is denied by pieces like Robert Louis Stevenson's 'Thrawn Janet', which includes a sustained and powerful use of Scots throughout. Scots, it seems, was continually on the verge of disappearing but remained persistent.

So what about the twentieth century? Certainly, whatever the realities of the situation there was a sense among writers at the opening of the twentieth century that Scots had degenerated into a language only used in the domestic sphere, and that as a consequence it did not provide a model for modern literary usage. In the period now known as the 'Scottish Renaissance' another revival of Scots language writing took place. Spearheaded by the poet Hugh MacDiarmid, a group of writers, including Lewis Grassic Gibbon and Nan Shepherd, sought to develop a form of literary Scots fit to tackle any subject and to engage with the European (and Modernist) concerns of the day. Not all of these writers tackled this issue in the same way, but all recognised that Scots to some extent needed to be brought out of its perceived parochialism and reinvigorated as a creative tool. For MacDiarmid, this involved writing in a form of language that did not attempt to represent Scots as it was actually spoken, but rather to employ a kind of 'ideal' or 'synthetic' Scots that drew upon vocabulary from all regions and all periods. The results are spectacular:

The Eemis Stane

I' the how-dumb-deid o' the cauld hairst nicht
The warl' like an eemis stane
Wags i' the lift;
An' my eerie memories fa'
Like a yowdendrift.

Like a yowdendrift so's I couldna read
The words cut oot i' the stane
Had the fug o' fame

An' history's hazelraw
No' yirdit thaim.[6]

Brilliant in its linguistic innovation and metaphysical complexities as this is, other writers of the period are perhaps more accommodating to their Anglophone readers. Lewis Grassic Gibbon, for example, writes at the outset of his novel *Sunset Song* (1932) that his aim is to offer a prose style where he captures the 'rhythms and cadence' of Scots. This is successfully achieved although Grassic Gibbon's novel also contains many Scots words.

MacDiarmid and the writers of the Scottish Renaissance had a profound effect on how Scots was viewed as a potential language for literary writing, and although writers later in the twentieth century were to launch their own 'renaissance' it was facilitated by those who had gone before them. For writers like James Kelman, Janice Galloway and Irvine Welsh, however, there was a further step to be taken: while MacDiarmid and his contemporaries may have legitimised writing in Scots they had not captured the speech of ordinary, particularly urban, Scotland, and too often they continued to maintain a hierarchy between an English narrative voice and speakers who employed a more colloquial form of speech. These writers sought to finally break down this hierarchy, offering an urban, demotic Scots that formed the very fabric of their narrative voice. James Kelman's Booker prize-winning *How Late it Was, How Late* (1994) offers a good example:

He had aye been a bit stupit. And there's nay cunt to blame for that except yerself. Ye aye come back to that same thing. Nay point blaming the sodjers if you've ladled into them in the first place; fuck sake man ye cannay blame them for giving ye a doing.[7]

The story of Scots is, then, one where the language is constantly described as receding, while clearly surviving, and of an ongoing re-imagining of how it may be used as a creative medium. So where does this leave us in the twenty-first century? As Bashabi Fraser has suggested, the linguistic situation in Scotland is now far more complex than it was in the twentieth century, and we can no longer talk about the languages

---

[6] Hugh MacDiarmid, 'The Eemis Stane', in *The Complete Poems of Hugh MacDiarmid*, ed. Michael Grieve and W. R. Aitken, 2 vols (Harmondsworth: Penguin Books, 1985), 1. 27.
[7] James Kelman, *How Late it Was, How Late* (London: Minerva, 1995), p. 15.

of Scotland as being English, Scots and Gaelic.[8] Indeed, as in Wales and elsewhere in the United Kingdom Scotland is now a multilingual community where many languages overlap, intersect and form new hybrids. However, just as it has adapted in earlier periods, writing in Scots has responded to this challenge and writers have emerged who recognise that this rich intersection of languages provides a creative opportunity. Fraser's own collection of poetry *Ragas and Reels* fuses Scots words with Indian ones to bring together the diverse experiences that now form part of modern Scotland. Similarly, Suhayl Saadi, Pakistani in origin but describing himself as

> English, British, Pakistani, Indian, Afghan, Sadozai, Asian, European, Black(-ish), Minority Ethnic, Male, Non-resident, twenty-first century person, fifteenth century being, Glaswegian, Middle-class, Writer, Seeker, Lover, Physician, Agha Jaan, Son, English-speaking, Music-loving, Left-leaning,[9]

writes in a complex hybrid prose that fuses English, Punjabi and Glaswegian Scots. His novel *Psychoraag*, for example, opens:

> *Salaam alaikum, sat sri akaal, namaste ji,* good evenin oan this hoat, hoat summer's night! Fae the peaks ae Kirkintilloch tae the dips ae Cambuslang, fae the invisible mines ae Easterhoose tae the mud-flats ae Clydebank, welcome, ivirywan, welcome, Glasgae, welcome, Scoatland, tae *The Junnune Show.*[10]

It is possible that the tradition of writing 'across and between' languages that has existed so long in Scotland may in part facilitate such developments. Cut free from its official status, writing in Scots becomes a space where alterity, in whatever form it takes, can find a voice, the space of Scots language writing becoming a space of creativity.

But what parallels, if any, can be found in the Welsh situation? English, as already noted, is a relatively young literary language in Wales. It can be seen as an example of a 'deterritorialised' language, like Kafka's Prague

---

[8]   Bashabi Fraser, 'Flavours from other shores: multiculturalism in Scottish poetry today', a conference paper delivered at the English: Shared Futures conference, Newcastle-upon-Tyne, 6 July 2017.

[9]   *Being Scottish*, ed. Tom Devine and Paddy Logue (Edinburgh: Polygon, 2002), p. 240.

[10]   Suhayl Saadi, *Psychoraag: A Novel* (Edinburgh: Black & White Publishing, 2004), p. 1.

German, and Welsh writing in English, bearing resemblances to other postcolonial literatures.[11] From its brief early appearances in the Middle Ages, Anglophone writing in Wales disrupts, distorts, enriches and plays with 'English', often drawing on an author's familiarity with the Welsh language. English is defamiliarised as grammar or orthography are reconstructed to reflect the syntax, idioms, or the sounds of Cymraeg (Welsh). In some texts, Welsh and English are used simultaneously in a toing and froing across and between the two (or more) languages.

This play of languages does not occur in a political vacuum, however. As Gayatri Spivak has argued,[12] translation and the 'contribution' of one language to another has political dimensions that change according to the shifting dynamics of power between the languages concerned. In the precarious case of Welsh, whose survival was very uncertain during the twentieth century, the relationship with the majority language can be fraught as well as creative. Living across and between languages is not without tensions.[13]

One of the earliest examples of Welsh writing in English exemplifies a number of these textual, linguistic and political features. 'Hymn to the Virgin' by Ieuan ap Hywel Swrdal (fl. 1430–80). It is written in full *cynghanedd* (lit. harmony) – a strict metre form – using Welsh orthography. The poet 'uses the English language in his awdl as he would Welsh, bending its syntax and rhythms to very alien purposes'. This, argues Tony Conran, is 'no *imitation* of a Welsh poem in English – it *is* a Welsh poem in English'.[14]

> O michti ladi, owr leding – tw haf
> at hefn owr abeiding:
> yntw ddy fest efrlesting
> i set a braents ws tw bring.

[11] Gilles Deleuze and Felix Guattari, 'What is a Minor Literature?', in *Kafka: Toward a Minor Literature*, trans. Dana Polan (Minneapolis, MN: University of Minnesota Press, 1986), pp. 16–27.

[12] Gayatri Spivak, 'The Politics of Translation', in *Outside in the Teaching Machine* (London: Routledge, 1993), p. 91.

[13] See Tudur Hallam, 'When a Bardd meets a Poet: Menna Elfyn and the Displacement of Prallel Facing Texts', in *Slanderous Tongues: Essays On Welsh Poetry in English 1970–2005*, ed. Daniel G. Williams (Bridgend: Seren, 2010), pp. 89–111, and Kirsti Bohata, *Postcolonialism Revisited: Writing Wales in English* (Cardiff: University of Wales Press, 2004), pp. 104–28.

[14] Tony Conran, 'The Hymn to the Virgin', *Welsh Writing in English: A Yearbook of Critical Essays*, vol. 1 (1995), pp. 5–22 (pp. 8–9) (my emphasis on 'imitation').

[Oh, mightly lady, our leading – to have / at heaven our abiding / unto thy feast everlasting / Ye set a branch us to bring (i.e. you set/planted a branch to bring us to the feast).]

The cultural tensions that motivated the poem were clear. It was written to assert Welsh linguistic and poetic skill, a form of 'writing back' to the Oxford elite: 'I shall compose a poem in English, in your own tongue,' says the poet, having challenged his contemporaries to beat him in a composition in a handful of European languages.[15]

Welsh syntax, grammar, idiom or – most often – a peppering of Welsh words would be common in Anglophone novels through the nineteenth century, from the anti-colonial *Twm Shon Catti* (1828) by T. J. Llewelyn Prichard through to the popular novels of Allen Raine. In his explosive collection of short stories, *My People* (1915), Caradoc Evans defamiliarised English in new and controversial ways. Evans's stories are indebted to oral story-telling and mimic Old Testament brevity and understatement. His English incorporates 'aggressive mis-translation'[16] of Welsh (such as the translation of Bod Mawr (Almighty God) as 'the Big Man') and gives the impression of borrowing syntax and idiom directly from Welsh: '"Boy bach foolish!" cried Katto. "What nonsense you talk out of the back of your head! Sober serious, mouth not that you have thrown gravel at Sara Jane's window!"'[17] Dylan Thomas's early short stories recall Caradoc Evans, and *My People*'s linguistic experimentation would influence James Joyce, who 'picked up on the peculiar blend of language'.[18] This synthesis of a distinctive Welsh English anticipates Hugh MacDiarmid and Lewis Grassic Gibbon's experiments with language and oral forms during the Scottish Renaissance.

If Evans's idiom was a modernist fusion of languages and registers for satirical purpose, other writers have adapted English to convey particular regional or working-class dialects. Niall Griffiths's rendition of Ceredigion's subcultures in *Sheepshagger* (2001) or Rachel Trezise's Rhondda or Mike Jenkins's Merthyr 'Wenglish' can be compared to the urban Scots narrative voices in Irvine Welsh's *Trainspotting* and James

[15] Quoted in Conran, 'Hymn', p. 5.

[16] John Harries, 'Introduction' to Caradoc Evans, *My People* (Bridgend: Seren, 1987), pp. 9–47 (p. 16).

[17] Evans, 'A Heifer without Blemish', *My People*, p. 58.

[18] Wim Van Mierlo, 'James Joyce and Caradoc Evans', *Genetic Joyce Studies*, Issue 7 (Spring 2007), <http://www.geneticjoycestudies.org/GJS7/GJS7mierlo2.html> [accessed 28 July 2017].

Kelman's *How Late It Was, How Late*: 'Ee wuz carryin / two bopa-bags / full o shoppin.'[19]

Some of the most startling and inventive 'bilingual' texts which fuse Welsh and English are to be found in avant-garde poetry.[20]

Partisan

rydw i am fod blydi i am
rydyn ni rydw i rody i
rodney rodney i am
rydyn am fod I am I am I am
rydw i yn Pantycelyn Rhydcymerau Pwllheli yes
/.../
roeddwn i'n fine yn y bore oherwydd
y heddlu not able anyway little zippo
lager considerable influence
tried to burn it not enough alcoalcohol
corner shop four-pack Diamond White Red Stripe
brns your heart out
/.../
ac yn nawr?
bod ar y satellite no defense
carchar poms yn saesneg
dim yn gallu handlo'r cymraeg
rîl traditional blydi welshman.[21]

These stanzas from Peter Finch's 'Partisan' illustrate the poem's playful yet urgent consideration of existence through language; the verb 'to be' is conjugated in Welsh, mutating into a slightly comic, if condescending, working-class identity: Rodney. The arson of bored post-industrial youth is here a degraded echo of nationalist protests (i.e. the burning of an RAF facility in Penyberth in 1936, which saw the founder of Plaid Cymru

---

[19] Mike Jenkins, title poem from *Barkin!* (Llanrwst: Gwasg Carreg Gwalch, 2013), p. 21. Jenkins uses a similar idiom for his short stories, though generally confines it to dialogue.

[20] Daniel G. Williams argues, though not in relation to Finch, that contemporary Welsh avant-garde 'poetry and national identity converge in a process by which formal and thematic experimentation reconfigures Welshness, and Welshness reconfigures the avant-garde': 'In Paris or Sofia? Avant-Garde Poetry and Cultural Nationalism after Devolution', in *Devolutionary Readings: English-Language Poetry and Contemporary Wales*, ed. Matthew Jarvis (Oxford: Peter Lang, 2017), pp. 115–56 (p. 126).

[21] Peter Finch, 'Partisan', *Useful* (Bridgend: Seren 1997), p. 46.

imprisoned, and the torching of holiday homes by Meibion Glyndŵr in the 1980s). A satire on contemporary Wales, the poem nevertheless rewards a bilingual – or semi-bilingual – reader.

In post-devolution Wales, writers fluent in both languages are working in, between and across Welsh and English. The coexistence of the two major languages of Wales is a recurring theme in the fiction and drama of writers such as Christopher Meredith, Fflur Dafydd, Ian Rowlands and Catrin Dafydd (no relation), to name but a few.[22] In the tense and emotive struggle for cultural and linguistic survival, there was a time when such border crossing might have been regarded as a cultural betrayal, and perhaps still is by some. But working across the language divide can also be a creative experience. Gwyneth Lewis, the first National Poet of Wales, describes the process of revising her own work, *Y Llofrudd Iaith* (1999) [the language murderer] into an English-language collection of poems, *Keeping Mum* (2003). She describes the result as 'translations without an original text',[23] and it is a phrase that could be applied to other works by authors writing in multiple languages

Alys Conran is one such writer. Her novel *Pigeon* (2016) is set in a contemporary, Welsh-speaking, post-industrial region of north Wales where English is a strange language to be articulated syllable by exotic syllable. *Pigeon* was published in English and Welsh simultaneously, though in fact both versions move across and between languages. The novel is about the excitement offered by new languages and the trauma of being forced into silence outside one's language community. Like his Urdu-speaking friend in the young offenders institute in Liverpool, Pigeon's native 'words made sounds and shapes that nobody could see', while his accented English marks his 'imperfection'. Both boys are vulnerable and silent, until Pigeon learns to wield 'pristine' English as 'a weapon' and 'a shield'.[24] It is an experience of isolation and vulnerability that is articulated and amplified in the words of refugees in Wales in *My Heart Loves in My Language* (2017).

The ongoing cultural fallout of the great linguistic shift that occurred in Wales during the last 150 years or so (and its attendant historico-political circumstances) is implicitly or explicitly a major concern of Anglophone Welsh writing. The various types of hybrid 'English' created in literature

---

[22] In academia the two literatures of Wales are increasingly studied together; see M. Wynn Thomas, *Corresponding Cultures: The Two Literatures of Wales* (Cardiff: University of Wales Press, 1999).

[23] Gwyneth Lewis, *Keeping Mum* (Tarset: Bloodaxe Books, 2003), p. 10.

[24] Alys Conran, *Pigeon* (Cardigan: Parthian, 2016), pp. 127, 131.

are comparable with the linguistic experimentation in Scotland and post-colonial writing more widely. While language remains highly politicised in Wales, post-devolution writers are both more ready to assume a multilingual audience and also to be creative with language in texts that nevertheless welcome in readers who might not themselves speak much or any Welsh.

In his poem 'Simultaneous Translation' Robert Crawford writes: 'Negotiators, opera-buffs, tourists: / This is where we all live now, / Wearing something like a Sony Walkman, / Hearing another voice every time we speak.'[25] The term 'Sony Walkman' probably now needs a translation of its own but as Google launch their own personal simultaneous translator the sentiment remains relevant. We all now inhabit a multilingual, translingual world, and clearly this launches a challenge to what 'writing in English' might mean. Scottish and Welsh writing, however, has always faced this challenge, and has responded to it in creative and innovative ways. As such it may provide a model for how 'English' might re-negotiate itself as a discipline in the heterogeneous space 'where we all live now'.

[25] Robert Crawford, 'Simultaneous Translation', *Talkies* (London: Chatto and Windus, 1992), p. 14.

Exploring Intersections between Creative and Critical Writing: An Interview with Elleke Boehmer

ELLEKE BOEHMER, DIYA GUPTA AND BÁRBARA GALLEGO LARRARTE

Elleke Boehmer, Professor of World Literature in English at the University of Oxford, is both a novelist, and a cultural and literary historian. Her critical and creative work published in 2015 focuses on the Indian Ocean cultural arena, teasing out its entanglements with empire and other global webs. The novel The Shouting in the Dark *(Sandstone Press, 2015) crafts a portrait of a lonely girlhood and looks at the suppression of women's voices through its narration of the inner life of a young woman in the 1970s, set against the political chaos of apartheid South Africa. Her cultural history,* Indian Arrivals, 1870–1915: Networks of British Empire *(Oxford University Press, 2015), considers the English metropole through Indian intellectual eyes, exploring the rich textures of contact between Indians and Britons on British soil at the height of empire through poetry and travel writing.*

Interviewers Diya Gupta and Bárbara Gallego Larrarte are doctoral researchers at King's College London and the University of Oxford respectively. Their conversation with Elleke Boehmer at Shared Futures *examined the points of contact between creative and critical modes of thinking and writing.*

Diya Gupta (DG): We'd like to begin this interview by considering how rare it is for academics to also be creative writers, particularly novelists – and yet you have received acclaim for both! Would you consider the critical and the creative as oppositional structures of thinking? Or are there intersections? Is it like changing hats?

Elleke Boehmer (EB): This is the question with which my work begins, or that lies at its nerve centre. I used to give a very different answer to this question to the one I give now.

In the past, I used to think that the two kinds of writing came from different parts of my experience and consciousness or 'brain'. In fact, I wrote creatively and critically at very different times of the day and of the week. The one kind of writing, the creative, seemed to have to be drawn up like water from a deep well, whereas the other kind of writing, the critical, often arose in interaction with the writing of others.

But, as time has gone on, I see that in fact the writing comes from the same place if sometimes along different channels: from the same perceiving eye or brain in interaction with different stimuli from the world, and of course with memory.

To get me to this much happier – or at least less fractious – space, new work in cognitive theory and communication, on literature as communication, has been very helpful. I'm thinking here of some of the recent work of Terence Cave, and also of communication theorists like Deirdre Wilson and Dan Sperber.

It has also been helpful that creative writing has found a place on university courses in literature, and in research ratings. Whereas before creative writing was dismissed as not meeting certain scholarly standards, perceptions of what counts as scholarship, and the critical and philosophical insights that might be delivered by creative writing, have fundamentally changed.

When I began as a lecturer at the University of Leeds in the early 1990s, for example, creative writing was perceived across the academy as something that one did in one's spare time, as a lesser mode of writing, as something not entirely respectable. It certainly didn't count for the (then) RAE. But now that has changed: published creative writing was (justly in my view) counted as a kind of exploratory research on its own terms for REF 2014. These changes have allowed me to make some peace institutionally with the different modes or roles of writing that run together in my brain, or in how I see my brain.

DG: It's interesting that you refer to these connections, as our recent reading of the two books, *Indian Arrivals* and *The Shouting in the Dark*, threw up a number of parallels between them. This suggested to us that you were probably working on the books at the same time, though the links are also quite subtle. For example, there's the idea of arrival that, of course, *Indian Arrivals*, is about. But also, has Ella – the main character whose perspective we inhabit – 'arrived' in the novel? Would you describe *The Shouting in the Dark* as a coming-of-age novel?

EB: Thank you for noticing this. It's a link that I hadn't yet spotted, and there definitely are others, though I should say they weren't always at the surface of my awareness as I was writing. They appeared largely in retrospect. But, yes, that is definitely a link between the two books – the idea of arrival – and the link speaks to those ways in which writing, whether creative or critical, autobiographical or historical, as here, moves and flows along related channels. There is, in this sense, at least as I experience it, no 'left brain, right brain' divide.

As to the idea of arrival, this was something that was very fruitful to explore, and I probably did so in both books in interaction with V. S. Naipaul's own memoir narrative *The Enigma of Arrival* (Picador, 1987). In particular, I responded to the idea that he investigates of cultural arrival – that is, those cases where the physical touching down in a new place is preceded by anticipated arrivals in the mind. Therefore, coming to the old cultural metropolis, London in this case, or arriving in a place that has been papered over with myth and story, like South Africa in the colonial imagination, can be seen as arrival for the first time yet knowing the place from before.

This is an experience that nearly all the educated travelling Indians I look at in *Indian Arrivals* had, travelling through the Suez Canal from 1879, or arriving in Europe and then London at the end of the nineteenth century. But it is also an experience that Ella and her mother in *The Shouting in the Dark* have as they travel between Europe and Africa. The moment of touch-down has been so heavily anticipated that it is always a second-hand, déjà-vu experience.

So yes, in that sense I'd agree with you that *The Shouting in the Dark* is a coming-of-age novel. It is about Ella arriving in her anticipated future, and claiming a place for herself in the world, in Southern Africa in par-ticular. But it is also a family drama with all the tensions and stand-offs pertaining to that form. And it is a book about writing and the formation of a writer, as is captured in this extract in which Ella discovers the power of writing –

Ella pulls out the drawing pad the air stewardess serving dinner gave her. The pad comes along with a pencil cunningly tucked into the spiral binding of the pad. On the first page she writes in English:
Either we fall out of the sky or we don't. Either way, no amount of crying will help.
She reads what she has written. She likes it: it makes sense and sounds wise. She has a picture of their plane up high in the sky, above the clouds, as if balanced on a pinnacle of thin air.
Something about this thought gives her perspective.
She writes a few more things.
Up in the air, *she writes.* Middle of a storm. Inside a bubble.
The effect is wonderful. Anything she writes down, whatever it is, one word after another, turns things quiet. What was noisy evens out, looks suddenly level and smooth. Mam lying there like a beast, *she writes,*

a dumb beast. *The disgust she felt at seeing her restrained ebbs away. Writing, she is both separate from herself and steady within herself. There, over on that side of herself, the part of her that is being written about still feels what, a moment ago, the rest of her was feeling. Here, over on this side, she is writing what happens. Here everything is at a distance but everything at the same time is under her control.*

She so much likes the effect of the writing that for the next couple of hours she goes on putting down words with her pencil, words like zoo *and* beast *and* hate. *Until long after the overhead lights have been switched off, she makes up sentences.* I hate to see her lying there like a zoo beast. *She wonders about the word* hate. *It comes without thinking about it. Maybe she doesn't mean it. But as she puts down the letters* h-a-t-e *it gives relief.* (pp. 102–03)

DG: That is such an evocative piece of writing! Is the extract based on your own experiences of the pleasure of crafting words?

EB: Yes, as I have probably anticipated, I approach writing very much as a craft, as something that involves making, shaping, piecing together and then, of course, re-shaping and revising. As in that passage, writing is so fascinating because it at one and the same time involves being in the ruck of the craft, as I see it, and yet removed from it, occupying the role of the creator who stands back, surveys what they have done, and then steps back in, to mould and refine the meanings made. As for Ella in the passage, writing involves both a poise and a stilling. Yet that poise or balance is full of energy pressing in on all sides. The challenge is how to control it, but also to be subject to it.

Perhaps this is where the juncture of the creative and the critical again invites attention. Writing as a critic or scholar, you do always have the voices of the tradition, or of other writers or critics resonating somewhere around the space in which you are writing. And yet you have to find a way of stilling those voices, or making a provisional truce with them, so that their potential judgement or critique doesn't overwhelm your own words and perspective. It's for this reason that revision and re-shaping is so important, to create a balance between the voices of tradition, and the new perceptions and experience you are trying to forge.

Bárbara Gallego Larrarte (BGL): Yes, and it seems that in both *Indian Arrivals* and in the novel the experience of crafting words, of constructing a narrative, often has the important function of working to counteract forms of oppression. You have argued elsewhere that the colonial process is not only characterised by exerting political and economic power, but that it also involves wielding 'imaginative command'.[1] When you focused on colonised perspectives in *Indian Arrivals*, did you discover counter-narratives different to those formed out of colonial power?

EB: Well, the counter-narratives of the late nineteenth century would probably have been more muted than those of the independence era. And yet sometimes, for a colonised writer to tell their own story was to produce a powerful counter-narrative. So that is a further parallel between the books, the recognition that telling your story to some extent resists and overturns the stereotypes that may be imposed upon you.

BGL: It also struck me that the novel has a distinct feminist reading. Ella seems to be trying to challenge the narrative of gender imposed on her, in large part by her father. He cautions her, for example, saying that 'Cheek is very ugly in a girl' (p. 37), or that she should prepare to 'slip backwards' as the boys take over, for 'It's what nature dictates. Women begin to concentrate on the things that come more naturally. The boys, the men, succeed instead' (p. 193). Writing is described as a process of empowerment. There is that poignant scene when Ella gets one of her poems published, and we read how 'The pleasure of seeing her very own words in print grabs her by the collarbones and pulls her upright' (p. 230). I found that description powerfully vivid, and I wonder if you see Ella's use of writing partly as a feminist act? In a previous interview you talked about the novel as 'crafting rage'.[2] Is this a distinctly gendered rage?

EB: Yes, gendered rage, it powers Ella's story, it drives her forward, this sense that it is wrong to be counted as lesser because of being different from boys. But this rage is important in another respect too, as it leads Ella to form common cause with others she sees as unjustly overlooked, in particular her parents' garden worker Phineas whom she falls in love with.

DG: Yet another parallel is that both the novel and the critical work are sea-facing. *Indian Arrivals* starts with Toru Dutt's poem about a beach –

Near Hastings, on the shingle beach,
    We loitered at the time

---

[1] Elleke Boehmer, *Colonial and Postcolonial Literature: Migrant Metaphors* (Oxford: Oxford University Press, 2005), p. 5.
[2] 'Feminism 4.0 – Debate with Naomi Wolf, Elleke Boehmer and more', <https://vimeo.com/141465995> [accessed 7 August 2017]

When ripens on the wall the peach,
  The autumn's lovely prime.
Far off, – the sea and sky seemed blent,
  The day was wholly done,
The distant town its murmurs sent
  Strangers, – we were alone.[3]

And Ella's first published poem, in Dutch, features herself on a beach, with the waves washing away her footprints. What about this image of the beach interests you?

EB: Again, thanks for pointing to the link, another one that isn't by design, or that I hadn't thought about consciously before, though it speaks to those interconnections of writing or writings we were already discussing. The beach interests me a lot, and that's obviously coming through here – the beach as interstitial zone, neither land nor sea, neither us nor them. The beach was one of the primary contact zones of empire, a place full of potential, for both positive exchange and trade, and yet also for violent encounter. The home beach or harbour was the place from where the coloniser-to-be set sail, directed to the wide horizon, with all the promise and the fear of the unknown that that represented.

Something of these associations are also, I guess, sparked in Ella's poem, and in those scenes where her father looks out to sea, and relives his days in the merchant marine, Ella standing nearby him.

But there's another interstitial place in the novel that's perhaps even more important at least for the unfolding of the story, and that is the verandah, the place where the father is most often seen: this too is a place of encounter, of memory, of exchange and story; of being neither inside nor outside, neither dark nor light.

DG: To experience such places of encounter, to understand the metropole, reading seems to become essential. You reveal very well in *Indian Arrivals* how the Indian literary imagination is shaped by reading English – for example, using Dickens as a literary lens to understand London. How, then, is reading an imaginative act? Can reading also be limiting or restrictive? In the novel, Ella is frustrated by the reference points available in her books: 'Everywhere you look, there are only English gardens, beautiful English girls with heart-shaped faces finding English love in English gardens,' she says (p. 145).

---

[3] Toru Dutt, 'Near Hastings', from *Ancient Ballads and Legends of Hindustan, 1876/1882* (Allahabad: Kitabistan, 1941).

EB: For me, as this might suggest, it is important to see reading as an active, not a passive activity. Reading involves an active engagement with what is being read. Ella in the novel is a reader, but an impatient one; she doesn't find enough to engage with in the reading materials available to her. But she does find enough of interest to go on reading, to persist. She is also a reciter, a performer, she collages together lines from poetry she enjoys, and her own lines. This, too, is a meaning-making process for her. Reciters are also readers.

BGL: I would like to talk a bit about the connections between narrative techniques in your creative and critical writing. I was very struck by your use of the definite article to refer to Ella's parents. Reading 'the father' and 'the mother' added a note of strangeness to the narrative – I found it very unsettling. It is such an effective distancing technique that I wondered if it perhaps afforded the critical distance of the academic to the novel writer? Is this further support that the creative and critical are closer than we think?

EB: Isn't it interesting how this question of the creative and the critical has formed one of the keynotes of this discussion, a thread to which we've kept coming back? On the definite article, certainly this represented a conscious decision, though its motivations came from the narrative itself, and had little to do with critical distance, though the usage did have to do with creating distance. I was interested in how the prose itself might hold the members of this family at arm's length. Though one of my editors didn't like it, and tried to persuade me otherwise, I was keen to keep on with the device. I wanted the reader to feel the estrangement that Ella also feels coming through in the language. It is another example of how writing, in this case creative writing, can actively engage the reader.

The definite article also connects to the translational second-language flavour I was trying to introduce to the prose. I was keen for the reader not only to share that sense of distance from her parents, 'the mother' and 'the father', with Ella, but also her sense of not being at home (of unhomed-ness) within English.

BGL: This sense of not being at home within English seems significant, not only for the colonial context, but also for your own experience of English as your second or adopted language. In the Epilogue to *Sharmilla and Other Portraits* (Jacana, 2010), you highlight how language brings to the foreground the condition of the migrant. You describe a feeling of 'linguistic outsiderness', of 'living in translation, on a borderline' (p. 175).

Could you speak, as a concluding thought, about how this outsider position has shaped your writing and how the English language in your work is shaped by other cultural awareness?

EB: It probably comes down to what it is to live bilingual, as I've tried to put it. Living bilingual (or trilingual) means that there is always more than one word hovering close by whenever we speak. Everything said has its echo in the other language, a different resonance and texture, a different aura of reference. Ella in fact experiences the two languages she inhabits as two different sensory worlds, one beige and soft, that's Dutch or Netherlands, one angular and purple-coloured, that's English.

This kind of double awareness provides incredibly fertile ground, I'd say, for the making of a story, where every new word represents a new possibility, another way of proceeding. It also represents an interesting way of creating characters, and managing the reader's relationship with the characters, either setting them at a distance or drawing them close. The father's language usage in the novel is demotic and salty, full of booming Dutch expletives, that is both quite bracing to read, or at least I hope so, and yet disturbing too. In a way, the Dutch textures of what he says allowed me to accentuate the violence of his speech and manner.

Throughout, it was interesting to explore how the story wound through different language worlds and to play on the reader's varying degrees of distance from those worlds. After all, none of us really occupy monoglot cultures; we always encounter layers and variations of dialect and register, or just different kinds of English. One reviewer even asked about a glossary, which I didn't mind, because it demonstrated that this reader at least had felt at certain points estranged from aspects of Ella's world. In this sense shared Ella's experience of feeling unhomed in English, at least at first, while also being increasingly alienated from her parents, even as she still understood their language and dreamed in it.

Integrating English

BILLY CLARK, MARCELLO GIOVANELLI AND ANDREA MACRAE

This chapter discusses the origins, activities so far, and future plans of the Integrating English project (http://integratingenglish.org). This project has aims that are very much in line with those of the English: Shared Futures project, since it seeks to celebrate the diversity of the discipline while also seeing the diverse range of activities it encompasses as unified. They are unified by their focus on how texts are produced, understood, circulated and evaluated. In this essay, we present a brief account of the origins and development of Integrating English, explain the project's approach to the nature of English as a diverse academic discipline and describe some of the activities we have carried out so far. We also highlight connections with English: Shared Futures, including some reflection on activities at the conference in Newcastle in 2017, and conclude with thoughts about how we see the future direction of the project. The main conclusions are that the view of English advocated by our project is timely, beneficial and suggests reasons for optimism about the futures of English.

Origins and Development

The project began in response to informal discussions with undergraduate students and university staff. Students approached more than one member of the project team asking about 'lang-lit' work. Some of these students had taken A-Level Language and Literature and moved on to BA programmes with titles such as 'English' or 'English Language and Literature'. They had noticed that the modules they were now taking each focused either on aspects of language or on aspects of literature. Very few, if any, genuinely involved 'lang-lit' work understood as work that included integrated linguistic and literary study. These conversations suggested that students were used to doing integrated linguistic and literary work at AS and A-Level. We later discovered that this was not an accurate impression. At this stage, we discussed these comments with colleagues in other HE institutions who pointed out that many of their programmes were combinations or had 'joint honours' structures. Here too, there appeared to be no more connection between work on language and on literature than there would have been if they had combined one of these with any other subject.

Discussing this led us to wonder whether anything could be done to encourage university programmes to offer more integrated programmes. As researchers working at the interface of linguistics and literary studies, we were aware of and valued the intersection of language and literature in English teaching and research, and were keen to find out ways in which we might champion and support a more integrated view of the subject in both schools and universities. We began by carrying out an investigation, funded by the Higher Education Academy, on what was on offer at school and at university and followed this with a one-day workshop at Middlesex University in June 2012. Speakers and delegates included teachers and students at schools and universities. We found that the situation was not the one suggested by the comments from students that motivated us. In fact, there was very little 'integrated' work at school and arguably more of this at university. At that time, the A-Level in English Language and Literature, often referred to as 'the combined A-Level', treated language and literature separately and there was very little real integration. Indeed it was often the case that different teachers delivered separate components of the course so that it was common for teachers to view themselves as either the 'literature' teacher or the 'language' one. The picture at university was more varied with some more integrated work, mainly within particular modules rather than across whole programmes.

We used the initial comments from the students and ideas and feedback generated from the Middlesex conference to develop our thinking around why we perceived integrated 'lang-lit' work to be a more useful way of conceptualising the subject in secondary and higher education, and to consider the benefits for students to encounter more integrated 'lang-lit' work, particularly involving activities that would be understood as falling under the heading of 'stylistics'. There are different views of what stylistics might encompass, but a broad view sees it as involving the application of ideas from linguistics and other disciplines in accounting for the production, interpretation and evaluation of texts.

Our initial work therefore focused on ways of promoting work that integrated linguistic and literary studies and activities. We considered how to promote this integrated approach to English to students and teachers at both schools and universities, and made plans for workshops and conferences. We were invited to help awarding bodies in the development of new qualifications for the 2015 A-Level reforms. This included the opportunity to reconfigure the existing AQA AS and A-Level English Language and Literature specifications so as to foreground the integration of language and literature and to draw explicitly on stylistics as an academic discipline.

As we went through this process, we developed a broader and more inclusive view of English. We realised that the very wide range of activities carried out in English can be seen as unified by an interest in texts (understood broadly to include anything that can give rise to interpretation processes and which involves at some level an intention to give rise to interpretations). The range of activities involved includes linguistic analysis, literary analysis and criticism, creative and more broadly professional writing and speaking, and work in a wide range of formats and genres. We also realised that this diversity is a strength, contributing to the vibrancy of the discipline as a collective endeavour and offering exciting opportunities for students as long as there is a creative focus on developing projects and not too much concern about boundaries between different areas.

The Diversity of English

As we proposed in a public statement of our view in an article in *Teaching English* (a professional magazine published by the National Association for the Teaching of English), we believe that taking a broad and inclusive view of English is good for the health of the subject and good for its students and researchers.[1] This view does not, however, rule out specialism or fairly narrowly focused activities, such as the analysis of a specific feature of a specific variety of English, the analysis of a specific text, the creating of a specific text, or the exploration of a cultural phenomenon or of an aspect of the context in which a particular text or texts is or was produced. In fact, we would argue that there is a unity in this diverse range of areas and activities in that they all have a shared interest in the discussion and analysis of texts.

We believe that this view provides a wide range of benefits. By pushing some of the boundaries within the subject into the background, we can encourage activities that are innovative and creative in a broad sense. For example, in the first edition of our undergraduate journal *Mesh*, Aisling MacAonghusa presents a video essay and accompanying written reflection

---

[1]   Billy Clark, Marcello Giovanelli and Andrea Macrae, 'Putting texts at the heart of English: English as a diverse but unified discipline', *Teaching English*, 6 (2014), 17–20.

on the hyperreality and architecture of Los Angeles as it appears in poetry and other works.[2]

Conceiving English as a diverse but unified subject therefore allows students and researchers to develop understanding of a wide range of topics and phenomena, and to develop a wide range of abilities. This view of English is also inherently interdisciplinary and facilitates further interdisciplinary work. Students on integrated English programmes are involved in a wide range of activities, becoming flexible and thoughtful researchers, practitioners and thinkers.

Current Activities

Our approach to English forms the basis for five strands of activity within the Integrating English project. These are: annual Continuing Professional Development events for English teachers; our online support for teachers, in the form of a website, *The Definite Article*; our undergraduate journal *Mesh*; research sub-projects and papers; and regular contributions to conferences and other events within the discipline to share the project's ideas, ethos and outputs.

Our Continuing Professional Development (CPD) events for teachers have been very popular. The fifth conference took place at Aston University in November 2017 (previous conferences were at Middlesex University, the University of Nottingham and Oxford Brookes University). We received support for these from host institutions, Cambridge University Press and the Poetics and Linguistics Association (PALA), and aim to make them free to attend.

These events usually involve a day of workshops, lectures and resource development sessions. The lecture-style sessions are predominantly delivered by academics who work in areas of English that integrate language and literature study, such as people who work in cognitive poetics, corpus literary studies and narratological stylistics. These guest speakers offer sessions and sample activities on aspects of literary linguistic study that directly occur in, or can support learning within, Key Stage 4 (typically GCSE level) and Key Stage 5 (typically A-Level) English teaching at schools. The workshops are more interactive, involving practical work with texts, but follow a similar approach to the lecture-style sessions in focusing on a particular area of literary–linguistic integration. In recent years we have also involved schoolteachers who have attended one of our previous CPD

[2] Aisling MacAonghusa, 'How to build Los Angeles: The fantastical structure of reality', *Mesh*, 1 (2017), <https://www.integratingenglish.com/mesh-journal> [accessed 15 October 2017].

events in co-delivery of some of the sessions, incorporating and feeding forward their and their students' experiences of work they have done in classrooms based on some of the ideas and approaches. The resource development sessions focus on group production of classroom activities and resources that explore the ideas engaged with the lecture and workshop sessions. These CPD events are always vibrant, creative and productive, and we receive consistently positive feedback and returning attendees.

Our aim in these events is to support teachers in developing their skills and knowledge in areas where language and literature intersect. While entrants to the profession come from a wide range of academic backgrounds, the majority of secondary English teachers have studied English literature as undergraduates and have little or no background in language study. Our previous research revealed that, while many teachers know where to go for research and scholarship in English literature and in English language, efforts to enhance and update their understanding of integrated English work such as in stylistics took them beyond their prior experience and out of their comfort zone. We therefore aim to ensure that our CPD events work to address this and to support teachers in this aspect of their work.

As part of the same endeavour, we provide content for *The Definite Article* (http://thedefinitearticle.aqa.org.uk), a website offering resources for teachers on areas of English study involving both language and literature. Our posts there include short digests of research articles, ideas for classroom activities, reading suggestions, and links to other news and resources. *The Definite Article* aims to address the research gap identified by teachers in our research and to provide teachers with recent research findings that are typically behind publisher paywalls and/or difficult to translate into meaningful classroom activities owing to their style and length. We have a strong presence on social media, with frequent recommendations, and have had extremely positive feedback from teachers. We use this feedback to plan for future resources.

In 2017, at the English: Shared Futures conference, we launched the undergraduate journal *Mesh* (http://integratingenglish.com/mesh-journal). This journal publishes work by current undergraduates or recent graduates that makes connections among strands of English. The first issue of this journal includes the work by MacAonghusa mentioned above, an essay combining research on book publishing history and author studies in an examination of the work of the writer Rose Blaze de Bury,[3] and

---

[3] Rachel Egloff, 'Rose Blaze de Bury and the 19th century world of publishing', *Mesh*, 1 (2017), <https://www.integratingenglish.com/mesh-journal> [accessed 15 October 2017].

a co-authored project presenting two innovative and challenging course designs and teaching ideas, focusing on news and social media and drawing together issues and methods from both linguistics and literary studies.[4]

The journal's remit stipulates only that submissions are innovative pieces that bring together or explore ideas relevant to two or more areas of English, for example, literature, linguistics, creative writing, drama, media and film, and teaching English (including as a foreign language). The journal welcomes submissions from both international and home-based students based in the UK or elsewhere. Students may submit their work in a variety of formats, including videos, photo essays, written essays, and reflective pieces and discursive pieces. The journal also welcomes reviews of works (for example, plays and exhibitions) that explore different aspects of English and therefore can contribute to debates about English as an academic discipline. Work is anonymously reviewed by the journal's academic editorial board, following processes typical of academic journals. *Mesh* provides a platform to share high-quality undergraduate output with a wider audience, and showcases and encourages some of the excellent work students are producing in intersecting areas of English studies.

As part of the Integrating English project we have also published position papers and research, looking particularly at the transition between school and university and the areas where language and literature meet. Our current research includes a project, funded by the British Academy and the Leverhulme Trust, examining how aware lecturers in English within Higher Education are of the 2015 reforms of the three A-Levels in English, what adjustments are happening within undergraduate teaching to better build on the new learning experiences and knowledge bases of students who have taken these A-Levels, and how communication about these kinds of reforms can be improved in the future. We will publish the results of this research in late 2018.

We have presented ideas from the project at a number of conferences and other events, including at a University English meeting (Oxford, April 2016), the Academics in the Classroom conference (Oxford, August 2016), the English Association conference (London, October 2015), the National Association for the Teaching of English annual conference (Newcastle, June 2015), and the iMean conference (Warwick, April 2015). More recently, we ran workshops relating to the project's themes at the English: Shared Futures conference in Newcastle in 2017. The next section

---

[4] Kathryn Jamshidi and Isobel Wood, 'Language and literature in the classroom: From theory to practice', *Mesh*, 1 (2017), <https://www.integratingenglish.com/mesh-journal> [accessed 15 October 2017].

discusses how we saw our ideas fitting and functioning in the context of the conference, and in the context of the discipline of English in 2017.

English: Shared Futures

The English: Shared Futures conference was an excellent fit for our project since the vision of the conference in celebrating the richness that the various strands of the discipline bring together very much aligns with our own. As well as officially launching *Mesh*, we ran two sessions at the conference, both of which brought together the various strands of English and aimed to engage participants in lively and productive dialogue about the nature of the subject. The first was a discussion-based seminar where we invited participants to consider questions relating to the sharing of good practice both within Higher Education English departments and between schools and universities. This session generated interesting examples of ways in which good practice can be shared. For example, discussion of within-department sharing included description of learning and teaching fora, peer observation with formative feedback, and a commitment to team-teaching that had a positive impact on student learning and colleagues' own professional development. Equally, participants shared their experiences of fostering relationships and practices with colleagues in the secondary sector, including a reciprocal 'guest lecture' arrangement to encourage understanding of the demands on students in each phase.

Our second session drew on our belief that different areas of the subject are connected by their commitment to and interest in studying texts. For this, we ran a close reading seminar where we invited participants to respond to a text, first drawing on their own methodological stance, and then sharing and discussing this with others working from a different perspective. This led to historical linguists, Shakespearean scholars, stylisticians, creative writers and discourse analysts working together to explore and discuss the extent to which we respond to and interpret texts in similar and different ways, and what that might mean for us both as researchers of texts and as teachers of close reading.

Overall, we felt that the conference provided a platform for sharing and considering the nature of our subject in inclusive terms. We were struck by how participants embraced the conference spirit by attending seminars and workshops beyond their own area of interest and by the wonderful job plenary speakers did in appealing to a broad audience and demonstrating the relevance of ideas within one area of English to others.

Integrating English in the Future(s)

So what's next for the Integrating English project? We plan, of course, to continue advocating a view of English as diverse but unified and to offer resources, including conferences and CPD opportunities for teachers and workshops and other activities for students at all levels. We hope that the undergraduate journal *Mesh* will receive more submissions and gain a wider audience. We continue to consider new initiatives to help English to grow and to celebrate its shared futures.

Employability in English Studies

JAMES ANNESLEY AND ROB HAWKES

In a UK Higher Education landscape increasingly shaped by tuition fees and high levels of student debt, Destinations of Leavers from Higher Education (DHLE) survey data, the NSS, and the TEF, the need to focus on the employability of humanities graduates has never been greater.[1] Prospective humanities students run the risk of being deterred from studying subjects that are not vocational, or might even forgo higher education for apprenticeship schemes. On the other hand, in seeking to present undergraduate degrees in English Literature, English Language, and Creative Writing as routes to specific forms of employment, we might risk undermining or damaging the qualities and values that mark English Studies degrees out as distinctive and appealing to both prospective and current students. In *The Singularity of Literature*, Derek Attridge defines 'instrumentalism' as 'the treating of a text (or other cultural artefact) as a means to a predetermined end: coming to the object with the hope or the assumption that it can be instrumental in furthering an existing project'.[2] Attridge goes on to present his book as 'an attempt to conceive of literature (and by implication other artistic products and practices) [...] as, in fact, defined by its *resistance* to such thinking'.[3] This essay seeks to identify and examine some of the employability strategies currently being implemented within undergraduate degree courses in English in the UK – focusing on the examples of two institutions in the North East of England – and to ask how and whether ensuring a sustainable shared future for our disciplines by continuing to attract students, while also enhancing students' prospects when they graduate, can be reconciled with *resistance* to the idea of literature (and, by extension, of a literary studies degree) as a means to a predetermined end.

---

[1] While 'employability' is far from an uncontroversial term, there is not space here for a discussion of its usefulness and/or drawbacks. For a significant intervention on the topic, though, see Tristan McCowan, 'Should Universities Promote Employability?', *Theory and Research in Education*, 13:3 (2015), 267–85.

[2] Derek Attridge, *The Singularity of Literature* (London: Routledge, 2004), p. 7.

[3] *The Singularity of Literature*, p. 7.

In order to explore these issues, let us turn first to Teesside University, which was cited in 2015 among a number of institutions engaging in 'pioneering work' in the integration of employability within the English syllabus.[4] In 2013, the revalidation of Teesside's BA (Hons) English Studies and BA (Hons) English Studies with Creative Writing programmes was seized as an opportunity to build on the strengths of the existing undergraduate provision by extending the embedding of employability in the curriculum. Alongside and, in many respects, bound up with an emphasis on the fostering of 'graduateness' underpinning the ethos of the new programme design, sits a principle of treating students as academic peers and fellow scholars. This approach sees all Teesside's second-year undergraduates presenting work at an academic conference, having first submitted abstracts in response to a call for papers, and – in place of a traditional dissertation – writing academic journal articles in the final year (also in response to a CFP). Furthermore, these programmes require students to engage in various forms of critical reflection at every stage (which are well-established forms of assessment in creative writing teaching but appear less frequently in literary studies settings), developing students' awareness of and ability to be articulate about the skills and knowledge they have acquired/will acquire through the study of English and Creative Writing. In broader terms, Teesside's programmes take an innovative approach to assessment, with traditional academic writing examined alongside other forms such as book reviews, critical introductions, group projects, annotated bibliographies and critical glossaries, blogs and online guides, presentations and learning journals, all of which foster transferrable skills and develop writing styles and techniques with a wide range of practical applications. Taken together, these aspects of the English curriculum at Teesside are designed to avoid the setting up of a false dichotomy between 'purely' academic pursuits – such as the acquisition of (and creation of new) disciplinary knowledge, of critical and creative thinking, and of learning for learning's sake – and the preparation of students for the world of work.

The centrepiece of the strategy for embedding employability in the curriculum at Teesside is the second-year core module 'English and the Real World', which is shared by both the English Studies and English

---

[4] Stephen Longstaffe, 'Employability and the English Literature Degree', in *English Studies: The State of the Discipline: Past, Present, and Future*, ed. Niall Gildea, Helena Goodwyn, Megan Kitching and Helen Tyson (Basingstoke: Palgrave Macmillan, 2015), pp. 83–99 (p. 85). Longstaffe also cites UCLAN, Oxford, De Montfort, Surrey and Cumbria as pioneering institutions in this respect.

Studies with Creative Writing programmes.⁵ The module, which ran for
the first time in 2014/15 and is currently in its fourth year of delivery, is
designed to engage students in activities with so-called 'real world' career
applications in mind and requires them to submit a portfolio of professional writing alongside a reflective report. The module content (and its
assessment strategy) thus enables students to develop and showcase the
advanced communication skills for which English graduates are rightly
renowned, especially in terms of an ability to adapt to the different styles
of writing required by a range of tasks and addressed to a range of audiences. The professional contexts the module focuses on include education,
marketing, publishing, and business, with sessions delivered by a team
of academic staff alongside visiting speakers including secondary school
teachers and PGCE students, and professional writers with experience of
book marketing. Each section of the module culminates in the submission
of an assessed element of the final portfolio. For example, the education
brief requires students to work in groups, to plan a series of lessons and
then to submit an individually assessed lesson plan. Groups must decide
on the level (Key Stage 3, GCSE, A-Level, etc.) and an overarching theme
for the lessons they plan. The topics and texts addressed must be appropriate for the age group chosen, and students need to provide evidence
of research into relevant exam boards, syllabi, and assessment criteria.
For the marketing element, students are asked to design a detailed book
marketing campaign for either a forgotten or neglected classic, an existing
book that could be marketed more imaginatively or effectively, or (with
creative writing students especially in mind) their own book or book-
in-progress. Alongside these more overtly 'real world'-focused tasks, the
module also incorporates an assessed element based within the context of
academia. This section of the module sees students required to respond
to a call for papers for *JET: The Journal of English at Teesside*, submitting
an abstract that forms the first stage in the planning of the final-year
major project (which, as noted above, culminates in the submission of an
academic journal article).

The inclusion of an academic writing project within the framework of
'English and the Real World' performs two important (and interrelated)

---

⁵ The module title 'English and the Real World' was originally chosen as a
tongue-in-cheek reference to the often-expressed idea that universities (and,
perhaps, especially university courses in the humanities) are removed from the
'real' world beyond the academy. Despite its only semi-serious intention, however,
the title runs the risk of reinforcing the dichotomy between 'real' and academic
work that the course overall seeks to deconstruct.

roles. First, it emphasises the idea that there is a 'real' world of academic work – of publishing research, of presenting at conferences, of responding to CFPs, and of writing articles, chapters and monographs – that the staff teaching undergraduate students are engaged in. Second, it enables students to identify the skills involved in responding to a call for papers, in writing an abstract for an article, and in planning a research project (responding to a brief, writing concisely and effectively for a specific audience, demonstrating an engagement with and expertise in a field of study, and planning a realistic and achievable project). Furthermore, it encourages the recognition that these skills are not *merely* applicable to academic work but to a wide range of other contexts.

The introduction of 'English and the Real World' and the wider embedding of employability within the English curriculum at Teesside presented a number of challenges, some of which have been addressed through incremental changes to the delivery and assessment of the module in each of its iterations since 2014/15. One of these challenges in the first year of delivery was a sense of reluctance among students to engage in activities that were not perceived to be in keeping with their idea of an English Studies/Creative Writing degree. Of course, this anxiety speaks very much to the resistance to instrumentalism with which we began. However, once students started to engage in (and often enjoy) the various activities undertaken during the module and, importantly, to see the ways in which the module content and assessed work represented different ways to engage in literary studies rather than a complete departure from them, much of this reluctance was overcome. On the other hand, some resistance came from students who already had a clear sense of their degree as the means to a predetermined end. For example, students already committed to the pursuit of a career in teaching were happy to engage in the lesson planning activity but were more likely to see the focus on marketing and/or business as unrelated to their career plans. Again, however, when students were encouraged to consider ways of linking these other tasks to their existing aspirations (the marketing project, for example, could be approached in terms of the marketing of a text aimed at schools), both staff and students began to recognise the (largely unanticipated) benefits of considering the common ground between the different assessed elements.

The module, thus, has increasingly sought to challenge a compartmentalised view of the career paths available to English graduates, while also resisting instrumentalism and the perpetuation of a false distinction between academia and the 'real world'. It is too early to assess whether 'English and the Real World' has had a significant impact in terms of

DHLE data (although, of course, relying on such statistics would entail instrumentalising the learning that has taken place, both on the part of students and staff). Nevertheless, one key benefit of the module and the wider programme approach (albeit one that is hard to quantify) has been an increase in confidence among students, both in their own (especially writing) abilities and about the wider 'value', applicability and versatility of their degrees. At a post-92 university with a high proportion of mature students and non-traditional entrants to higher education (who often lack the social and cultural, not to mention economic, capital that inspires self-confidence in many of their counterparts at other institutions) this is by no means an insignificant achievement.

Newcastle University's School of English Literature, Language and Linguistics also has a tailored careers module for students, 'The Cultural Industries Placement'. Offered as an option to final-year undergraduates, the module starts with taught sessions aimed at helping understand the skills they have already acquired on their degrees and at preparing them for 60 hours of work placement at local film companies and arts organisations, theatre companies like Northern Stage and Zendah, the charity Changing Lives and ITV Tyne Tees. As such, it offers meaningful work experience to students looking to build their CVs. Asked to write a reflective blog about their experiences and produce a critical essay about the commercial and cultural contexts that inform the activities of the sector, there is a mix of the practical and the analytical in what, since its launch in 2006, has been an innovative and successful module that has seen a number of former students now employed at the organisations where they originally undertook placements.

There are, of course, limits to what can be achieved with a module like 'The Cultural Industries Placement'. The most obvious is capacity. In a small city like Newcastle, there are only a certain number of potential placements, and the result is that the module can only accommodate around twenty students each year. As it happens, however, it is rarely oversubscribed, a reality that speaks to a related concern about all optional modules of this kind, namely that they only attract students who are already starting to career-plan. The irony is that students who elect to swap traditional honours-level teaching for a placement module are a self-selecting group, individuals who are perhaps least in need of the kind of training and experience that such a module offers.

A similar challenge faces the same School's work with its Alumni Advisory Group. Set up to help advise on employability, the School of English, Literature Language and Linguistics' Alumni Advisory Group draws on the experience of former students working in business, banking, publishing, the law and the media, and those running their own businesses. With a broad remit, the group convenes in Newcastle a couple of times a year for meetings that give academic staff a chance to learn more about the experiences of graduates after graduation. In the past, the Alumni Advisory Group has run careers talks for students, sessions that the school has filmed for its designated Employability web page. Though these events and the bank of materials created have been valuable, the issue again has been the extent of student engagement and the fact that, as with 'The Cultural Industries Placement', students likely to attend an extra-curricular alumni meeting on a busy Wednesday are individuals who are already well on the way to thinking constructively about employability. The challenge for the school, as it is for all institutions offering degrees in English, is to offer employability skills and experience for all students, not just those who are motivated, already have experience and/or already have the kinds of familial connections that will help them find placements.

It was the experience of working with the Alumni Advisory Group and work on 'The Cultural Industries Placement' module that encouraged the school to extend its employability offer by giving all students real opportunities to reflect on their skills and gain relevant experience. Creating a core module, with employability at its heart, along the lines of that offered at on Teesside's 'English and the Real World', was one option. Many staff were, though, uncomfortable about their ability to deliver effective employability teaching. Alongside that, they also felt that creating a compulsory focus on employability within the degree made teaching overly instrumental and pandered to the sense of the student as customer. As at Teesside, Newcastle students were also concerned that they would, in their words, 'lose' time that could be devoted to learning about Literature, Language and Linguistics, and that a compulsory careers module would dilute the amount of subject content on their degrees. In this regard, both students and academic staff were gesturing towards the kinds of concerns raised by Tristan McCowan in 'Should Universities Promote Employability?' when he asks whether 'the incorporation of employability might undermine the university's [...] functions in a qualitative sense', and suggests that the 'orientation of course content to the needs of current employers might encourage a change in relationship to knowledge among students (and possibly academic staff), towards a valuing of learning only in so far as it can provide an immediate, tangible and most probably economic benefit'.[6]

---

[6] 'Should Universities Promote Employability?', p. 280.

With all of this in mind, the school started looking at alternative models and found some of the most interesting in university-wide initiatives. The University of Edinburgh, for example, runs a Festival of Creative Learning focused on a February week with a strong careers and employability emphasis. Exeter University has The Exeter Award and the exFactor Employability and Professional Day, a day that 'aims to get you to start thinking about what motivates you, what your interests and values are, the skills set you already have and what you need to develop in order to help you succeed after graduating, whatever you decide to do'.[7] In similar terms, Newcastle University's Careers Service runs its own university-wide Creative Careers events, events that sit alongside its NCL+ award and a suite of work placement modules open to all honours-level students.

All successful in their own ways, these initiatives do however have common weaknesses. Engagement can be patchy and will, as with other kinds of extra-curricular employability work, often speak to those already taking steps to build careers. More than that, there is the sense that these offers are not quite tailored enough to the specific demands of students taking English degrees. Generic by design, this strength is also a weakness, one that only more subject-focused work on employability can remedy. In this context, then, the School looked to design employability activity that aimed to satisfy a range of criteria as follows: it needed to be tailored to the demands of English undergraduates, while open enough to speak to the huge range of career opportunities available to them; it needed to generate broad engagement from staff and students, without relying on the inevitably partial nature of the academic capacity for teaching employability among lecturers in our subject; it could not cut into teaching time, but it did need to be bedded into the teaching year so as to ensure it was not seen as an option; it needed to help build on our successful partnership with alumni, drawing on their experience in ways that would really help students; above all the work needed to be meaningful, both in terms of the opportunities afforded for self-reflection and in terms of the practical nature of the experience gained.[8]

It was with all this in mind that the School designed 'Employability, Enterprise and English', a stand-alone event run in partnership with

---

[7] 'eXfactor: employability and professional development day', Career Zone, *University of Exeter*, <https://www.exeter.ac.uk/careers/events/exfactor/> [accessed 17th October 2018].

[8] Films made at the events can be viewed here: http://www.ncl.ac.uk/elll/careers/triple-e/.

Newcastle University's Careers Service. Timetabled for all stage 2 students across a day in the early spring, the event looks to bring all of the students in the cohort together to work in teams with alumni and careers trainers on a real-life work challenge with the results then pitched to panels of judges. Run off-campus at a city-centre conference venue, the event has a professional quality to it, one that sets out to mirror the kinds of experiences graduates are likely to face when attending a selection day for a major employer. To add to the professional texture of the event, Newcastle University's Careers Service enlisted the support of Accenture, a company with a significant presence in Newcastle. In contributing, a half-dozen or so members of Accenture's consulting team mentor student teams as they plan their pitches and join in the final judging. Accenture also contributes to the design of the task, spinning ideas out of current consulting projects (recycling and waste for Newcastle City Council; health awareness among young people for the NHS). Through Accenture's involvement, students benefit from engagement not just with a real-life professional situation, but also from contact with a group of professionals, many of whom are recent graduates with humanities degrees.

While some students, and some academic staff too, have raised questions about the involvement of a large organisation like Accenture, arguing that this provides an overly corporate context, the majority welcome the involvement of the firm, recognising that in helping establish a professional ethos for the event and in modelling the kinds of careers humanities graduates *could* pursue, it adds significantly to the experience of students. The fact that Accenture has helped design tasks focused on improving public sector work has also helped to address questions about the corporate emphasis.

Having run twice, and having been nominated for an Association of Graduate Careers Advisory Award in 2016, the event is now an established and successful part of the school's work. Building the confidence and experience of stage 2 students, 'Employability, Enterprise and English' gives students the chance to use their skills in team-working and presentation to respond to creative business challenges at an event that asks them to step beyond the familiar content-based work of their degree. Meaningful contact with colleagues from the Careers Service, alumni and other professionals is an additional benefit, exposing students to the model career stories of a range of humanities graduates. Underwriting this success is the event's central place in student timetables and a strong communications effort on the part of the school that aims at ensuring engagement. Students are not being asked to take time away from their studies, but to see that the event was bedded in alongside their existing programme. With networking opportunities built in and a greater sense of cohort identity developed, the events also make a broad contribution to the student experience, even as they build skills in employability. The focus on stage 2 students at the start of their second semester was also a strength. At the exact mid-point in their study, students had enough freedom from the pressure of their final year to be able to enjoy the event and enough time left on their degree programme to be able to learn from the experience gained in useful ways *before* graduation.

There are of course weaknesses with this kind of event. In separating the school's careers focus out from the core of the undergraduate curriculum, many of the benefits of the integrated model used at Teesside are lost, and there is the risk that 'Employability, Enterprise and English' sets up a conceptual divide between the world of work on the one hand and English Studies on the other. The broad-based nature of the employability day is another possible weakness. In aiming to appeal to a lot of students, it creates challenges for those who already have clear career plans, and who feel, as the evaluation questionnaires made clear, again like Teesside, that they would have preferred something more bespoke. As far as the school is concerned, the event also involves significant costs both in terms of money (venue hire, refreshments for students, and travel and accommodation for alumni all add up) and time and as such there is pressure each year to find funding and to demonstrate value for money. Positive feedback from students, alumni, careers service colleagues and academic staff, national recognition at the AGCAS awards for excellence and the palpable energy and enthusiasm of participants on the day all, however, offer clear evidence of the benefits brought by 'Employability, Enterprise and English' to the undergraduates and the event is now an established part of the school's year

Outlined above and explored in more detail at panel discussions at English: Shared Futures, the work done at Teesside and Newcastle not only exemplifies the range of approaches to Employability in English being offered across the UK but also throws some of the challenges into relief. On the one hand, there are broad questions about instrumentalism and the value of employability within humanities degrees; on the other, there are the specific pressures placed on individual schools by the need to recruit students and enhance their experience even as colleagues deliver against public measures that have data linked to employability factored in. More than that, whatever their views on the employability debate, there is a shared commitment to delivering meaningful opportunities to students, a commitment that creates a positive pressure to provide high-quality support for the development of their skills, competencies and confidence. Whether evidenced in the career stories of graduates or in DHLE data, there is little doubt that graduates with degrees in English Studies have real opportunities to build successful and fulfilling futures, futures underwritten by the kind of teaching and events offered at Teesside and Newcastle.

Creative Living: How Creative Writing Courses Help to Prepare for Life-long Careers

PAUL MUNDEN

> Our aim is to produce students who, having experimented with and developed their writing, are effective writers who are prepared and able to pursue their careers as they choose, whether that is on a conventional graduate track, within the creative industries, freelance, self-employed or a 'portfolio' worker.

This and other comments below are taken from *Beyond the Benchmark*, a research report into creative writing in higher education commissioned by the Higher Education Academy.[1] It is typical of the (anonymised) responses received from those teaching on creative writing courses across the UK when asked specific questions about the career support and professional development provision for students.

The responses suggest that UK universities are highly active in preparing students for the world of work. This is not to say that the courses themselves are career-focused; quite the opposite. The prime attention of the vast majority of creative writing courses is on *writing*, unaffiliated to specific walks of life – or the prospect of financial remuneration. They do however incorporate a wonderful variety of professional guidance, much of which is derived from initial input by the National Association of Writers in Education (NAWE). That input was generated by Arts Council England promoting professional development within the arts, and the establishing of NAWE's 'Writer's Compass' as a resource for writers at all levels. NAWE worked closely with universities, sometimes visiting and offering talks and seminars with a careers focus, and produced a useful planning handbook, *Getting to where you want to be*. Increasingly, universities have started to build in their own provision, some of it substantial.

---

[1] Paul Munden, *Beyond the Benchmark: Creative writing in higher education* (York: Higher Education Academy, 2011), pp. 10–34.

'Why Not Be a Writer?'

This headline, found in a variety of newspaper advertisements over the years, attempts to lure would-be writers to commercial, non-academic writing courses. It equates writing with being published. In higher education, by contrast, publication is seen as one potential, positive outcome for students, but nowhere is it in evidence as the *sole* purpose, or even the prime one. Of course, a number of MA courses are designed to support students in the production of a major work, and tutors inevitably offer what assistance they can in progressing that work towards publication:

> The big commitment we make to all our students on graduation is that if they follow through on the feedback we've given, act on their own personal development plan, complete their full-length work and then come back to us, we will knock on doors, put calls in, and do our best to get them to an agent or publisher. The onus is on the student to do the high-quality work first, though.

Another university offers 'an annual series of visits from agents and publishers' and 'an agent mentoring scheme that pairs every graduate with a literary agent for four months at the end of the course'. Typically, though, university writing tutors make very different claims:

> I describe our purpose as the intellectual, personal and professional development of our students, and the teaching of specialist skills in craft and technique. We reward innovation, artistic ambition, experiment and risk.

> The purpose is to allow students to explore their potential and discover where they fit in the writing world, and if it is something they will continue with for pleasure or as part of a portfolio career.

The aspiration for graduates is that they leave equipped not only to make a living, but also to take a leading role in creating the culture they wish to inhabit. As Maggie Butt, former Chair of NAWE, states, they are positioned to do this across a remarkably varied spectrum of occupations:

> Our students are coming out of university with all the skills which constitute true 'graduateness'. And more. Often they have delved deep into themselves and faced their demons. They have experienced the joy, and despair, and hopefully, they develop their ability to write well, to express themselves with clarity and vividness in a range of genres; a skill which can be applied to writing a good business report, as much

as to writing fiction, and satisfaction which comes with any creative activity. They are Humanities students in the broadest sense; they have stood in the shoes of others by reading their poetry, plays and prose, and by the imaginative act of creating fictional characters of their own ... A small minority choose the writer's life, perhaps going on to post-graduate study, aiming to become recognized as playwrights, novelists or poets, and usually supplementing their income with some other 'day job'. Some of our students have gone directly into work as professional writers, journalists, advertising copywriters, script-writers, dramatists. Others have chosen to use the insights and skills they've gained as teachers, PR people, art therapists, web-site designers, book editors, sub-editors, TV researchers, literary agents, librarians... parents.[2]

That last word, 'parents', seems especially important, speaking of people's lives – and their valuable role within the world – beyond the sphere of work. Another respondent to *Beyond the Benchmark* makes a similar point when suggesting that creative writing graduates cope particularly well with 'joblessness':

> A temptingly amusing headline for the critics, the true implication is the important, high level of inner resourcefulness with which Creative Writing graduates are fortified: in learning to construct a variety of human narratives within their studies, they are perhaps better equipped than most in finding their own personal ways through even the most difficult of times.

Adaptability

At the Changing the Conversation conference of 2013, organised by the ArtWorks alliance of which NAWE is a member, it was generally agreed that flexibility should be a fundamental characteristic of the creative arts graduate, brought about by the essential nature of the teaching across the degree in its entirety. It might nevertheless be useful for students to be made explicitly aware of this highly valuable aspect of their education. They are, in their writing studies, constantly solving problems, working out how to adapt their growing set of skills to address issues of narrative structure, character development, emotional crises and resolutions, and the complexities of communicating all of that with sensitivity, yet also power.

[2] Maggie Butt, quoted in Paul Munden, 'Sharing the art, craft and imagination', *New Writing, the International Journal for the Theory and Practice of Creative Writing*, 8:3 (2011), 215–37.

It is also important to recognise how, in all of the above, students are taking control. This is replicated in everything they do *in association with* their writing:

> They are directors of the medium, not a passive part. Every year it is the students themselves who raise money for an anthology and promote it – a punk DIY ethic: don't expect people to do things for you; that would be falling for an old lie. You have to re-invent readership every single year, and [our programme] is a mechanism for this. We don't sit back.

Some modules require students 'to engage with external projects, and to identify opportunities for work and professional writing relating to their aspirations on graduation, then to produce CVs, submission and job application letters'.

> The value of writers setting up their own projects is increasingly recognised, partly for educational and career-based reasons but also as an act of community, which some programmes put to the fore.

Many universities help to arrange placements for their students. One has '30 publishers, agents and writers' organizations offering placements to our students, mostly at M level'. Some 'connect with schools, local authorities, galleries, museums and libraries' (ibid.). Several have fruitful connections with local theatres, and one cites a particularly useful relationship with the Royal Shakespeare Company:

> The Writing Centre offered [a rehearsal space] as well as the opportunity for directors to work with university staff. We hosted an international playwright in residence, writing a new play as well as teaching. The English Department of course has Shakespeare experts – but no previous link with the RSC. It is now a very positive thing to have live contact with actors and directors. It counters the idea of writers working alone.

Some programmes put the onus on students 'to make connections of their own, with an entrepreneurial requirement even built into their course'.

> We create creative, flexible, literate, resourceful people. That's preparation.

A Degree of Precarity

So much for positive thinking, but are creative writing courses really worth the money? This has become a new variant on the 'can creative writing be taught' question:

> Why teach a skill that, for centuries, has been practised without formal training by extraordinary poets, essayists and fiction writers? Does the economy really need people with critical sense or aesthetic sensibility? Moreover, should universities be charging fees to educate young people in a social/cultural practice that is unlikely ever to deliver income-earning capacity?[3]

In current times, in a way that continues to escalate, the sheer investment involved aligns university education to speculative, financial success. Jen Webb explains:

> a widely-held expectation of any contemporary university degree is that it will open doors to a lucrative career: the expense and effort of university study being repaid by better work, and – over a lifetime – a significantly higher earning capacity than is available to those who have avoided tertiary education.

She goes on to say:

> Creative Writing is not alone in this respect (science graduates are not necessarily able to make a career in science; history graduates rarely win employment as historians); and after all, in an era of massive industrial and technological change, there are no assured professions; rather, as is often said in the sector, *we are training students for jobs that don't as yet exist.*

Webb's comments are derived from her research into the employment of creative arts graduate careers,[4] which suggests that they 'earn significantly less than their fellow graduates, but it doesn't bother them as much as might be expected'; they 'report much higher levels of overall satisfac-

---

[3] Jen Webb, 'Writing and the global economy', *Writing in Education*, 72 (2017), 25–30.

[4] DP150101477, 'Working the Field: Creative Graduates in Australia and China' (2015–2017), and DP160101440, 'So what do you do? Graduates in the Creative and Cultural Industries' (2016–2018), both funded by the Australian Research Council Discovery Program.

tion than do the more highly paid lawyers and accountants and doctors'. Personal satisfaction is however only part of the equation. Far from being self-centred, or pursuing work of little value to anyone but themselves, creative writing graduates have a strong sense of community and social purpose, which universities (and governments) would do well to recognise. Webb quotes Jennifer Westacott, Chief Executive of the Business Council of Australia:

> 'Universities should not be just about producing accountants and lawyers, they should be producing leaders and good citizens'; and that this is where the Humanities (which includes Creative Writing) comes into the picture. Ethical people; thinking people; people who understand human behaviours in a globalized culture, and who are not perplexed by change.[5]

This returns us to the older purpose of higher education, enabling individuals to discover their own interests and sense of purpose in the world, before successive governments decided – in parallel to their rebranding of literacy as *functional* literacy – that any form of study was to serve their purpose in shaping a workforce. Their thinking was fundamentally misguided, based on a poor grasp of the changing world – and how human beings prefer to make their place within it. Moreover, human beings want to effect further change, not become cogs in a failing machine.

Speakers on this subject at English: Shared Futures were brought together by NAWE from the US and Australia, as well as the UK, and their comments were expanded in an issue of *Writing in Education*. Randall Albers, from Columbia College, Chicago, states:

> We cannot afford to let a division between town and gown obtain. We need not see ourselves as capitulating to careerism or the captains of industry in order to give our students skills that enable them to survive and write.[6]

This challenges the 'anti-arts' comments made by Nicky Morgan, former Secretary of State for Education in the UK, including her statement that 'the subjects that keep young people's options open and unlock the door

---

[5] Jennifer Westacott, 'The True Value of Humanities', Business Council of Australia Media & Speeches (4 November 2016), <http://www.bca.com.au/media/the-true-value-of-humanities>.
[6] Randall Albers, 'But Can You Get a Job? The Dual Mission of Creative Writing Programs', *Writing in Education*, 72 (2011), 31–37.

to all sorts of careers are the STEM subjects (science, technology, engineering and maths)'.[7]

Albers describes various student success stories – and considerable attitude – in contradicting Morgan:

> These people, who represent a wide range of careers and career stages, speak to the value of Creative Writing training, and all of them assert that they wouldn't have traded that training for anything. One said, 'I can't imagine my life without it.' Another: 'You might say everything ELSE I studied was a waste of time.'

Paul Hetherington, another ESF panellist, from the University of Canberra in Australia, also contradicts Morgan when he says of creative courses that 'They provide knowledge about "spin" and rhetoric, sincere and insincere speaking, and enable students to express themselves in more fluent and nuanced ways.'[8] Creative writing students 'are able to speak back to the rhetoric and "spin" that dominates so much of the current news cycle, because they have tools to construct alternative ways of speaking. These are highly useful and important skills.' Hetherington goes on to suggest that universities should do more to set the matter right:

> Employees who are skilled in and confident of their capacity to use written and verbal language tend to make good communicators. They are able to complete written tasks more quickly and to a higher standard than people without such skills and confidence. One challenge for the future is for universities to communicate to employers how useful these skills are, and how broadly they may be applied to problem-solving and team-building in the workplace, which may partly be achieved through the further development of successful internship programmes.

Randall Albers set out four clear things that need addressing:

> First, we need to talk to our students about alternative careers – or even better, let alumni working in a variety of such careers speak directly to them at Career Nights about their skills and the application of those

[7] Richard Garner, 'Education Secretary Nicky Morgan Tells Teenagers: Want to keep your options open? Then do science', *Independent* (10 November 2014), <http://www.independent.co.uk/news/education/education-news/education-secretary-nicky-morgan-tells-teenagers-if-you-want-a-job-drop-humanities-98523 16.html>.

[8] Paul Hetherington, 'Sincere and Insincere Speaking: Preparing Creative Writing Graduates for Lifelong Careers', *Writing in Education*, 72 (2017), 8–43.

skills during their work lives. Second, we need to do expanded research on successful Creative Writing graduates working in multiple fields, including those that are most cutting-edge, in order to get clues about alternative professions and possible new professions of the future. Third, we need to reflect continually upon our pedagogical approaches to teaching the complex act of writing and the flexible application of skills developed in this process to the ever-evolving jobs of the future. Fourth, we need to de-stigmatize alternative careers and treat them with the same respect as traditional Creative Writing professions – perhaps even using 'adjunctive' rather than 'alternative' in order to show that writers through the ages (or at least since the demise of patronage outside of the university) have nearly always found ways of working that day job along with their ongoing creative pursuits.

Conclusion

I began by playing down the importance of publication, but the award of the 2017 Nobel Prize for Literature to a former creative writing student, Kazuo Ishiguro, may be the single most significant event in the recognition of creative writing's value. No longer can it be said that nurturing creative writing within a higher education environment has no effect. I recall Malcolm Bradbury (one of Ishiguro's tutors at the University of East Anglia) describing (at a Great Writing conference in Bangor, 1998) how he urged Ishiguro to move beyond competent stories of suburban Bristol and dig deeper. *An Artist of the Floating World* was the result. The criticism often levelled at creative writing courses, that they result in a homogenous if accomplished product, is clearly flawed.

There is of course a danger in citing publication success as a measure of the value of a course; if, for instance, 5% of graduates go on to achieve major publication success, that might equally be described as a 95% failure rate. 'Ultimate' success, however, such as a Nobel prize, and where the roots of the writer's unique development can be traced in this way, seems important to acknowledge.

I may have made claims in this chapter for creative writing study being particularly useful. I believe that, but would not necessarily wish to champion its value above other, equally worthy fields of study. What is most important to recognise, perhaps, is that immersion in any field of study will have a significant effect on an individual's outlook on life and modus operandi.

Creative writing has been considered here mainly as a field in its own right, but the focus of the English: Shared Futures conference was of course on the interaction between the three English disciplines. Knowledge of each benefits the other. My own literary career, having studied English Literature at university, began by answering an advertisement in the *TLS* and working (unwittingly) as a reader for Stanley Kubrick; I ran poetry workshops for next-to-no financial reward before doing the same for university adult education departments, and then working for NAWE; I got lucky and gained work for the British Council as 'conference poet' – all of which I reflected upon when I finally came to undertake a Professional Doctorate by Public Works, which in turn gained me a position at the University of Canberra, and new publishing contracts. Yes, precarity has featured large, but always with compensating rewards.

I have been writing this essay in the days after a family funeral. I mention that as I think it represents the manner in which the job of writing, no matter *what*, is related to one's larger life; the title of this essay is significant. My study of literature and creative writing, and my subsequent work with words have been of real benefit to me as I have coped firstly with the bereavement, and then with the task of assembling this essay in difficult circumstances. There are many, many ways in which writing and living are creatively entwined.

Practice at Large: How Creative Writing can Enhance University Research Environments

CORINNE FOWLER AND HARRY WHITEHEAD

'I don't at all favour the institution known as the "creative writer on the campus",' opined F. R. Leavis in 1967.[1] 'What next?' linguist Roman Jakobson remarked, when he heard Vladimir Nabokov had been offered a Harvard professorship, 'shall we appoint an elephant to teach zoology?'[2] Like King Cnut, their helplessly raised hands failed to hold back the tide. Creative writing (hereafter CW) maintains an uneasy relationship with its academic mother subject, English, 'rather like welcoming Heathcliff into the family', in Nicholas Royle's British 'elephant' equivalent.[3] Beyond this uncomfortable duality as academic sub-discipline and object of study, however, Royle recognizes that CW attracts students, connecting its rapid expansion in many minds to the marketization of Higher Education.[4]

A success story, yet often eyed still with suspicion then, CW has gradually carved out a distinct academic identity for itself. This essay outlines the subject's genesis within English Studies, and describes the ways it has come to describe its own research paradigms. It considers how the subject is currently securing its future in Higher Education. We discuss how the University of Leicester's CW research centre, the Centre for New Writing, has adapted to the wider academic research environment. Notwithstanding the subject's business value to institutional managers, we show how it provides many opportunities, both to serve the wider writing community, and to design innovative research projects with colleagues from other disciplines. Archaeologists, archivists, historians, geographers and medical researchers are awakening to the power of imaginative writing and beginning to understand its potential for delivering considerable public benefits.

---

[1] F. R. Leavis, *English Literature in Our Time & The University: The Clark Lectures 1967* (London: Chatto & Windus, 1969), p. 69.

[2] Cited in D. G. Myers, *The Elephants Teach: Creative Writing since 1880* (Englewood Cliffs, NJ: Prentice, 1996), front-quote.

[3] Nicholas Royle, cited in Gerard Wood, 'First Novel by Nicholas Royle: Review', *The Guardian*, 4 January 2013.

[4] Wood, 'First Novel'.

Understanding 'Creative Practice'

Sociologist Laurel Richardson 'was taught ... not to write until I knew what I wanted to say'; instead, she finds 'I write *in order to* learn something that I did not know before I wrote it.'[5] The late author and screenwriter Alain Robbe-Grillet believed the

> function of art is never to illustrate a truth – even an interrogation – known in advance, but to bring into the world certain interrogations not yet known to themselves... When we ask [the writer] why he has written his book, he has only one answer: 'To try and find out why I wanted to write it.'[6]

Of course, any scientist conducting laboratory experiments understands this. It is the *doing* of science that brings knowledge. Social scientist, scientist, and creative writer all recognize the value of practice to understanding.

Indeed, writing practice as knowledge contribution lies at the heart of how CW justifies its existence in Higher Education (HE) research. As the National Association of Writers in Education's revised Research Benchmark Statement (still in draft form at the time of publication) notes, 'The most common mode of Creative Writing research is creative practice... The process of artistic practice and its resulting output are perceived as contributions to knowledge' (NAWE n.d., p. 1). The first defining principle of the QAA, the Quality Assurance Agency for Higher Education's, 2016 maiden subject benchmark describes how CW 'focuses on the production of new writing by students and critical reflection on that practice'.[7] The Australasian Association of Writing Programs and the American Association of Writers and Writing Programs both stress 'practice'.[8] So fundamental has the notion of practice as research in CW

[5] Laurel Richardson, 'Writing: A Method of Inquiry', in *Handbook of Qualitative Research*, 2nd edn, ed. Norman K. Denzin and Yvonna S. Lincoln (Thousand Oaks, CA: Sage, 2000), p. 924.
[6] Alain Robbe-Grillet, *For a New Novel* (Evanston, IL: Northwestern University Press, 1963), p. 14.
[7] QAA Subject Benchmark Statement, Creative Writing, The Quality Assurance Agency for Higher Education (2016), p. 5.
[8] For an overview, see Harry Whitehead, 'Emergence: Creative Writing Theory and Practice-Led Research', in *New Ideas for the Writing Arts: Practice, Culture, Literature*, ed. Graeme Harper (Cambridge: Cambridge Scholars Press, 2013), pp. 95–112.

become that its practitioners in HE too often ignore or remain ignorant of its very particular cultural/historical origins and evolution.[9]

Creative Practice Evolves

CW is often described as a recent subject or, at least 'still developing'.[10] If we leave aside the implication that older subjects might have ceased to do so, CW has in fact been taught in HE since its generally acknowledged origins in Harvard composition classes in the 1880s.[11] If the term 'creative writing' may not have come into use pedagogically until around 1925,[12] these classes nonetheless considered literature 'as if it were a *continuous experience* and not a mere corpus of knowledge – as if it were a living thing, as if people intended to write more of it'.[13] CW's subsequent development within progressivist and 'creativist' pedagogical movements of the early twentieth century has been too widely documented to dwell on here. By 1929, H. D. Roberts remarked in the *English Journal* that 'a creative-writing movement [is] gaining a foothold in the curriculum'.[14]

The Iowa Writer's Workshop graduate degree program's formal opening in 1936 marks the moment when this movement positions itself clearly in the Anglophone world's universities (Soviet CW programs began a little earlier, with the opening of the Maxim Gorky Literature Institute in Moscow in 1932).[15] Iowa proved the ur-model for the subject as it spread through the US, and then beyond. Firmly embedded in English as CW was and remains, Myers describes how Norman Foerster, an Iowa founding father, saw it as literary criticism's 'natural ally ... Creative writing was *an effort at critical understanding* conducted from within the conditions

---

[9] See Harry Whitehead, 'The Programmatic Era: Creative Writing as Cultural Imperialism', *ariel: a review of international literature*, 47 (2016), 1–2 (Special Issue: 'Experimental Writing in a Globalizing World').

[10] QAA 2016, p. 5.

[11] See *The Elephants Teach*, and Mark McGurl, *The Program Era: Postwar Fiction and the Rise of Creative Writing* (Cambridge, MA: Harvard University Press, 2009), p. 199.

[12] 'Creative writing' is considered first to have been foregrounded as the title for an academic subject in the celebrated educationalist, William Hughes Mearns' then widely disseminated pedagogical work, *Creative Youth* (New York: Century, 1925).

[13] *The Elephants Teach*, p. 4.

[14] H. D. Roberts, 'Editorial', *English Journal*, 18 (1929), 345–46 (p. 346).

[15] Harry Whitehead, 'Soviet Creative Writing Programmes and the Personal', unpublished paper, 2017.

of literary practice' (our italics).[16] Iowa's blend of literary practice with a
very particular formalist criticism meant an overriding focus on craft and
structure rather than critique of content.[17] As the subject expands beyond
the Anglophone Global North's universities and around the world, these
highly particular cultural/historical origins remain prevalent, yet often
poorly articulated.[18]

Despite the subject's comparative antiquity in the US, it arrived more
recently in the United Kingdom. At HE level, it emerged first in David
Craig's undergraduate class at Lancaster University in the 1960s, then in
the UK's own 'ur-program' at the University of East Anglia in the early
1970s.[19] Craig's colleagues derided his course as 'Yankee'.[20] Importing
many American CW pedagogical paradigms as the subject did, still, UK
CW drew on other arts subjects to articulate its defining research principles. 'Practice-led research' became for many years the dominant catch-all
phrase. The term's conceptual origins lie in attempts by fine art and design
to define their own research processes in the late 1970s and early 1980s.
However, it was Christopher Frayling who make practice-led research the
central descriptor for research production in art and design.[21] At least
until 1992, the 'applied research' artists undertook had more often been
understood as 'professional practice',[22] and hence essentially vocational.
Frayling's model devised three modes of arts research: research *for* practice
(activities supporting the artist in her work), *through* practice (creative
drafting and editing), and *into* practice (e.g. observations of artists at
work).[23] In its 2008 incarnation, NAWE's research benchmark considered '[t]he most common mode of Creative Writing research [to be] that

---

[16] *The Elephants Teach*, pp. 128, 133.
[17] See 'The Programmatic Era', *passim*.
[18] 'The Programmatic Era', p. 362.
[19] See Michelene Wandor, *The Author is Not Dead, Merely Somewhere Else:
Creative Writing Reconceived* (London: Palgrave, 2008).
[20] Wandor, *The Author is Not Dead*, p. 10.
[21] Christopher Frayling, *Research in Art and Design*, in Royal College of Art
Research Papers No. 1 (London: Royal College of Art, 1993); *Practice-based
Doctorates in the Creative and Performing Arts and Design* (n.p. [UK]: UK Council
for Graduate Education, 1997).
[22] Judith Mottram, 'Asking Questions of Art: Higher Education, Research and
Creative Practice', in *Practice-Led Research, Research-Led Practice in the Creative
Arts*, ed. Hazel Smith and Roger T. Dean ((Edinburgh: Edinburgh University
Press, 2009), p. 235.
[23] See Whitehead, 'Nomadic Emergence' for a critical appraisal of its continuing
influence.

of creative practice, which is often referred to as "practice-led research"'.[24] NAWE's newly revised research benchmark moves on to offer the wider umbrella term 'creative practice research'. This form of research uses 'a *range* of methods, approaches and styles, *including* – channeling Frayling – 'those variously labelled as practice-led research, research-led practice, practice-based research and practice-as-research'.[25]

At what point does a subject finally grow up? From Harvard composition classes to the 2017 English: Shared Futures conference represents a journey of 140-odd years. Surely CW is at least approaching middle age. Perhaps the perception of its ongoing nascency lies with a certain 'soft, fat, sassiness', in Moxley's painful description.[26] Has CW rested indolently on the laurels of its own exponential success, 'providing a haven from academic challenge and ... intellectual rigour'?[27] While discussions about CW's epistemological distinction from other subjects continue, such fundamentals remain – as yet – limited in their articulation.[28] Creative writers are preoccupied with writing creatively. Still, Harper notes that the 'primary epistemological ammunition ... for Creative Writing in the academy *must* be the declaration of a viable and systematic pedagogy'.[29] Donnelly believes the 'emergence of the workshop as an independent entity, or academic specialisation, at the graduate level [was] the point at which Creative Writing becomes a discipline'.[30] The workshop's focus on drafting, peer review, and re-drafting, of course, offers practice as the key ordnance in Harper's epistemological ammunition.

---

[24] National Association of Writers in Education (NAWE), *Creative Writing Subject Benchmark Statement* (available at www.nawe.co.uk) (2008), p. 11.

[25] National Association of Writers in Education (NAWE), *Revised Creative Writing Subject Benchmark Statement* (unpublished at time of writing), n.d., p. 1.

[26] Joseph Moxley, 'A Writing Program Certain to Succeed', in *Creative Writing in America*, ed. Joseph Moxley (Urbana, IL: National Council of Teachers, 1989), *passim*.

[27] Moxley, 'A Writing Program', p. 263.

[28] Whitehead, 'Nomadic Emergence'.

[29] Graeme Harper, 'Responsive Critical Understanding: Towards a Creative Writing Treatise', *New Writing: The International Journal for the Practice and Theory of Creative Writing*, 3:1 (2006), 1.

[30] Dianne Donnelly (ed.), *Does the Writing Workshop Still Work?* (Bristol: Multilingual Matters, 2010), p. 49.

Defining Creative Practice for the Wider Academic Environment

We have seen how CW's focus on practice evolved, and how the notion of creative practice as research came to be articulated in UK Higher Education. To return to our starting point, as Richardson and Robbe-Grillet described it, the actual process of the imaginative act of writing itself generates new knowledge. However, new knowledge about form – the art of writing – is one thing, yet how may it contribute to new knowledge of content or subject matter? Of course, there is no topic toward which a writer may not turn her attention. CW is innately interdisciplinary, hybrid in content and often form. It attempts to invoke diverse realms of experience. Among an almost infinite variety of subject materials, creative practice research can 'use source-based methods, relying upon the use of documentary evidence, interviews, case-studies and artefacts'.[31] Creative practice research can be presented as fiction and/or poetry, creative non-fiction, memoir, biography, graphic novel, critical writing. It can experiment in genre, form, content and presentation. For NAWE, CW 'is not primarily a vehicle for what may be termed 'factual' knowledge, but a synthesizing process that brings about both knowledge and emotional awareness through imaginative interpretation and representation of experience'.[32]

Shared Futures: CW and the Impact Agenda

Research impact is an increasingly prominent feature of the Research Excellence Framework (REF), comprising 25% of the final score in REF2021. Correspondingly, HE institutions are actively seeking ways to promote and support impactful activity, identifying potential case studies to present in 2021. Universities invest time and money in preparing impact case studies. Case studies are currently based in individual units of assessment, but future REF exercises are likely to require institutional-level case studies to demonstrate interdisciplinary work with demonstrable public benefit. The impact agenda uniquely suits CW, since creative practice may profitably involve itself in other academic subjects' research both as investigation *and* impact. It offers the potential to discover as yet unseen research directions, draw together seemingly random elements and, through the imaginative play of its practice, discover new potential directions for the production of knowledge.

[31] NAWE n.d., p. 2.
[32] NAWE n.d., p. 2.

With the strengthening institutional presence of CW, colleagues from other disciplines are awakening to the subject's scope for delivering significant public benefit. Archaeologists, archivists, historians, geographers, scientists, medical and many other researchers are realizing that CW can attract new audiences for academic research, accessing additional constituencies of potential beneficiaries. Recent examples of interdisciplinary collaboration – drawn from our own experience at the Centre for New Writing – include 'Affective Digital Histories'.[33] This AHRC-funded project engaged writers to attract the public into newly digitized archives about industrial Leicester from the 1970s to the present. Working closely with the university's special collections manager Simon Dixon, the writers explored, recovered and re-imagined evidence of Leicester-based factory workers in the city's newly conceived Cultural Quarter. The Centre for New Writing commissioned and published[34] eight pieces of creative writing in five literary forms. The project came into being when the Centre director was called to a meeting by the Special Collections manager in response to an AHRC call. The researchers at the meeting were drawn from Local History, Management, Museum Studies and Sociology. They had attended previous meetings and discussed their desire to engage the public with the archive and to capture the affective dimensions of post-industrial urban change. Creative writing, as it was pointed out, was uniquely able to research the archives, and to capture and explore the formerly untold stories of people's relationship to buildings that undergo change. This, the researchers found, was the missing element that brought the project together and enabled it to be funded.

Entirely by chance, the Affective Digital Histories project coincided with royal history-in-the-making when the University of Leicester discovered the remains of Richard III under a car park. Contrasting with this national celebration of 'history from above', the project's newly commissioned writing – in the words of one contributor – 'reframes our collective knowledge of people whose lives rarely register in either local or official histories of post-industrial spaces'.[35] Later collaborations have included 'Life Cycles',[36] a research-driven methodology devised with the Diabetes Centre to discover whether sedentary people – so far immune to health warnings – can be inspired literally to get on their bikes by commissioned

[33] www.affectivedigitalhistories.org.uk.
[34] Corinne Fowler (ed.), *Hidden Stories* (Leicester: AHRC, 2015).
[35] Carol Leeming, cited in *Hidden Stories*, p. 6.
[36] <https://www2.le.ac.uk/departments/english/creativewriting/centre/the-essence-of-cycling>.

writing that evokes 'cycling culture'. Meanwhile, the Sole2Soul project[37] facilitated writing across the generations and increased footfall to a boot and shoe exhibit in Harborough Museum. Another 'Artificial Intelligence' project[38] aims to communicate the social benefits of AI to overthrow its Orwellian image. Colonial Countryside,[39] a child-led writing and history project involving one hundred children, teaches primary pupils to produce short personal essays about English country houses' Caribbean and East India Company connections. The children's essays will reach live and digital audiences, including the National Trust's five million members. Such work has clearly evolved in response to the opportunities raised by the research impact agenda.

It is in these choppy waters that institutional agendas and value systems meet. Discomfortingly strategic though they may be, such projects are meaningful to research directors and university leadership teams. In a world of climbing research targets, swelling marketing departments and shrinking English units, there is a place for pragmatism as much as for scepticism. Unjust as it is, making the case for literature becomes a matter of survival as much as idealism. Literature has always had a material dimension. In practical terms, joining forces with academics – particularly outside the Arts and Humanities – does not merely draw resources towards CW activity, but – more meaningfully – serves the literary environments in which universities are geographically based. Such projects help to diversify literary voices beyond the metropolitan mainstream.[40] Through the agency of proactive teaching and research staff, universities can make a significant contribution towards creating thriving literary cultures in cities throughout Britain. In the University of Leicester's Centre for New Writing, the focus has been on regionally based BAME writers who, as is argued elsewhere, 'suffer disproportionately from the commercial and cultural logic by which writing has historically been deemed worthy of national and international readerships'.[41] The projects described above offer an implicit answer to the

[37] <https://www2.le.ac.uk/departments/english/creativewriting/centre/sole 2soul-narrate-curate-rejuvenate>.
[38] <https://www2.le.ac.uk/departments/english/creativewriting/centre/artificial-intelligence-commission>.
[39] <https://www2.le.ac.uk/offices/press/press-releases/2017/july/child-historians-to-explore-english-country-houses2019-colonial-connections>.
[40] These words are drawn from the University of Leicester's Centre for New Writing 'About' statement.
[41] Corinne Fowler, 'A Tale of Two Novels: Developing a Devolved Approach to Black British Writing', *Journal of Commonwealth Literature*, 43:3 (2008), 75–94.

fundamental and enduring question: what is creative writing and who it is for?

Conclusion

The obvious objection to CW approaches that conform to the impact agenda is that such projects adopt instrumental, rather than aesthetic, approaches to the subject. Yet aesthetics need not be framed in opposition to approaches that acknowledge that creative writing environments thrive on material investment. Craft, in any case, remains uppermost in the discipline's discourse about itself.[42] Strategic thinking ensures that universities uniquely contribute to flourishing local writing environments. Academics can offer writers new material, in the form of recent research in a host of areas. Writers reframe research questions, reinterpret archives and share public platforms. These collaborative shared futures potentially deliver enduring benefits to academics and writers alike.

[42] See 'The Programmatic Era', *passim*.

'And who can turn away?'
Witnessing a Shared Dystopia

SERAPHIMA KENNEDY

Take a suitcase
full of your thirsty mountains,
they will thrive in that rain.

Pack the voices of your neighbourhood
in a musical box, firmly locked
for the long journey.
Choman Hardi[1]

For this is the place the world ended.
Miroslav Holub[2]

Yes, and who can turn away?
Claudia Rankine[3]

Two days before the fire at Grenfell Tower, I found myself at the scene of
the London Bridge attacks. I was retracing the steps of a family journey
along the riverbank, taken two years before when my younger sister visited
from Canada.

The attacks took place on 3 June 2017, while the country was
getting ready for a snap general election and the English: Shared
Futures committee was in the final stages of preparation for our conference in July. I was out of London at the time. By the time I
returned, on 12 June, the election had passed and we had become used
to seeing crowds of mourners at vigils and multi-faith ceremonies in
Westminster, Manchester and London Bridge. I had known about,
but not set out to find, the tributes, flowers and prayers, the pink
and yellow Post-it Notes covering the concrete isosceles monument

---

[1] Choman Hardi, *Considering the Women* (Glasgow: Bloodaxe, 2015).
[2] Miroslav Holub, *Centres of Cataclysm*, trans. George Theiner, ed. by David
Constantine, Helen Constantine and Sasha Dugdale (Glasgow: Bloodaxe/Modern
Poetry in Translation, 2016), p. 58.
[3] Claudia Rankine, *Citizen* (Minneapolis: Greywolf Press, 2014), p. 33.

outside London Bridge station, and the banks of flowers on the pavement in front of Evans Cycles.

In the cobbled alleyways around Stoney Street the police cordon was still in place. Chipboard covered up shattered windows, and parts of the road were marked off with blue and white police tape. I wandered into the cool stone interior of Southwark Cathedral and found myself sitting in a service of thanksgiving. The church was busier than I'd ever seen it, with volunteers and local residents speaking to each other animatedly in corners, signposting people to the garden, or the service, or just stopping to sit quietly. I felt the air reverberate with shock as members of the church and the local community came together to pray and weep, along with tourists who – like me – had not planned to take part. I listened to the tales of horror and courage, saddened yet grateful that no one I knew had been affected.

*

Later that year, in November, I took part in a reading for *The Rialto* magazine at the Poetry in Aldeburgh festival. The poet Richard Osmond was also performing. We had been published in the same late summer edition of the magazine, and inevitably both reflected on the events of those seemingly endless, dangerous hot months.

Richard's stunning sequence of poems told of his experience of being caught up in the London Bridge attacks, mixing translations from *Beowulf* and the *Qur'an* with his own reflections. In his poem, 'Beowulf 710–720', he wrote:

Grendel came creeping
under cover of mist
carrying the full wrath
of God on his shoulders:
a reaper, come to snatch
a handful of mankind.
Through the fog
he saw the beer hall lit up…
in bright gold before him.[4]

By the time I read Richard's poem in November, I couldn't read the name 'Grendel' without substituting 'Grenfell' – even as I type this my fingers reach for the *f* instead of the *d*, add another *l* at the end of the

---

[4] Richard Osmond, 'Beowulf 710–720', in *The Rialto 89* (Late Summer 2017), ed. Edward Doegar, Will Harris and Michael Mackmin, p. 5.

word. Grendel/Grenfell had already carried 'the full wrath/of God' and
'snatched a handful of mankind.'

*

In 'Rock, Paper, Scissors', Richard spoke of the chance decision that
led him and his friends, 'eight hours into Rob's stag,' to Katzenjammers
'authentic German bierkeller/under London Bridge,'

> where we would
> listen to an oompah band, eat sauerkraut,
> drink litre steins of Paulaner Dunkel
> and (though we didn't know it yet)
> be held in the basement by police
> for our own protection
> as terrorists attacked the door outside,
> see bloody victims hurry down
> the stairs to shelter in the bar,
> watch paramedics treat
> slash wounds to the throat and
> stab wounds to the stomach[5]

*

My poem, 'Budget', appeared a couple of pages after Richard's sequence
in the same edition of *The Rialto*. I wrote from a position of shock – from
far back, rather than up close:

> tonight we must use all our tools
> deep breaths   diazepam   watch the world
>
> from far away   clutch at loved ones and pay
> attention to the orange sky[6]

'Budget' was written quickly in the weeks after Grenfell. The language in
this poem is simple, the sentences broken. I did not have words for some
of the things I had seen, and did not know how to write about them
anyway. It felt coarse to reach for metaphors.

When *The Rialto* emailed their acceptance, I was out shifting donations
in Kensal Road, the streets buzzing as if they were in a time-lapse film. I was
by no means a first responder, but I'd been in the area, trying to find people

---

[5] *The Rialto 89*, p. 6.
[6] *The Rialto 89*, p. 8.

I had known in my previous life working in housing, on estates across the road, next to, around the corner from Grenfell Tower. I'd written a furious piece for *The Guardian*, and accompanied a couple of supply trips to hotels where the displaced were staying. The first funerals had taken place – or at least, memorials in accordance with religious rites where bodies had not yet been recovered. When I closed my eyes, I saw the missing posters that plastered the streets of north Kensington. My clothes smelled of smoke.

I wrote 'Budget', an attempt to write about Grenfell at a remove, or 'watch the world/from far away'. The poem talks about 'water, hair straighteners' – referring to the mountains of bottled water in the streets, and the essential items given out, along with food, underwear, clothing of correct sizes, and cash to buy food. You might not think that hair straighteners are essential, but for some people they are what makes them feel more human. These kinds of items were donated by well-wishers, and helped those who wanted to go to work the next Monday. Many survivors and displaced people had run from their homes in their pyjamas, without debit cards or cash, or any form of ID.

*

Unlike Richard's poem, 'Rock, Paper, Scissors', which gives a close, first-person account of seeing 'slash wounds to the throat and/ stab wounds to the stomach', I found it difficult to get too close to what I'd seen because it was not my tragedy. It's only now, looking back at the events of the summer, that I see the two experiences as linked.

*

This essay is neither a scholarly article nor an account of what it was like to observe the aftermath of the fire at Grenfell Tower. That is not my story to tell; it is the story of multiple shared communities of people, a local and national tragedy with national and even international consequences. It is also the story of individuals whose lives are still badly affected by the sudden rupture of their day-to-day existence, the loss of loved ones, homes and communities.

I can only present this as a personal essay in which I pick out fragments, magpie-like, of literature, memory and theory that have run through my head in the months since. In writing about a shared past, I hope to point a way towards a better shared future.

*

In his 2017 PEN Pinter Prize lecture *Songs for Dead Children: Poetry in Violent Times*, the poet Michael Longley talks of a chance meeting with

the cameraman who filmed the bloody aftermath of the Kingsmill mas-
sacre in January 1976. Ten textile workers were 'machine-gunned' by the
side of the road home on their way home from working in a factory at
Glenanne:

> A policeman said the road was 'an indescribable scene of carnage.'
> That scene was viewed on television screens around the world. By pure
> chance I met in a Belfast pub the following day the English cameraman
> who had filmed the bloody aftermath. I asked him how he managed in
> such a nightmare. He replied: 'I take out my light meter, and I focus
> the lens.'[7]

The printed booklet of Longley's lecture must have gone to press in late
May 2017, or early June, because in it he makes reference to victims of
the Manchester bombings:

> The songs from the children's street games reverberate down the decades
> and sound, in my imagination, for the children killed in Manchester
> in May this year. The deaths of children – always 'innocent victims' –
> epitomize the shame of political violence.[8]

Longley writes of the way in which the Troubles echoed through his
poetry over many years, and through the writing by his contemporaries.
He writes of being 'haunted' by the death of Patrick Rooney, a nine-year-
old boy who was the first child to be killed in the Troubles in August
1969. 'In helpless response,' he says, he wrote 'Kindertotenlieder':

> There can be no songs for dead children
> Near the crazy circle of explosions,
> The splintering tangent of the ricochet,
>
> No songs for the children who have become
> My unrestricted tenants, fingerprints
> Everywhere, teethmarks on this and that.[9]

He writes, 'Patrick Rooney haunts me to this day.' When I read this
poem now, I read it forwards as well as backwards. For me, it points to
the forensic examinations at Grenfell Tower. I see 'teethmarks' and think

---

[7] Michael Longley, *Songs for Dead Children: Poetry in Violent Times* (London:
Faber & Faber, 2017), p. 15.
[8] *Songs for Dead Children*, p. 4.
[9] *Songs for Dead Children*, pp. 3–4.

of dental records. The word 'fingerprint' leads to police officers carrying out fingertip searches on bent knees.

*

I say Longley's lecture 'must have' gone to press in late May, because *Songs for Dead Children* makes no mention of the London Bridge attacks, or of the children who died in the fire at Grenfell Tower. Of course, this may be a deliberate choice. Perhaps it is not useful for the focus to shift. The link between Manchester and the Troubles is a direct and clear line tracing the history of public death and 'the shame of political violence', between political decisions and the lost lives of children.

Terrorism is not the same as fire. In the dark constellation of era-defining tragedies, we must be sensitive to the specificity of grief, not to assimilate or drown out individual voices in easy comparisons.

*

And yet, I cannot help but make those links.

What happened to those caught up in the Manchester blast was not my personal tragedy – but it was a national tragedy, felt by us all. It was an act of violence aimed at innocent teenagers, mostly girls, who could have been me, myself, my sister, my sister's daughters.

*

That is to say, it could have been anyone.

*

But it was not anyone. It was a particular set of people, in a particular location, at a particular time.

*

The 'songs from the children's street games' reverberate also in the play-grounds of north Kensington, where eighteen children are known to have died. The Grenfell nursery was located in the base of the tower. I imagine it smoke-filled, waterlogged, falling apart, like the 33 flats that did not burn.

**

Five days after the fire at Grenfell, I stood beneath the Westway, an elevated dual carriageway that traverses London from Shepherd's Bush to Paddington, bisecting Bramley Road, and then Ladbroke Grove.

The streets were wild with cars, as relatives drove around looking for news. It was hot, the air was still thick with smoke, and I was overwhelmed by the hastily photocopied colour posters of the missing, taped to bus stops, railings and shop windows between Shepherd's Bush and Westbourne Park.

*

All of the images were heartbreaking, but there was one that stood out: a three-year-old girl, pictured in a party dress and gold hat. *She died because she lived in social housing,* I thought. She died, along with her parents, and her auntie, who was simply visiting.

I found myself praying, although I am an atheist. I promised her that I would do everything in my power to make sure she was never forgotten.

*

Rock, paper, scissors. When I got home I heard sirens: the Finsbury Park Mosque attacks. I went to bed with my windows flashing: blue/red/blue/red.

**

In *The Generation of Postmemory: Writing and Visual Culture After the Holocaust*, Marianne Hirsch raises questions about the 'ethics and aesthetics of remembrance' in the aftermath of tragedy. Thinking about Susan Sontag's 'pain of others', she asks,

> What do we owe the victims? How can we best carry their stories forward, without appropriating them, without unduly calling attention to ourselves, and without, in turn, having our own stories displaced by them? How are we implicated in the aftermath of crimes we did not ourselves witness?'[10]

These words came to haunt me in ways I could never have anticipated, both in the early hours of the morning of 14 June and in the hot, dust-caked aftermaths, when the pavements of north Kensington were filled with locals who were desperate and grieving, and cars sped around street corners as if in a video game. I couldn't remember which disaster movie, or dystopic fiction it was supposed to be. The idea of the 'Big Society' felt like a cruel joke.

---

[10] Marianne Hirsch, *The Generation of Postmemory: Writing and Visual Culture after the Holocaust* (New York: Columbia University Press, 2012), p. 2.

Here it was, a dystopia from which the authorities were almost entirely absent. Here it was, what happened when you strip society down to its bare bones.

**

I should note, here, that there are many people who contributed far more to the relief effort at Grenfell than I could. My efforts were anonymous, peripheral and tentative. I felt limited by my strange position as someone who'd worked for the organisation responsible for the building, and then again as a suddenly very public writer introduced frequently as a 'whistle-blower' or 'journalist'. I was, of course, neither of these: I kept telling people I was a poet, as if that would make me seem normal.

*

In that first week, I found a local resident who I'd been in regular contact with a couple of years before. She looked like she hadn't slept in days. I told her about the article I had written, how I wasn't sure if it was the right thing to do. I told her I was sorry for what she was going through. She said, 'Maybe that's what you can do now. Writing.' I took that as my lead. (Later, I questioned whether I had made this up. It seemed too convenient. But I don't think so. I remember standing in the estate gardens, the heat.)

*

I have always believed that writers have a duty to highlight stories of injustice, that the voices of those who have suffered at the hands of the state should enter the record and be heard. Journalism is often a valuable way of ensuring this happens. Grenfell has made me re-examine some of my assumptions about this.

In situations where personal stories become public property, those directly affected by bomb blast or house fire can find themselves fighting for the right to tell their own stories.

*

In the initial aftermath of Grenfell, volunteers reported seeing media outlets offering children cash for stories, even as people remained unaccounted for.

An inquiry into the Manchester bombings will look at the role of the media, how they treated victims and relatives after the bombings. One relative talks of being 'hounded' by journalists who found his address, before his relative's body had been officially identified.

Victims of public tragedies such as Grenfell are caught in a tight bind, one in which the desire for truth and accountability may compete against the desire to be left alone to grieve or rebuild in private. They may also find themselves at the hard edge of competitive sympathy ('why are they getting more money than the victims of the Manchester bombings?'), internet trolls ('aren't they all illegal immigrants?'), and real-life saboteurs.

*

While preparing for English: Shared Futures, I myself was pursued by journalists. I remember trying to patch a colleague into a conference call, only to find an Irish radio station on the other end of the phone. Speaking out comes at a price. For the victims, that price is the picking over, in the public sphere, of their families, incomes, backgrounds.

*

I read about the idea of 'competitive memory' in Michael Rothberg's book *Multidirectional Memory: Remembering the Holocaust in the Age of Decolonization*[11] in which he asks 'What happens when different histories confront each other in the public sphere? Does the remembrance of one history erase others from view?' For Rothberg, memory is *multidirectional*, 'productive, and not privative'. He is talking, of course, about collective memory – something that is complex even from a distance of many years.

*

What is the response to injustice? How should a good victim behave? How should a good *writer* behave?

*

It has only been six months.

**

What is the difference between terrorism and fire? Between indifference and war? Is it a difference of degree? Of intent?

*

Surely, there can be no equivalence?

*

[11] Michael Rothberg, *Multidirectional Memory: Remembering the Holocaust in the Age of Decolonization* (Stanford: Stanford University Press, 2009), pp. 2–3.

'They asked us to go to another room and lock ourselves in and said they'd be coming to get us.'

These were the last words of B's sister in law, K (not their real initials). She died in the fire at Grenfell Tower, along with her husband and all three of her children.[12]

*

B told me these words one day after I met him at the opening of the Grenfell Tower Inquiry, but I met him on the hottest day of 2017, exactly one week after the fire, during a Channel 4 news broadcast.

I listened as a senior firefighter talked about attending the scene, about having to bring in ladders from Surrey because they didn't have one high enough in London. I remembered standing at the base of the tower as the light on what looked like a toy crane went out and the water was turned off.

In the news programme, I watched B, obviously shell-shocked with grief, struggle to make his voice heard over the noise of people arguing.

The producer hadn't told me that it would be a town hall-style debate; if they had, I wouldn't have taken part. Politicians, police officers, civil servants, volunteers – some of whom popped up and then disappeared in the weeks after the fire, some of whom remained, carrying out vital work with survivors, the bereaved and the local community – all of them arguing wildly so that he could not speak over them. No one from the local authority attended.

*

Since then, I have sat in meeting after meeting, listening as people describe what it is like to be homeless, to have lost everything, or to have been on the phone with those who were trapped.

One man, who I'll call T, lost two relatives in the fire. At one memorable council meeting, he told the local authority of the practical difficulties that come with burying multiple members, including young children, of the same family.

'How many bodies should you put in a coffin?' he asked. 'This is a question that no one should have to answer.'

*

[12] Some names, initials and identifying features of relatives have been changed.

T's family were social housing tenants and lived in Grenfell Tower. They are no longer living.

My family are social housing tenants in the same borough and live in a street property in the more prosperous south. They are still alive.

*

The poet Aracelis Girmay writes, 'What to do with this knowledge? That our living is not guaranteed?'[13] I do not know what else to do with this knowledge other than to make sure the world knows about it. I imagine I will be writing about Grenfell, in some form or other, for the rest of my life.

*

In the weeks after the fire, while everything was frantic, the suffering of people in the local community was overwhelming. It was easy to feel powerless. I kept hearing the words of the poet Carolyn Forché, who travelled to El Salvador in the 1980s, rolling through my head like a refrain:

> It is
> not your right to feel powerless. Better
> people than you were powerless.[14]

*

Better, because they were children?

*

Better, *because* they were powerless? No.

*

Better, because they had potential, and we will never know what they could have achieved.

*

They were powerless, and so I must not be. It is not my right.

**

[13] Aracelis Girmay, 'On Living', in *Kingdom Animalia* (New York: BOA Editions, 2011), p. 30.
[14] Carolyn Forché, 'Return', in *The Country Between Us* (New York: Harper Perennial, 1981), p. 20.

I have been thinking about dystopias. About how the ruins of the past enter the present and the future.

My own life is built on such stories: the migration of people after war, dust on their hands. The story of my grandmother scrabbling at the rubble after her house was bombed in Crofton Park. 1941, her five-year-old daughter killed by a bomb that crushed their home. My grandmother's daughter – my aunt – is listed in the Book of War Dead.

*

But we are not at war.

*

'I take out my light meter, and I focus the lens.' In his poem, 'Midnight, Dhaka, 25 March 1971', Mir Mahfuz Ali writes:

I am a hardened camera clicking at midnight.
I have caught it all – the screeching tanks
pounding the city under the massy heat,
searchlights dicing the streets like bayonets...
I click on, despite the dry and bitter dust...[15]

He is talking, of course, about what it is like to witness a war. But the difference between war, domestic terror, or a preventable fire may be a matter of degree or intention to those who experience them directly. For anyone else – those of us lucky enough to have lived our lives without gunfire or smoke – it is an abstract.

*

I count the floors down from the top – six floors down and the flames are still burning. A woman next to me says, 'Dental records. Only way you know them now is through their teeth.'

I shortcut the main road and head down an alleyway where one or two news crews are still gathered. I am counting the floors that are still on fire as I move around the tower block. Ten floors down, twelve floors down. Fire is visible inside every window of the building. Fifteen hours after it started, and the whole building is burning.

A drizzle of water, tiny against the black tower, spurts from a crane that only reaches halfway up. The water stops. The lights on the crane go out.

[15] Mir Mahfuz Ali, 'Midnight, Dhaka, 25 March 1971', in *Midnight, Dhaka* (Glasgow: Seren, 2014), p. 7.

**

'How difficult is it for one body to feel the injustice wheeled at another?'
writes Claudia Rankine in *Citizen,* her deconstruction of race in America.[16]

*

'I used to have a life,' one survivor told the council. 'But you have turned
me into a beggar.'

*

I am supposed to be writing about a shared future. But I don't know
what the future looks like, now. What future we can have. The place of
language in it. Each day I think about what it means to write, and who I
am writing for. There have been many times when I have had no words
to respond to people's suffering. I can only think that their future must
be better than this.

*

I thought that the procedures would have worked. I imagined that the state
would be there for those who were injured. Remember images of the army
being sent in to help with flooding in Yorkshire? There would be a plan.

*

There was no plan. Or, if there was, it was wholly insufficient. It is important to ask why.
    The phrase 'institutional indifference' has been used repeatedly by sur-
vivors and the displaced, and now taken up by the media. It refers to the
altitude of both local and national government to citizens affected by the
five, many of whom had previously raised concerns about safety.

*

Do you believe that the state exists to support and protect the lives of its
citizens? That's what I thought.

*

Who decided that it was acceptable to wrap buildings in flammable materials? Was it you? Was it *you* who thought the fire brigade didn't need
cranes big enough to tackle a high-rise building?
    I didn't think so.

---

[16] *Citizen,* p. 116.

*

'The world is wrong. You can't put the past behind you.' Claudia Rankine, *Citizen*.[17]

*

What good are words, in these circumstances? Who has the right to write about this? And what if I can't help but tell you what I saw?

*

'Yes, and who can turn away?' says Rankine.[18]

*

'They live. There is nothing left
to do   but live.'[19]

*

I put on my shoes. I put on my shoes and lace them up. I take out my pen. I don't know what else to do but write.

[17] *Citizen*, p. 63.
[18] *Citizen*, p. 33.
[19] Girmay, *Kingdom Animalia*, p. 30.

English and the Public Good

SARAH DILLON

The phrase 'English and the public good' immediately calls to mind the long history of arguments which claim that reading imaginative literature improves us. These arguments can be traced from, for example, Philip Sidney's 1595 'Apology for Poetry', through the Romantics and the Victorians, to modern-day cognitive science and psychology. Sidney argues that stories convey their moral truths through their art, and that this medium exceeds the power of history or philosophy to teach men to act virtuously. Edmund Spenser wrote that the aim of publishing *The Faerie Queene* was to 'fashion a gentleman or noble person in vertuous and gentle discipline'.[1] This argument for the moral or improving value of literature is usually in tension with a belief in its aesthetic beauty, creating a conflict between the demand to instruct or educate and the impulse to entertain and delight. This tension can be found in John Dryden's dialogic 'An Essay of Dramatic Poesy' (1668), or in the nineteenth-century struggle between didacticism and aestheticism, positions perhaps best denoted by John Ruskin's commitment to the moral value of art and literature on the one hand, and Walter Pater's advocacy of 'art for art's sake' on the other. In the twenty-first century, scientists have entered the debate, attempting to provide evidential proof of the morally improving value of literature. In a much-reported article published in *Science* in 2013, David Comer Kidd and Emanuele Castano claimed to have proved 'that by prompting readers to take an active writerly role to form representations of characters' subjective states, literary fiction recruits ToM [theory of mind]'.[2] Very few news outlets reported their qualification – 'but we see these findings as preliminary and much research is needed'; nor has the media widely covered the fact that in 2016 another group of researchers published an article scientifically challenging Kidd and

---

[1] Edmund Spenser, 'A Letter of the Authors Expounding His Whole Intention in the Course of this Worke: Which for That It Giueth Great Light to the Reader, for the Better Vnderstanding Is Hereunto Annexed', in *The Fairy Queene*, ed. Thomas P. Roche, Jr. (London: Penguin, 1987), pp. 15–18 (p. 15).

[2] David Comer Kidd and Emanuele Castano, 'Reading Literary Fiction Improves Theory of Mind', *Science*, 342:6156 (18 October 2013), 377–80 (p. 380).

Castano's claims because the results of their experiments proved not to be replicable.[3]

There is no doubting that Kidd and Castano's intentions were good. Their research and enthusiastic public dissemination of it was clearly driven by a commitment to providing evidential proof to support rhetorical defences of literature. The site of this defence in cognitive science and psychology is, it seems, located in proving the power of literature to improve us by developing our empathetic skills.[4] But there are many problems with the moral improvement defence of literature, whichever form it takes, and whether rhetorical or scientific: the question of whether or not it is in fact true; its neglect or repression of other important values of literature, for instance, pleasure, transportation, escape; and the fundamental role that literature plays in challenging and disrupting dominant moral and ethical codes. Spenser may have said that the aim of *The Faerie Queene* was to 'fashion a gentleman', but the content of his epic poem provides nuanced challenges to the established gender roles of his day.

I do not think that reading literature makes us better people, more moral, more empathetic. Nor do most of the literary scholars I have asked about this. As a group of people who read for a living and who move in professional circles made up of other people who read for a living, our collective view on this ought to carry some weight. It can be summed up in this (admittedly very 'in') joke:

> Two literature professors are having a drink after work. One says to the other, 'I have definitive proof that reading literature doesn't make you a better person'. 'What's your proof?' asks the other. 'Today's departmental meeting,' replies the first.

I would welcome a study of the power of literature to increase theory of mind, empathy, or moral probity which compared English scholars to a control group of the general population. I suspect there would be very little difference in results.

[3] Maria Eugenia Panero, Deena Skolnick Weisberg, Jessica Black, Thalia R. Goldstein, Jennifer L. Barnes, Hiram Brownell and Ellen Winner, 'Does Reading a Single Passage of Literary Fiction Really Improve Theory of Mind? An Attempt at Replication', *Journal of Personality and Social Psychology*, 111:5 (2016): e46–e54.

[4] Kidd and Castano's article includes a thorough literature review of studies on literature and empathy. The work of Keith Oatley is perhaps most prominent in this field. See, for instance, Maja Djikic, Keith Oatley and Mihnea C. Moldoveanu, 'Reading Other Minds: Effects of Literature on Empathy', *Scientific Study of Literature*, 3:1 (2013), 28–47.

But this does not undermine the fact that literature does have power, and I locate that power in literature's ability to intervene and disrupt through its specific medium and modes of engagement with the world. Literature's value lies in its ability to challenge, from the smallest to the largest level.[5] At one end of the spectrum, one word, line or paragraph can pose a challenge to understanding, forcing us to study it, to read it again, to learn new words or new uses of language, challenging us to reflect on the words we use and how we think. At the other end of the spectrum, its stories and the tacit knowledge they convey can intervene in the world, challenging the dominant order of the day. If literature did not have that power, why would there be such a long history of literary censorship? Why would PEN exist? For totalitarian regimes that seek to close down thought and constrain freedom of expression in order to sustain their power, literature and the imagination are some of the first things to be controlled: we see this in real life, in the history of China or North Korea; we see it played out in fiction in novels from Yevgeny Zamyatin's *We* (1924) to George Orwell's *1984* (1949), from Margaret Atwood's *The Handmaid's Tale* (1985) to Madeleine Thein's *Do Not Say We Have Nothing* (2016).

Such regimes also seek to control the press and the academic freedom enshrined in universities. I am writing this essay after a week of astonishing attacks on the latter from the current UK government and populist press, in which my own university and in fact my own English Faculty have featured prominently.[6] These events present a new context in which we must think about the future of the discipline of English (as opposed to the body of creative work that is its subject). Such thought must now take place in the context of the radically shifted political and social climate of the UK since the referendum on membership of the European Union, and of the US since the election of Donald Trump. The most prominent existing defences of Universities, of the Humanities, and of English studies were all written before this shift: Stefan Collini's *What Are Universities For?* (2012), Helen Small's *The Value of the Humanities* (2013) and Rick Rylance's *Literature and the Public Good* (2016, and

---

[5] For a fuller rejection of the position that literature has to be informative or morally improving, see Joshua Landy, *How to do Things with Fictions* (Oxford: Oxford University Press, 2012).

[6] For a useful summary of recent events, see Andrew McRae, 'This is not normal: universities in the news', *Head of Department's Blog*, 29 October 2017, <https://headofdepartmentblog.wordpress.com/2017/10/29/this-is-not-normal-universities-in-the-news/> [accessed 30 October 2017].

therefore presumably in press before the EU referendum and the US Presidential vote).[7] Whilst these works remain crucially important, they are all responding to a pre-2016 climate in a mode primarily of defence; in a more threatening cultural and political environment, we need to move from defence to intervention. There is also a tendency to conflate English understood as 'literature' with 'English' as the *study* of works of imaginative literature, that is, 'English' as the interpretative activity known as literary criticism that we carry out in our university research and teaching. A good example of both defensive rhetoric and such conflation is Sarah Churchwell's 2014 opinion piece in the *Times Higher Education*, 'Why the Humanities Matter?'[8] Through probing Churchwell's piece, and outlining where and why I disagree, I want to offer a new vision for the future of English studies and its public good after 2016.

Churchwell's piece oscillates between arguing for the importance of literature and other arts, and arguing for the importance of study of them. 'Literature, history, art, music, languages, theatre, film – and yes, television and computer games – are the stories through which we express our humanity', she says: 'we understand ourselves and our world through the telling of stories.' The morally improving aspect of her argument is contained here in the choice of expression – she is not arguing that telling stories is what makes us human (Jonathan Gottschall has done an excellent job of that in *The Storytelling Animal* (2012)), but that we express our *humanity* through them. This is a different argument, with all the moral probity that the word 'humanity' as opposed to 'inhumanity' carries. While I agree that telling stories is an irreducible human trait, those stories can just as well express the inhumanity that always already inhabits our supposed 'humanity', making us realise just how evil, narrow-minded, violent, or unjust so-called 'humanity' can be. They can reveal how many exclusions the 'our' of 'our humanity' entails, of minorities within the human as well as of all life classed as non-human, with those two categories sometimes overlapping. The 'art is morally improving' argument becomes explicit when Churchwell asserts that 'visual dramas teach us sympathy, empathy, pity, encouraging us to break out of our solipsistic shells'. This takes us back to

---

[7] Stefan Collini, *What Are Universities For?* (London: Penguin, 2012); Rick Rylance *Literature and the Public Good* (Oxford: Oxford University Press, 2016); Helen Small, *The Value of the Humanities* (Oxford: Oxford University Press, 2013).

[8] Sarah Churchwell, 'Why the Humanities Matter?', *Times Higher Education*, 13 November 2014, <https://www.timeshighereducation.com/comment/opinion/sarah-churchwell-why-the-humanities-matter/2016909.article> [accessed 30 October 2017].

the debates of the first half of this essay, but also does not acknowledge the fact that visual dramas can teach 'us' different things, depending on who that 'us' is. For instance, Hollywood cinema teaches men that they have a right to dominate and control, to lead and to destroy, whereas it offers women, as feminist theory has argued for decades, only the position of object, or of masochistic voyeur of the objectification of her own sex.[9] The recent exposure of widespread sexual harassment and misconduct in Hollywood, ignited by the revelations regarding Harvey Weinstein, have only brought to mainstream light what feminist film critics, viewers and actresses have always known about the gender inequality and sexual exploitation of the Hollywood film industry, on and off screen. Much art, visual or textual, does not teach many people sympathy, empathy or pity but rather highlights and enforces for such people the exclusions of a culture that still presumes a universal 'us'.

Churchwell moves from this humanistic argument for the value of creative production to a defence of the Humanities as a discipline of study. 'The humanities', she says, 'are the study of what makes us human, of what it means to be human.' I have the same concerns as above, regarding this statement, but more than this, the move itself is problematic, as a scientist noted in a revealing comment posted on the online version of the article: 'the essay conflates two things the enjoyment of culture and the study of it. I enjoy a lot of cultural activities and indeed, I would agree that culture is a defining aspect of humanities without which life would be intolerable'; what the commenter remains unconvinced by is the argument for the worth of studying them in an academic context. Unfortunately, Churchwell does not provide a strong argument for this beyond the fact that we develop and teach critical thinking skills – which indeed we do – and the more elliptical assertion that 'the humanities conserve and safeguard those aspects of our being that intersect with the meanings of human existence beyond industry'. This latter defence makes sense when understood in the context in which Churchwell was writing: Churchwell's piece is clearly responding to the marketisation of UK universities and the top-down introduction of quantitative measures of value and success which a priori discriminate against the modes of knowing offered by the Humanities and our objects of study.[10] Such marketisation, which continues apace under the current

---

[9] The seminal essay on this topic remans Laura Mulvey, 'Visual Pleasure and Narrative Cinema', *Screen*, 16.3 (1975), 6–18. See my *Deconstruction, Feminism, Film* (Edinburgh: Edinburgh University Press, 2018) for a theorisation and performance of the possibilities for feminist spectatorship in the twenty-first century.
[10] For a good evocation of feeling at that time, see Alex Preston, 'The War Against

government, has produced battlelines: 'us' Humanists, staunch and honourable defenders of what it means to be human, versus 'them', defined by Churchwell as 'the instrumentalists and technocrats who decide our society's priorities'. It has put the Humanities on the rhetorical defensive. I believe that if the Humanities, English studies included, is to flourish, this narrative has to change. We need to adapt and evolve in order to demonstrate in powerful and palpable ways our value and importance, our contribution, as the title of this piece has it, to the public good.

In the first instance, we have to challenge the very name of our discipline and the problems that lie within it, entwined as 'English' literature is with our country's history of colonialist expansion and exploitation. Which aspects of 'humankind' do the stories we study pay attention to, and how do we diversify both our modes of study and our objects of study so that our work might have value to the diversity that in fact constitutes 'the public', both our own student bodies and the population outside the academy? We also need to be continually aware that the benefits our academic discipline offers are not the same as the benefits our subject-matter offers, and we need to formulate new ways of showcasing and celebrating (not defending) the former. To do so, we need to move from rhetorical defences of English studies to action and engagement. We need to think hard, to use the harmful misnomer that has been used to name this, about our 'impact'. When public engagement and impact have become so inextricably associated with the marketisation of higher education and the quantification of value that has precisely been blamed for the devaluing of the Humanities, it might seem strange to turn to them as the site of action and resistance. But in them lies, I believe, the most powerful future of our discipline. The clumsy introduction of impact into the REF, driven as HE policy so often is by thinking about the sciences with little thought given to how non-sciences might respond to the agenda, has done incredible harm to academic perception of impact in the Arts and Humanities. But in my recent experience, the impact agenda is changing the environment in which we work in positive and productive ways, creating platforms, networks and changes in mindset that offer a brighter future for English studies and the Humanities disciplines in general.

One solid example of this is the collaboration between the AHRC and BBC Radio 3 on the New Generation Thinkers scheme, which is networking national broadcasting with academia in a way never done before. More and more academics are now able to make programmes

Humanities at Britain's Universities', *The Guardian*, 29 March 2015, <https://www.theguardian.com/education/2015/mar/29/war-against-humanities-at-britains-universities> [accessed 30 October 2017].

informed by their research, contributing to the BBC's mandate to enrich people's lives with programmes and services that inform, educate and entertain, and bringing academic literary criticism and original scholarship to a public audience. Indeed, my career in broadcasting, as well as that of other literary scholars such as Shahidha Bari, were launched by the scheme. Even those academics who are selected for audition but do not make the final cut are networked with BBC producers in a way never possible before. An ecosystem of communication between academics and the BBC is developing; it is no longer 'us' academics and 'them' broadcasters.

More widely, from an early stage in their research project planning, academics now think about how they can share their work with the public. The possibility of doing so is enhanced by the creation of local and national festivals that showcase Humanities research, for example, the Cambridge Festival of Ideas and the national Being Human Festival, launched in 2014, of which Churchwell is the Director. It is no longer 'us' academics and 'them' members of the public. And things are beginning to change in Whitehall. To give another personal example: last week I delivered a talk at a workshop with other Humanities academics – both scholars and practitioners – the AHRC, the British Academy, representatives from charitable bodies and representatives from the Department for Communities and Local Government, the Department for Digital, Culture, Media and Sport, the Department for Work and Pensions, and the Cabinet Office. The workshop was an open conversation about how the Arts and Humanities, including English, can make a contribution to the work of government. The results of the conversation were illuminating. Government departments are beginning to draw up and publish 'statements of need' outlining the key areas in which they require input from academics and other external bodies – they are thinking carefully about how these might be phrased so as not to exclude, a priori, Humanities disciplines. And they listened to the case we made for the importance of English and other Arts and Humanities subjects as interpretative sciences that do not produce data but other forms of knowledge that are equally valuable and important in determining decision-making about our country and its inhabitants. It is no longer 'us' academics and 'them' policy makers. Through initiatives such as these, AHRC policy training programmes, and the new 'Research impact at the UK Parliament' online hub, lines of communication are now opening.[11]

---

[11] The hub is available at http://www.parliament.uk/research-impact.

I am not suggesting by this that all our problems are over and that the value and importance of what we do for the public good is self-evident to everyone all of the time. But what I am proposing is that it is no longer appropriate for us to engage in the world from a position of embattled defence. In a radically different post-2016 climate, in which exclusive focus on quantitative value has led to the financial crisis and its repercussions, to a populist swing in many countries, and to a world in which the most common phrases in conversation and the media are words only coined in the past twelve months – fake news, post-truth, alternative facts – then if we truly believe in what we do (and I do truly believe), we have to step out into the world: we have to intervene, analyse, comment, engage and inform. We have to use the idea of impact to empower ourselves and so others. For English to flourish in the future, we have to evolve and adapt. This means adapting what we do: becoming more public-facing and more interdisciplinary; being prepared to bring our skills and knowledge to bear on collaborative projects; and, sometimes, being prepared to be responsive in our choice of research topics to the pressing issues of the times. But it also means dropping the 'us' and 'them' mentality and recognising that we have the power to intervene in, and change for the better, our environment. In evolutionary biology, this is called 'niche construction', the way 'human beings [...] modify significant sources of selection in their environments, thereby codirecting subsequent biological evolution'.[12] As I argue elsewhere, by homology, the idea of cultural niche construction provides one model for understanding how politicised action and resistance can effect change.[13] If we can alter the types of narratives that are successfully replicated by modifying sources of selection in the cultural environment, for example, it becomes very clear why diverse representation in university English departments, in publishing, and in the literary press is an urgent necessity. As English scholars, we *can* change the world, or at least little bits of it, and trying to do so will be for our own, as well as the public, good.

[12] Kevin N. Laland, John Odling-Smee and Marcus W. Feldman, 'Niche Construction, Biological Evolution, and Cultural Change', *Behavioral and Brain Sciences*, 23 (2000), 131–75 (p. 131).
[13] See my essay, 'On the Politics of Adaptation: *Cloud Atlas* and Narrative Evolution' (in preparation) for a fuller argument about how the biological theory of niche construction provides a homology for the way in which we can change our environments in order to change the narratives that are successfully replicated within them.

'Can Wisdom be put in a silver rod? / Or Love in a golden bowl?' On Not Defending the Humanities

SIMON KÖVESI

While it certainly had a celebratory and affirmatory atmosphere, it is important to be clear that the English: Shared Futures conference was born of uncertainty about the future of English.[1] That discipline-specific concern is a major constituent of ongoing debates about the state and status of the humanities and arts across English-speaking universities globally. So many 'defence of the humanities'-style polemics have been written across the past few years, that I have long worried that our subjects are becoming defensive by default, nervous by character. Rather than resolving to be hard as nails in trying times, we are in danger of feeling institutionally, systemically, hard done by. In turn, I worry that our response as a community in English and beyond can appear grotesquely self-important and brittle. As a Head of Department – constantly concerned about getting student bums on lecture theatre seats – I wonder then about how attractive our subject might be to the wider world. How attractive is it to be seen as entrenched, defensive, or even *arch*? Does anyone want to come into English, or support it, because we moan about how embattled we are as we proclaim our own significance, cultural superiority and sheer status?

It might be that some of what we do to argue for the humanities is self-harming. Self-declaring polemics that 'defend the humanities' penned by those who are ostensibly most secure in their profession – and I include myself in that bracket – might be damaging to those principles we in the humanities think we live and work by, though I hold those principles to be anything but homogenous.

[1] This essay was originally commissioned in autumn 2017 by the *Palgrave Campaign for the Humanities*, the 'Spotlight' section of which is a collection of essays in which Palgrave authors consider the humanities and what can and should be done by way of analysis and advocacy. I thank Ben Doyle and Verity Bingham at Palgrave for their kind permission to rewrite and reprint the essay here. See *Palgrave Macmillan's Campaign for the Humanities*, <https://www.palgrave.com/gp/campaign-for-the-humanities/spotlight-on> [accessed 11 July 2018].

This essay is not a 'defence' of the humanities. I don't want to mount a 'defence of the humanities' because I do not wish to imply that my humanities-based critical practice is an inviolate, pristine militarised citadel, all classic lines and Doric columns, with barbed wire atop the private, inward-facing, excluding, college wall. I don't want the humanities to be a stolid assertion that is beyond critique. A 'defence' might imply that. It might also suggest that I have a secure idea of what it is I would be defending. Regardless of the opposing forces rumoured to be 'attacking' the humanities, regardless of the professional responsibility you might demand, or the sense of critical and pedagogical history I ought to extol, I still cannot grasp a secure idea of what the humanities is, or what it is for. Not because I don't think it is anything, or for nothing, but because I think it encompasses everything. Probably, somewhere among my motivational devils here is that I want you to think I resist definition so that I appear more radical than a secure foundation in the shape of knowledge would allow me to be. English Literature scholars like to appear radical, don't we? In reality, like most of you, I am probably not quite so radical – reliant, comforted and paid, lucky as I am, by what the humanities mean institutionally, hierarchically and economically. If I write a polemic, I do so from a pretty safe position. The inviolate, pristine militarised citadel of the humanities secures that privilege for me. A little intellectual embarrassment is the biggest risk here – as it is for most 'defences' of our subjects. I do not write from a precarious position, because actually my humanities practice is secure (which was certainly not the case for all colleagues at English: Shared Futures). That material reality troubles the radicalism and resistance I seek from my subject. If you are lucky, your subject of English is good capital.

Of course I appreciate that humanities are being undermined on many fronts – fronts propelled by capitalising versions of value in an entirely economic and monetary sense. Like most of my colleagues, I remain deeply concerned about the monetisation and commercialisation of higher education, the functionalism of education in general, and about what debt and crass vocation-seeking do to the valuation of the humanities in higher education – and I am aware of the effects from the classroom through to the executive boardroom. It would be weird – irresponsibly naïve even – if I wasn't concerned about this set of trends. But there have been so many defensive and brittle articles about these aspects of the 'attack' on the humanities, that I want to use this opportunity to push in a different direction: to look at the humanities and wonder what it – or they? – might enable.

Writing this essay makes me less sure of what the humanities is, not more secure that I know it to be something worth 'defending'. The word 'humanities' pushes into the light the irritating fact that as a conceptual umbrella, indicating the broad categorisation of a sweeping set of disciplines, 'humanities' does not mean as much to me as 'art' or the even narrower habits of 'literature' (usually, at this juncture, defences of the humanities seek to draw security by defining the term on the basis of learned tradition and classical reference points, as if that helps secure our tent in the storm). And literary criticism, which is what my narrow slice of activity is called, is neither art, nor meaningfully does it require the label 'humanities' in anything other than in its institutional organisation (universities, libraries, publishers, funding bodies). I hope I am not deliberately seeking to cause trouble for the sake of it, nor resisting categorisation because – in puerile self-regard – I don't want my work to be defined (you cannot box me in, I won't be tied down – that sort of thing). But still the words that categorise our work have to mean something particularising to our cause, to mean much. And if we are to defend them, if we are to cluster underneath the words on a banner of continual protest, these categories have to mean everything.

I want my discipline category to include rubble, to own detritus. I want it to be grounded, sub-cultural, insecure, furtive, on edge, subterranean, adult, dangerous. The critical humanities as a threat, not a duvet. The self-immolating speaker of Dostoevsky's *Notes from the Underground*, not a cock-sure hero of a pap genre thriller. Though we can talk about both, we must tend towards complexity, towards paradox, towards the anti-hero, towards the marginalised and the minoritarian. I want to attack the disciplines myself. I want my words to be variations of attack, not defence. I want my words to be attacked. I want the 'process' of the humanities to be varied and discomfiting and awkward and immeasurable and playful and irresponsible and celebratory and unsustainable and explosive and unsettling and wasteful. Critical indiscipline, rather than academic discipline.

I want this kind of messiness and resistance to orthodoxy, because so many other academic areas have given up the ghost – or (to be kinder) have had to sustain themselves by actual products, by tangible outputs beyond the book or the article – bridges and roads, new drugs, treatments, buildings, software, environment, maps, policy, processes, formulae. In the humanities, we claim to be free: and we claim to be agents of freedom, yet we are the greatest critics of freedom's assumptions and implications and distortions. Language is metaphor. We know that claims to freedom are rhetorical device. We are aware of how little freedom anyone has in organised societies. Yet we ourselves write the word 'freedom' on university branded paper. We ask – what does freedom mean? And so we criticise ideological prisons as well as those built by the stones of law in which our fellow humans dwell. We irritate. We claim to be radical and edgy from within the safe havens of elite institutions. And we argue because the argument is there to be had. We might not storm the Bastille, but we talk a lot, restlessly, about doing so. Constant agreement threatens supine complacency. Do we argue for a living? Someone has to ask questions, or else society is reduced to machinic processes of acquiescence. We seek truth, yet in English literary critical work we revel in fiction. Humanities has no territory, because we are liberated in our critical practice, and we write beyond the walls of ownership, from behind the safe walls of university life, if we're lucky. We occupy an irresolvable and paradoxical situation as humanities scholars, and the resultant discomfort must be a necessary constituent of our work. Discomfort – and not defensiveness – should be the outward-facing characterisation we present. We worry away at the 'crisis' in the humanities: but are worry and crisis driving forces of humanities scholarship?

I want argument. Because to my mind, literary criticism – after investigation, balance and proof – is argument. Argument in process; sifting and moving; lifting and probing; destroying, reassessing, renewing, modernising *and* antiquating. I like old stuff, I like new stuff, but I like mixed up old-and-new stuff best, because it is troubling, and provokes questions. Because it is not pure. Purity is a myth of the totalitarian, of the scientist, of the ideologue. Poetry is dirty. As Gadamer has it, humanities research is always a compromise between truth-seeking and the contingencies of the scholar's prejudice; being self-reflexive about our own prejudices is a core social hope offered by humanities scholarship.[2]

The literary-critical end of the humanities spectrum is sustained not by declaration of fact or by assertions of fixed value, nor by normalisations, but by sceptical questions that seek to prod, probe, find evidence for and against, quiz and yes – sometimes – demolish. Variation, fluctuation, imagination, qualification, daydreaming, procrastination, deferral. A book delivered too late and with a different objective than that planned – because it was always written as experiment. No discernible ends in sight. No end.

I am not an architect. No one needs to live inside any of my ideas, and no one looks to them for food or cure, and they would be foolish to do so.

---

[2] Hans-Georg Gadamer, *Truth and Method*, 2nd rev. edn, trans. Joel Weinsheimer and Donald G. Marshall (London and New York: Continuum, 2004), esp. pp. 268–310.

If I contribute at all, I contribute questions. I join an ongoing argument. I don't want that argument to close down or close off unless it is boring or stale or becoming accepted, and if so, I should leave it behind. If we humanities people see a wall, we dig underneath it, or we push through it, or we walk along it, or we jump over it – all by asking: what is a wall? What is the history of walls? What is the power that built the wall? What territories does it assert and deny? Yet I am not building anything; I am free to not build, to not assert ownership, to quiz definitions and not to make them. I can criticise a system without suggesting another system to replace it – because in my job as a critic I am free of responsibility, free of care, free of determined outcomes – though the risk is that the subjects are free only to diminishing extents. I know humanities to be important, but I resist defining its social function, resist turning it into a project, or policy, or a full-spectrum system. We revel in fragments, in bits and pieces, in the irritations of the stuff of culture being 'out of place'.

I have morality through the humanities precisely because I question ethical practices, question authority, question rhetoric – lift up the ideological stone to see what lurks beneath. And then realise that stone and insects beneath form a metaphorical mess that obscures and manipulates. So I question myself and my motives, and the styles I adopt. Everything has an agenda. Me too.

Although it seems in reality I do not – I like to think that I resist doing anything designed to be measurable by those who maintain that economic or social or educational value are the end points of all academic and intellectual endeavour. Who gave such people – such ideologies, such mindsets – control? We did – and we do every day we write or answer an email along those lines. These people are us. And these are the ideologies and mindsets we work and think by. What impact do you have? What is your economic value? Fill in this spreadsheet and enumerate the precise number of four-star research outputs in your unit of assessment. What do I have to measure and offer for my tenure portfolio? My ideas have so far amounted to 78cm of silver rod and I have filled 2.6 golden bowls with the love in my books.

Can wisdom be put in a silver rod, or love in a golden bowl? Well, yes William Blake, it seems we have allowed it to be so. And we are ashamed when we teach radical art or radical politics; but shame is awareness, is insight, is opportunity. Glossy, powerful, established systems govern us – those self-same systems we sought to drive, when we first saw them in the car showroom of academic ambition. Even if there is no palpable humanities castle to defend, still we make the case for the humanities' significance every time we argue, every time we expose our words. And we wreck the purpose of the humanities every time we rest on our laurels, every time we measure it or count it or convert it into money, or every time we feel *superior*. So let's argue. Let's expose our own prejudices and elitisms. Opposition for opposition's sake. Planes of being, not hierarchies of deference. Sentences without verbs. Opposition is true friendship, but I don't want us to be smug in agreement over constant opposition either.

Are the humanities free? Does study of and through the humanities free people? Does it unshackle in practice and on purpose? Does it actually hold the powerful to account – and are we brave enough to want it to do so? Who are the powerful in the humanities? Is the profession all about earning potential, about paying off debt, about providing articulacy and succour to powerful orthodoxies of money and hierarchy, about feeding the machine – the hospital, the university, the career, the livestock pen, the abattoir – of capital? Why do we constantly need to 'defend the humanities'? There is real danger in these defences being so *dull*: we step out into a battle none cares for except us, and we look behind us to see what legions we can draw on, and all we see are our colleagues suddenly dissipate into careerist clerks, recede into risk-averse bureaucracy. Sometimes when I think of the humanities, I feel like the ghost of Akaky Akakievich searching for his overcoat, in the frozen mist of a Gogol farce.

But I can see myself better, for having read Gogol: my snobbery, my jealousy, my greed, my insignificance in the face of bureaucracy, and my desire to be legitimised by that same bureaucracy. I can see the pomposity of my role within higher education's arcane labyrinth. To repeat: as academics we have to question the humanities, not defend it. Lift it out of the bell jar, because it only flourishes for us when we start chewing on it, squeezing the juice from it – to see what it really tastes like. We have allowed systems of value and processes of codification that are entirely alien to – and which run counter to – our own liberating sceptical purposes, to invade our classrooms, and to colonise our own value systems, in practice, on paper, in meetings, on spreadsheets – in the words and modalities we pass on to our students. We have allowed our ideas to be measured in silver rods. Learning outcomes are golden bowls. What is the precise outcome that any student will get from studying this sonnet in this session, for these two hours? What is the measurable socio-economic impact of your research into the ancient origins of the Finno-Ugric languages? What star-rating will I give this journal article on sexual politics in the fiction of Nell Dunn? How will the economy be boosted by *yet another* book on a parochial peasant poet who died in an asylum in 1864?

Even answering such questions, direct, is to risk submission to their ethical logic – to grant them a moral authority over us – an authority that we ourselves have voted in, that we ourselves have had a hand in, that we ourselves have thought through and written down and passed on and overseen. Such questions of value we all feel a guilty urgency to express, before our managers come knocking, or so that we can fill in that grant application, or tick that box in the CV. I have done so myself, innumerable times, and have supervised – even *compelled* – others in doing the same. I am that foul hydra – an academic and a manager. I skip gaily from a meeting in which *without hesitation* I talk about academic and administrative colleagues as 'resource', immediately to a seminar where I try to inculcate ideological concern at the implications of Arthur Morrison's description of the poor as 'rats' in *A Child of the Jago*. The paradoxes – the raw hypocrisies – in being a humanities scholar in an institution fed by marketised cash and student debt are dizzying.

If not on our chartered corridors, then at least in our subject areas – surely, *desperately*? – we must allow ideals: in the literary-critical arts we can read them, we can make them up, we can fabricate idealised spaces and utopias of no-space, allow the accident and chance of passion and intrigue and reading in libraries and fickle association to construct possible idea-worlds. Do we do that when we 'defend' the humanities? Or are such public defences from the elect essentially admissions of our supine state, and mere echoes of a sad defeat that happened many moons ago?

Want to see a bracing debate about the future of the humanities by the great and the good of our most esteemed institutions? £20 please. There is no such thing as a free canapé. Dare we in the sceptical humanities attack the ideologies, the assumptions, the rhetoric and the discourse – that generate the moral logic of the questions themselves – and the questioners? Do we need to dig beneath such questions, or else knock them down, or else leap right over them, to prove the value of what we do, to prove our real 'contribution'? We should do so not as a mob, not all in the same 'professionalised' direction – but all over the place, from all manner of provocative modes and lifestyles. I don't want to agree with the other essays in this collection. English agreeing with itself about what it is and where it should go and what its purpose is? Who would that benefit? I don't want to be in a club of mutual justification. It is important that we all disagree. I don't want you to like this essay. I write it to dig you in the ribs, to annoy you and myself. Intellectual satisfaction is a bourgeois dead end. We should be awkward, ungainly, misfits, imposters, disagreeable.

We need to do the business of humanities not by acquiescence to and concurrence with polite professionalised practices, but through dissent and disagreement and disagreeableness. If we feel we have made a 'contribution', we then need to question the nature and purpose of contribution, the system that values it, and our ethics within it. I now must question why it is I need to express it all like this, from my position of privilege and socio-economic comfort, sitting here in the secure warmth of the Bodleian library (see – they let me in – and I mention it to impress you!), surrounded by the products of 'people like us' (that is, book-writers like me, I want that to be true, I do so want to be in this book club, want my name on one of those hard-wearing spines – but why?). I love libraries, but they raise my hackles too. Anything that feels sanctified, precious or ordered is likely to be a form of established power.

Why do I have to care? Liberal arts? Codified. Humanities? Roboticised. Your brain? Just a computer.[3] So keen were we academic humanities scholars for the establishment and its finance gods to accept our seriousness that we forgot to make up our own rules, or to offer our own metaphors for the way the brain works, or the way intellectual life should be valued.

We need to take responsibility for the systems of power to which we submit, and we need to realise that for the most part, while we might benefit from that submission as individuals, we also lose something worth defending as a collective. From this itch of paradox – of bad faith even – and in the refreshing self-knowledge of our compromise and our messiness and our complexity, we must begin our questioning. That's what the humanities afford, and irritating questions must be a foundational guarantee in the study of English.

[3] This popularly accepted modelling of the brain-as-computer has been resisted of late in scientific fora, by a Blakean Romanticist no less: see Jon Roberts, 'The Objects of Consciousness: A Non-Computational Model of Cell Assemblies', *Journal of Consciousness Studies*, 24:1–2 (2017), 228–53.

'Something Real to Carry Home When Day Is Done': The Reader in Future

JANE DAVIS

During the last five years of my twenty years as a teacher of literature, largely working with adults in the Department of Continuing Education at the University of Liverpool, I began to want *something else*. I had no idea what that *something else* would be, but it would be something with literature, which had been for me both a life-saver and life-maker. I was increasingly conscious that this life-giving resource was not being utilised by many people who, like me, might have great need of it.

Such people might be people like my mother, who had died at the age of fifty-one from alcohol-related diseases. She was a keen reader-escapist, consuming acres of novels by Georgette Heyer, Dennis Wheatley and Dick Francis. These are books which, like drugs or alcohol, take you out of yourself and put your head somewhere else. I read them when I was a young teenager, because we had them in the house, but later, reading became something more than escapism. It's not been fashionable at any point in my life to think of books as moral teachers, but in the absence of parental guidance (Mum was usually in the pub and my father was not around) books offered clues on how to live a life. My relationship with literature deepened as, over a fifteen-year period, my mother drank herself to death, and I, propelled by unconscious necessity and fuelled alternately by hard work and lucky breaks, gathered a few qualifications and got myself to university to read English. In my third year I flourished under a brilliant teacher, Mr Brian Nellist. I went on to complete a PhD, became a university teacher and grew into someone with a life away from drugs and alcohol. I put quite a lot of that down to the input I had from great books.

In my years of university teaching, I read, as Dickens says in *David Copperfield*, 'as if for life'. George Eliot, Wordsworth, Milton, Dante, George Herbert, Iris Murdoch, A. S. Byatt, Doris Lessing, Tolstoy, Shakespeare, Thomas Hardy, Charlotte Brontë, Mrs Gaskell, Saul Bellow, Dostoevsky and Bernard Malamud all helped me build an adult self. I brought my needs to the Continuing Education classes I taught and developed a way of teaching based on close reading informed by personal response, a style and content wildly at odds with the prevailing mode of theory-based literary thinking. My husband Philip Davis, and my teacher, Brian Nellist, continued to teach literature as they had always done, as a direct personal experience, but apart from them, the general tenor of 'English Literature' seemed to me unreal, self-indulgent and ultimately pointless.

In my Continuing Education classes I read literature as myself, through my own eyes, trying to apply to it to my own life and my own moral problems. I did that in the company of legal secretaries, unemployed philosophers, ex-dockers, librarians, nurses, barristers, people existing on benefits, midwives, housewives, failed undergraduates and a retired medic, Dr Betty, who attended my classes for ten years as she went through the long, arduous process of dying as a single professional woman with no family near. I watched Betty use literature as a way to understand what was happening to her during this difficult time: I saw literature and the social life of our classes provide a kind of meaning and connection that Betty did not find elsewhere, not from her distant family, nor her Church, nor her social service care support package. And it wasn't just Betty. Perhaps most of us, a community of regular readers attending, teaching and learning in these classes, were to a greater or lesser degree using literature as a practical tool for life.

My need for *something else* resulted, in 1997, in *The Reader* magazine, which I created with Dr Sarah Coley and Dr Angela Macmillan, who taught alongside me in the Continuing Education programme. 'A magazine about writing worth reading' says the strapline on the first, blurry, badly proof-read issue. It was backed by The English Association North, which Philip Davis ran from the Liverpool School of English at that time. In that first Editorial, Sarah and I wrote:

The Reader has come into being to continue and extend the work and sense of community generated by literature classes in Liverpool University's Continuing Education programme. For ten years now, since the part-time M.A. in Victorian Literature was created to provide serious, personal, high-level study for the experienced lay reader in the North West, our classes have tried to provide the reading public with accessible, informal but challenging courses of study. And over the years, tutors and students alike have realised that something else has happened in or through such courses. A loosely-woven yet very real community of readers has been born. It is a community brought together through what amounts to a shared hunger. In Saul Bellow's novel, *Herzog*, the eponymous hero – a Continuing Education lecturer in the throes of a nervous breakdown – writes in another crazy letter to his boss,

The people who come to evening classes are only ostensibly after culture. Their great need, their hunger, is for good sense, clarity, truth – even an atom of it. People are dying – it is no metaphor – for lack of something real to carry home when day is done.

Anyone who has been to Continuing Education classes will have seen, and felt, this hunger for themselves. What is real, what will give us satisfaction, is not easy to come by or to find. That's why our reading life can be so useful and rewarding, if we follow our instincts for what to read seriously enough to make reading a kind of expression of our deepest selves. When Herzog's life and learning mesh, he gets better.

It's interesting looking back now to see the words 'community', 'deepest selves' and 'better' in this early expression of what The Reader is and does.

The Reader magazine, though, was not *something else* enough. I knew that only certain people would ever become part of this Continuing Education community. For people in pubs, like my mother, for people in rehab like the friends of my youth, for people in mental health in-patient wards, or for people suffering old age like Dr Betty, but lacking her considerable personal, professional and financial resources, the meaning and community provided by these classes was unimaginable.

Things crystallised one day when I was driving to the university to teach Wordsworth's 'Ode: Intimations of Immortality'. It was spring and there were daffodils lining the path to the door of an ex-council house opposite the traffic lights where I had stopped in North Birkenhead. The daffodils were dancing, and the door was opened by a younger woman in her pyjamas with a baby, perhaps a year old, on her arm. He seemed to leap up with joy at the sight of the older woman and I thought, 'the babe leaps up on his mother's arm', a line from the *Immortality Ode* I had been reading earlier that day. At exactly the same moment that the line came into my mind, a thought also exploded: that child will never read Wordsworth. He'll never think 'the babe leaps up' or know 'The Daffodils'. He can't have this stuff that has made a life for me. He will get a bad education, not including any of the joy and usefulness of poetry, and he'll end in a dead-end job, or in prison, and be hurt by life.

The lights changed and I drove off. Within months, I'd set up a five-week summer outreach project called 'Get Into Reading'. The first session took place in a community education centre on the other side of that set of lights.

I brought a story, 'Schwartz', by Russell Hoban and the Tennyson poem 'Crossing The Bar' to that first group. Among the seven or eight recruits who'd come along to try getting into reading were two young mothers who were not fully literate. As a university teacher of literature I had no idea that vast swathes of the UK population – about 28% across all populations, and over 57% in prisons – are not literate.[1] I read the story aloud, as a way of getting round that problem, thinking, I'll read it, and we'll stop every now and then and talk.

That became the model for Shared Reading: someone reads aloud, we stop to talk about what is read and then read on.

The story worked well, and, strangers that we were, we began to be able to talk to each other a little about work or not working, and being creative or being stuck, about drug-use, music and personal guilt, the things that swirl around in Hoban's story. Later, as I read 'Crossing the Bar', one of the women in the group began to cry. In twenty-odd years at the University, I had never seen anyone moved to tears by a poem, but here we were, in a room in a community centre in Birkenhead, and a woman was crying.

> Sunset and evening star,
>   And one clear call for me!
> And may there be no moaning of the bar,
>   When I put out to sea,
>
> But such a tide as moving seems asleep,
>   Too full for sound and foam,
> When that which drew from out the boundless deep
>   Turns again home.
>
> Twilight and evening bell,
>   And after that the dark!
> And may there be no sadness of farewell,
>   When I embark;
>
> For tho' from out our bourne of Time and Place
>   The flood may bear me far,
> I hope to see my Pilot face to face
>   When I have crost the bar.

In that group, and in two other such groups, people cried when I read this poem. Why?

---

[1] https://www.rt.com/uk/357676-literacy-britain-adults-oecd/. Over half (57%) of people entering prison were assessed as having literacy skills expected of an 11-year-old, <http://www.prisonreformtrust.org.uk/Portals/0/Documents/Bromley Briefings/Summer2017factfile.pdf>; Skills Funding Agency (2016), OLASS English and maths assessments: participation 2015/16 (London: SFA).

My dad died last year and it reminds me of him, said one woman. My daughter died six weeks ago, said another. It reminds me of my father, he died when I was fourteen, another told me. That line about the tide, 'but such a tide as moving seems asleep' reminds me of when we would walk together and the Mersey would be high and full...

Of course, I knew that literature was personal, and had experienced that myself, both close-up in private, and at some distance in my university teaching, but now without the screen of 'teaching', without 'university course', without 'classroom', the stuff of feeling was exposed as live ammunition: powerful emotional things could and would happen because of the words coming to life in our minds. After the woman whose daughter had died got through the session, crying all the while, a man, an ex-welder, leaned across the table and took her hand. 'Well done, kidder,' he said. I knew at that point that I had stumbled into something extraordinary, and The Reader's mission has grown from that tender place. This was the *something else*.

Three readers gave testimonies to the power of Shared Reading at the English: Shared Futures Conference with me in Newcastle in 2017, and are representatives of thousands of people who attend or lead Shared Reading groups every week across the UK and in six European countries, New Zealand and Australia. Kevin Robertson was one of the three, and his testimony spoke of the impact of meeting Shared Reading in an addiction-recovery setting:

> I was told about the Reader group and imagined a group of us sitting around listening to someone reading a book to us, it sounded a nice way to spend a couple of hours. As I was on another 'try anything to stop drinking' buzz, I decided to go along. It therefore came as a shock to me when I found out actually what happened in the group. We all had a chance to read, we all listened, we stopped every now and then to talk, to express our thoughts on what we had just read. I was hooked and it soon became a favourite activity of mine during the week.
>
> It wasn't on its own the thing that changed my life, but it was a major part of it. With other treatments and a commitment on my part, my life was slowly turned around. What the group gave me was a place, a safe place, to have a voice.
>
> But the first thing, when you read literature, you get these first impressions and you can't lie about them.

Kevin, who has recently trained as a Reader Leader, is one of thousands of people, previously non-readers of literature, who now read together with others on a weekly basis. His sense that Shared Reading gave him in the first instance a place 'to have a voice' is one shared by many participants over the last decade or so. There are hundreds of thousands of people who do not have a chance to exercise their voice – people in recovery, perhaps, like Kevin, but also people in Care Homes, people sleeping rough or in institutions, people doing time in the criminal justice system or simply, like the baby I saw at the North Birkenhead traffic lights, unlucky enough to be born in an area where poverty will blight life, health and educational chances. While we're working on the big fixes our social systems need, Shared Reading can offer an immediate opportunity to achieve joy and meaning and 'something real to carry home when day is done'.

But it may be that the big fixes must begin as small changes. Kevin speaks about the fact that literature demands or calls up a truthful response in him. This is the basis for real growth and change, and I recognised in Kevin's words my own experience and the experience of many hundreds of others with whom I have shared reading over the last twenty years. A man in a Drug Rehab said to me, 'for two hour a week I have meaning in my life'. His words echoed in my memory for a long time (my thought: two hours' meaning is not enough!), and have led to a big new development at The Reader.

The Reader span out from the University and became a charity and social enterprise in 2008. Now we are building the International Centre for Shared Reading at Calderstones Mansion in Liverpool. Calderstones is a community based on Shared Reading, powered by volunteers and social businesses. We hope our reading community will become a model for many smaller communities across the country as we build a movement of readers over the next five or ten years. It is our ambition to make Shared Reading part of the fabric of life, so that people like Kevin, like myself, like my mother, like Dr Betty can have the opportunity to join a Shared Reading group wherever they live. For example: there are about 20,000 Care Homes in England, many of them failing to provide stimulating engagement for residents. Shared Reading can help here, as Rose, who is 77 and has been a Care Home resident for three years, testifies:

> We're all pleased about you coming! We feel like somebody cares. We didn't know what to expect when we first started the group, but what we got was lovely! I mean if you didn't come, we'd have nothing to think about. It's surprising what it does to the mind. Your mind starts wandering when you're unhappy, it wanders too much. After you've been and we've read these poems, I think it helps a lot. Everything in your mind seems clearer. I often think about them after you've left.

It puts something in your mind. It doesn't always come straight away but the mind starts thinking. When we all get together and start talking, it makes you feel important [laughs]! Because we're learning something every time. It makes you think you're not as daft as you think you are.

This is the only time we talk, you see. The rest of it is always in there [points to head] and we're not happy. Everything that's been happening in the group has been very true. Real. And this stuff that's written down makes you feel different. We like to listen to these things – they mean something.

Bringing it out [puts her hand on her chest]. It brings out what's been gathering here [hand on chest]. Not leaving it there. Leaving it there makes you unhappy. Bringing it out with the group. Whatever's been bothering you. We're getting old, aren't we, we're getting old. And we like to know you're coming here because it brings back memories in a way. It's important not to chase them away – remember them! You start thinking about what life's been like and you think 'this is very important'.

But talking about these poems, I think it helps. They've got a lot to say these poems about life as if, that's the way life's got to be. It can't be good for everybody. We hope it is, but it never is, is it? These poems mean something don't they? They mean something because you can't wait to hear them, read them and think about how it's been a bit like the life we've had.

I imagine how it would be if every Rose had weekly visitors bringing poems and stories. I imagine 20,000 pairs of Literature students visiting those 20,000 Care Homes each week.

To bring such a future about The Reader plans to use the structures developed by successful movements like Guiding and Scouting: dedicated individuals volunteer to run weekly groups in local places, other volunteers support those weekly groups, while a small paid staff coordinates the programme, raises money and ensures safety. We are building the structure needed for such a model and want to work with universities, colleges and schools to recruit people who love reading and care about creating a better world. We need to recruit Reader Leaders who will commit themselves to running weekly groups, and we need skilled organisers to help develop the support systems as Local Organisers. If you'd like to help create something real to carry home when day is done, visit www. thereader.org.uk.

Afterword

STEFAN COLLINI

Oh Christ, not another bloody conference! Who needs them? And a mega-conference, to boot: even more papers I don't want to hear and even more people I don't want to meet...

I am not – how shall I put it? – a natural conference animal. Some mixture of intellectual impatience, inability to sit still for long periods, and a resistance to all that promiscuous nodding and agreeing has led me largely to shun such events. But, as a result of some fatal brew of duty and delusion, I had let myself in for this one, and anyway there would be the consolations of Grey Street and Newcastle's surprisingly rich legacy of 1820s and 1830s architecture, as well as the chance to see more by going running with one of my fellow-panellists. And once I was there, I thought I might as well go to as many sessions as possible: as in other areas of life, hope retains an astonishing capacity to triumph over experience.

This is not a conversion narrative. I didn't suddenly see the light, and I will admit to sneaking out to a nearby Caffè Nero at one point, partly just to have (better) coffee, but partly to escape for half an hour from the obligation to be so nice to everyone. But I did notice that even I, least promising of recruits, seemed to be getting caught up in the spirit of the thing, and I made sure I was back in time for the beginning of the next session.

My choice of which sessions to attend was dictated by an unsteady combination of intellectual inclination and self-improvement. That I went to sessions called things like 'Broadcasting English' and 'Literary criticism in an age of radical politics' may have been predictable, but in the end I spent even more time going to sessions on 'employability', 'funding', 'early-career opportunities', and so on. I have had, by any standards, an extraordinarily fortunate career, holding tenured posts in excellent universities during better times. People like me need to hear from, and not just about, those whose circumstances have been dramatically less favourable, not as a kind of voyeurism or slumming, but to keep us real and to chasten our sense of what it takes to go on teaching English as a member of British academia's growing precariat.

But although there were despatches from the trenchiest of trenches, the mood was not apocalyptic or whingeing, yet nor was it wilfully upbeat or sunny. It was reflective, argumentative, and above all collaborative: 'How should we be thinking about this...?' or 'Here's the way I've experimented with this...', and so on. I was also struck by the imaginative, even emotional, resilience on display: here were dozens of examples of ways of nourishing an intellectual and aesthetic life by turning a once-familiar bit of our sprawling subject into something less recognizable and more intriguing, endowing it with that additional meaning that comes from making a topic one's own. I suspect most academic disciplines allow their practitioners some such satisfactions – they provide, even if unofficially, some existential glue to hold together otherwise scratchy and anomic bits of our daily lives – but 'English' may offer to do this is in a more immediate and less disguised way. There was a strong feeling across the sessions that this was a 'lived' subject.

I caught glimpses, often in surprising places, of something that had survived from those childhood years when burying oneself in, or puzzling over, things written in books seemed more real than so-called real life, something that had survived through the long years when graduate education and fragile employment had done their best to turn us into technically proficient CV designers and article manufacturers. The conference provided the opportunity to be reminded of this and to register that the loves and identifications that had beguiled us into this strange way of life, as well as the frustrations and resentments that so bruise those feelings in our everyday institutional existences, were not so solitary or idiosyncratic after all. And despite myself, despite my ingrained Scrooge-like resistance to joining in conventional collective celebration, I found something oddly, well, heartening about this tangible mood. No one seemed to have given up on our putative 'shared futures', even though some sessions involved exceedingly gloomy forecasts of the political and financial weather. Yes, these were 'interesting times', in the sense used in the Chinese curse, but, more emphatically, this was an interesting and indispensable subject to be part of.

So: an oversized self-help group, a low-key revivalist meeting, a distracting departmental away-day? No, not quite any of those things, though such gatherings must end up meeting more needs than even the most ambitious organizers could ever enumerate in advance. A lot of what went on was more focusedly intellectual and specific than that: 'here are some new sources, new perspectives, new ideas about X or Y – what do you think?' Some was simply practical and useful: 'here's how we've done it in our department – details are available through this link'. And some of it, as ever, was unashamedly performative: 'I'm really rather good at what I do and I'd quite like to get a better job.' But holding it all together was the shared sense of recognition of why we care in the ways we do, and a reminder of the extremely improbable truth that these things – literary criticism and textual editing, creative writing and theatre practice, analyzing language and studying linguistics, teaching in schools and in adult education, studying Irish or Welsh or Scottish literature, promoting reading or contesting various kinds of illiteracy – do, just about, make up a single 'subject'. And though we mustn't say it out loud, of course, it was also a reminder that those who cultivate this subject are far from being dispirited helots or unautomated marking-machines or failed Morris Zapps, but are a quirky, wordy, funny, clever bunch.

It was all quite surprising, really. Like other kinds of orgy, it's probably not something that can be repeated too often, but words such as 'success' and 'triumph' were incautiously murmured by no small number of the departing participants, and not just when they were thanking the heroic organizers. I hope I managed to maintain a decent façade of grumpy scepticism throughout, and I trust it wasn't too obvious that I was rather glad I'd come. But I have to admit that, on the train home, I even found myself thinking that actually the coffee hadn't been that bad, either.

Index

Miller, Arthur, 10
  The Crucible 117
  Death of a Salesman 10
Milton, John 201
Mitchell, David 94
MLA, 92, 93
  MLA Commons 92
Modernist studies 59, 60
Modernists 2
Mondal, Anshuman 121
Mondal, Lewi 58
Monograph 95, 96
  pre-eminence of 95
  print run and sales 2005–2014, 97
Moody's credit agency 76
Morgan, Nicky 168
Morrison, Arthur 208
Mort, Helen 2
Moxley, Joseph 175
Mukherjee, Ankhi 124
Mullan, John 2
Mummery, Tom 31
Murdoch, Iris 210
Mussel, James 86

Nabokov, Vladimir 171
Naipaul V. S. 138
National Association for the Teaching of
  English (NATE) 146, 149
National Association of Writers in
  Education (NAWE) 3, 162, 164,
  167, 172, 174, 176
National Trust 178
Nellist, Brian 210–11
Neoliberalism 34
New Generation Thinkers 199
New Historicism 40
New York Times 109
New York University 109, 110, 112, 116
Newcastle 1, 119, 217
Newcastle City Council 159
Newcastle University 1, 156, 158, 159,
  160
Newfield, Chris 1
NHS 74
Nobel Prize 169
Norse 127
North Korea 196
Northern Stage 156
Notes and Queries 87
Nottingham University 46

O'Brien, Dan 180
Ofqual 18

OFSTED 7
O-level 8
Olufemi, Lola 54
Oluwaseun 54
Open access 71, 83, 84, 88, 89–92, 97,
  98
  cost of gold open access 91
  resource properly for PhD
    students 72
Open Book Publishers 91
Open University 104, 107
Orwell, George 196
Osmond, Richard 181, 182
Outreach 27, 29
Oxford Brookes University 147
Oxford Journals 84, 85, 88
Oxford Scholarly Editions Online 102
Oxford University Press 102, 103

Paddington 185
Paris 110
Paynel, Olive 119
Pedagogic Criticism 40–50
PEN 196
Penyberth 133
Peripeteia 31
Peston, Robert 4
PhD, award of to be celebrated 57
  employment data 62
  excellent training for many things 63
  not serving future carer 61
Philology 46
Physics 3, 79
Pine, Joseph 36, 37
Plagiarism 9
Plaid Cymru 133
Poetics and Linguistics Association 147
Pope, Rob 104
Populism 201
Postcolonialism 119
Practice-led research 175, 176
Pravinchandra, Shital 121
Precariat 62
Precarious employment 6
Precarity 166, 170
Prescott, John 51
Prichard, T. J. Llewelyn 132
Priestly, J. B., *An Inspector Calls* 10
Private providers 74
Project Gutenberg 94, 101, 102
ProQuest 102

QAA 172
QR (Quality related) funding 75